THE POETRY OF

Heinrich Heine

THE POETRY OF
Heinrich Heine

SELECTED AND EDITED WITH AN INTRODUCTION

BY FREDERIC EWEN ❧ THE POETRY

TRANSLATED BY LOUIS UNTERMEYER, HUMBERT

WOLFE, EMMA LAZARUS, MARGARET ARMOUR,

AND OTHERS, INCLUDING 110 NEW TRANSLATIONS

BY AARON KRAMER ❧ ❧ ❧

CITADEL PRESS   Secaucus, New Jersey

TO THE MEMORY OF TWO SOLDIERS
DAVID McKELVY WHITE
LIEUT. LEONARD E. KURZ

PREFACE

The present edition of the poetry of Heinrich Heine was undertaken in the belief that there was need for a comprehensive one-volume selection which would do justice to the many-sided genius of that great writer. It was felt that while many of the traditional versions of his poems were admirable, the time was ripe for a modern rendering, suitable for contemporary readers.

The present volume retains a number of the standard versions of Heine's poems. But the greater portion of the verse here offered represents a new translation prepared for this volume by the gifted American poet Aaron Kramer. It is with regret that we have been compelled to omit the important "Atta Troll," but space permitted the inclusion of only one of Heine's long poems, and "Germany—A Winter's Tale" was selected as being most timely and representative.

The editor wishes to acknowledge the generous help of many friends: Joseph M. Bernstein, Dr. Francine Bradley, Dr. Lyman R. Bradley, Dr. Philip S. Foner, Dr. Arthur Geismar, E. Louise Malley, Isidor Schneider, and the officers and staff of The Citadel Press.

FREDERIC EWEN

New York
June 1969

CONTENTS

Heinrich Heine: Humanity's Soldier
   by Frederic Ewen   3

Poems and Ballads
   BOOK OF SONGS
      Prologue   53

   Young Sorrows

            DREAM PICTURES
      Im nächtgen Traum hab ich mich selbst geschaut   55
      Was treibt und tobt mein tolles Blut?   55

            SONGS
      Morgens steh ich auf und frage   57
      Lieb Liebchen, leg's Händchen aufs Herze mein   57
      Schöne Wiege meiner Leiden   58
      Anfangs wollt ich fast verzagen   58

ROMANCES

Poor Peter 59
The Two Grenadiers 60
Don Ramiro 61
The Minnesingers 66
Journey by Water 66

SONNETS

To My Mother, B. Heine 67

Lyrical Intermezzo

Prologue 68
Im wunderschönen Monat Mai 69
Aus meinen Tränen spriessen 70
Die Rose, die Lilie, die Taube, die Sonne 70
Wenn ich in deine Augen seh 70
Lehn deine Wang an meine Wang 71
Es stehen unbeweglich 71
Auf Flügeln des Gesanges 71
Die Lotosblume ängstigt 72
Du liebst mich nicht, du liebst mich nicht 73
Ich grolle nicht, und wenn das Herz auch bricht 73
Die Linde blühte, die Nachtigall sang 73
Sie haben dir viel erzählet 74
Ein Fichtenbaum steht einsam 74
Aus meinen grossen Schmerzen 74
Und als ich so lange, so lange gesäumt 75
Manch Bild vergessener Zeiten 75
Hör ich das Liedchen klingen 76
Ich hab dich geliebet und liebe dich noch! 76
Sie haben mich gequälet 77
Wenn zwei von einander scheiden 77
Vergiftet sind meine Lieder 77
Ich hab im Traum geweinet 78
Der Traumgott bracht mich in ein Riesenschloss 78
Am Kreuzweg wird begraben 79

Homecoming

The Loreley 79

Als ich, auf der Reise, zufällig   80
Wir sassen am Fischerhause   81
Du schönes Fischermädchen   82
Der Wind zieht seine Hosen an   83
Wenn ich an deinem Hause   83
Das Meer erglänzte weit hinaus   84
Still ist die Nacht, es ruhen die Gassen   84
Ich stand in dunkeln Träumen   85
Sie liebten sich beide, doch keiner   85
Mensch, verspotte nicht den Teufel   85
Herz, mein Herz, sei nicht beklommen   86
Ich wollt, meine Schmerzen ergössen   86
Mein Kind, wir waren Kinder   87
Du bist wie eine Blume   88
Du hast Diamanten und Perlen   88
Wie dunkle Träume stehen   88
Doch die Kastraten klagten   89
Der Tod das ist die kühle Nacht   90
Sag, wo ist dein schönes Liebchen   90
Mir träumt': ich bin der liebe Gott   90
The Pilgrimage to Kevlaar   92

The Journey to the Harz

Prologue   95
Mountain Idyll (II)   95

The North Sea

Coronation   97
Twilight   98
Sea Greeting   99

NEW POEMS

New Spring

Prologue   102
Ich lieb eine Blume, doch weiss ich nicht welche   103
Leise zieht durch mein Gemüt   103

Gekommen ist der Maie 103
Der Schmetterling ist in die Rose verliebt 104
Was treibt dich umher, in der Frühlingsnacht? 104
Die schlanke Wasserlilie 105
Sag mir, wer einst die Uhren erfund 105
Mit deinen blauen Augen 106
Ich wandle unter Blumen 106
Wie die Nelken duftig atmen! 106
Es war ein alter König 107
Der Brief, den du geschrieben 107
In meiner Erinnrung erblühen 108
Die holden Wünsche blühen 108
Sterne mit den goldnen Füsschen 108
Spätherbstnebel, kalte Träume 109

Miscellaneous

SERAPHINE

An dem stillen Meeresstrande 110
Dass du mich liebst, das wusst ich 110
Wie neubegierig die Möwe 111
Sie floh vor mir wie'n Reh so scheu 111
Das Fräulein stand am Meere 112
Auf diesem Felsen bauen wir 112

ANGELIQUE

Ich halte ihr die Augen zu 113
Wenn ich, beseligt von schönen Küssen 113
Während ich nach andrer Leute 114
Schaff mich nicht ab, wenn auch den Durst 114

HORTENSE

Wir standen an der Strasseneck 115

CLARISSA

Überall wo du auch wandelst 115

FRIEDRIKE

Verlass Berlin, mit seinem dicken Sande 116

KATHARINA

Gesanglos war ich und beklommen   116
Ich liebe solche weisse Glieder   117
Jüngstens träumte mir: spazieren   117

Tragedy   119
Tannhäuser   119

Romances

The Adjuration   126
The Unknown   127
King Harald Harfagar   128
Childe Harold   129
Sir Olaf   129

To Ollea

Wander!   132
Old Fireplace Piece   132

Poems for the Times

Night Thoughts   134

ROMANCERO

Histories

The Battlefield of Hastings   136
The God Apollo   140
Charles I   144
The Asra   145
Geoffrey Rudel and Melisande of Tripoli   146

Lamentations

Woodland Solitude   148
Old Song   152
To the Angels   153

The Light Goes Out 154
An Evil Dream 154
Enfant Perdu 155
Annual Mourning 156

POEMS 1853-1854

Babylonian Sorrows 157

TO LAZARUS
Wie langsam kriechet sie dahin 158
Mich locken nicht die Himmelsauen 159

POSTHUMOUS VERSE

Love Poems

Wenn junge Herzen brechen 161
In the Morning 162
To Jenny 162
The Song of Songs 163

Miscellaneous

Testament 165
Warning 166
Where? 166

The Mattress Grave

The Dying Man 167
Mein Tag war heiter, glücklich meine Nacht 168
Den Strauss, den mir Mathilde band 168
Ich seh im Stundenglase schon 169
Hallelujah 170
For the Mouche 172
Es kommt der Tod—jetzt will ich sagen 176

Germany

Departure from Paris   179
Germany: A Winter's Tale   181

Songs of Protest

Du bist begeistert; du hast Mut   243
The Silesian Weavers   244
Ich hatte einst ein schönes Vaterland   244
The Slave Ship   245
Anno 1829   249
Anno 1839   250
To Georg Herwegh   251
Germany   251
October 1849   252
Tendency   254
Promise   255
The Emperor of China   255
Reassurance   256
Adam the First   257
1649—1793—????   258
King David   259
Hymn   260

Hebrew Melodies

Princess Sabbath   263
Prologue: The Rabbi of Bacherach   268
Disputation   268
Belshazzar   281
Donna Clara   282
The New Israelite Hospital in Hamburg   285
Jehuda Ben Halevy (Four Selections)   286

Notes   299
Index of First Lines in German   305

Heinrich Heine

HUMANITY'S SOLDIER

HEINRICH HEINE
?≈ *Humanity's Soldier*

BY FREDERIC EWEN

HEINRICH HEINE WAS BORN IN DÜSSELDORF on December 13, 1797, and died in Paris, on February 17, 1856. His life-span thus embraces one of the most exciting periods of modern European history—Napoleon, the Congress of Vienna, the Revolutions of 1830 and 1848. Since he was no indifferent onlooker on world events, his works reflect and interpret them sensitively. He was a Jew, and a German. He was brought up in the Rhineland, which was the first of the German states to feel the impact of the French Revolution and the advent of Napoleon. Wherever the French armies advanced, the walls of medievalism fell. The six and thirty kings who had ruled the German states with the sleepy security of feudal sovereigns and had been supported by a privileged landed aristocracy, a complaisant clergy, and a submissive, predominantly agrarian population, were powerless to oppose the tide of new ideas brought by irresistible armies. They fell—as the medieval fortresses of their ancestors before newly discovered gun-powder. The new revolutionary laws which were promulgated broke the power of the landed aristocracy and the clergy, effected the redistribution of the land, abolished serfdom and the payment of tithes, established legal and religious equality.

By 1809, Austria and Prussia were completely humbled, and the German states were replaced by three political units: the Rhine Confederation, the Kingdom of Prussia, and the Austrian Empire. All were under the sway of Napoleon. Strange phenomenon! Not all of the victories of Prussia combined had done as much for Germany as this foreign domination! In the words of the German historian, Franz Mehring, "It introduced Germany into the orbit of the modern civilized nations."

To the Jews it appeared as if Messiah had come. They achieved the status of citizens. Ghetto walls were broken down. For the first time since the fifteenth century, Jews were permitted to enter the city of Cologne, where the French commissioner said to them: "All traces of slavery are now abolished . . . You shall account to God alone for your religious beliefs, and as to your civil status, all men stand equal before the law." What humiliations they had hitherto been exposed to! Let Ludwig Börne describe them for us as he saw them in Frankfurt before the Emancipation:

"On Sundays, they were not allowed to leave their street, lest they be beaten by drunkards. Before their twenty-fifth year they were not allowed to marry, so that their offspring might be strong and healthy. On holidays they could not take a walk outside of the gate before six o'clock in the afternoon, for fear that the excessive heat of the sun might harm them. They were prevented from using public sidewalks and were forced to betake themselves through the fields, so that their agricultural talent might be stimulated. If a Jew crossed a street and a Christian called out: 'Mach mores, Jud!', the former had to take off his hat and through his courtesy cement more closely the love between the two religious groups."

Not to mention the special taxes, the restriction of occupations, and other such unpleasantnesses. Now and then an exceptional Jew had achieved the status of *Schutzjude*, of a "protected" or "privileged" Jew. Such had been the case of Moses Mendelssohn. But for the other Jews, their faith was, in Heine's impish words, not a religion, "but a calamity."

It is not at all likely that young Harry Heine, as he was then called, understood much of what was happening. By the time he had reached the age of understanding, many things in the Rhineland had changed

—and not for the better. But during the twenty years the French administered that region, the middle classes and peasantry achieved a degree of freedom they had never known before, and the Jews a sense of self-respect along with their title of citizens. The Rhineland was close to France. It was never to be completely free of French influences and ideas, and being industrially and economically more advanced, it remained one of the most liberal centers of Germany.

HEINE'S CHILDHOOD WAS A HAPPY ONE. His father, Samson Heine—the family name had originally been Bückeburg—was not the romantic figure his son was later to describe, but he was a kindly, soft, somewhat weak man who loved the pleasures of life much more than the drudgeries of his dry-goods business. He was not affluent when he came to Düsseldorf, but Peira van Geldern fell in love with him, and despite the opposition of her parents and the local rabbinical authorities, she married him. They settled in the Bolkerstrasse, which their first-born son was destined to make immortal.

Peira (or Betty) Heine was the strong member of the family. She may not have been as intellectual as her son pretended. But she was none the less a daughter of the Enlightenment, read Rousseau, and took a prominent—her son sometimes thought a too prominent and decisive—interest in the education of her children. Her temper was eminently practical. She despised poetry as so much romantic nonsense, and planned distinguished worldly careers for her son Harry— which she altered from time to time to suit historical necessities. They ranged all the way from a brilliant ambassadorial post to the more commonplace, though no less powerful, position of a banker, à la Rothschild. That these dreams were all doomed to frustration was not the mother's fault.

Heine was alert, eager, and bright. After a preliminary tutoring at the hands of a Frau Hindermans and a Jewish *melamed* in a private Hebrew school, he entered the local lyceum at the age of seven. The latter was housed in a Franciscan convent. The course of studies, though in the main directed and conducted by priests, was modeled on the French curriculum and was astonishingly liberal. Heine was never to forget the excellent impression made on him by Rector Schallmeyer, who combined the best qualities of the French Enlightenment with the thoroughness of a Catholic priest, and who set the young boy an example of tolerance he was later to repay by a noble literary tribute.

Harry studied Greek, French, and Hebrew, as well as many other subjects, and proved to be so promising a pupil that the Rector—and his mother, too—were convinced Harry would go very far if he ever took holy orders.

Under his very eyes, historical events succeeded one another with lightning speed. When he was nine, he witnessed Joachim Murat's entry into Düsseldorf as Napoleon's vice-regent. When he was fourteen, he saw Napoleon riding down the lime-tree avenue of the royal gardens. Not long thereafter came the frightful debacle of the Russian campaign and the retreat from Moscow. Then Leipzig, Elba, the Congress of Vienna, Waterloo, and the inglorious finale on St. Helena . . .

1815. IT SEEMED AS IF THE CLOCK OF HISTORY had been turned back half a century. "Legitimacy" was in the saddle again, and the Congress of Vienna began to undo all the work of the French Revolution and Napoleon. The victors set about to divide the spoils and they consecrated their piracy with the aura of holiness. England, Russia, Prussia and Austria were now the dominant powers. The Holy Alliance, that unholy partnership of Russia, Austria and Prussia, proclaimed the gospel of obedience and adjured all subject peoples "to abide by the solemn truths taught by the religion of God, our Saviour." It was not the first time, nor was it to be the last, that the name of the Crucified One was invoked to sanctify the enslavement of nations. Europe was now to be tranquillized—if necessary, at the point of the bayonet. In Vienna sat Prince Metternich, the brain of the Holy Alliance, the satanic physician who meant to cure Europe of her infernal malady—freedom.

The watch-dogs of reaction were set loose. The great crusade against all liberal ideas began. Wherever men rose up to free themselves—in Italy, or Portugal, or Spain,—there the Holy Alliance sent its armies to crush them.

The patriotic zeal of the Germans, who had rallied to expel the French invaders and to crush Napoleon, was to be rewarded in a peculiar manner. When he was in sore need, crushed and humiliated, Frederick William III of Prussia had promised his people a constitution and a parliament. As a matter of fact, between 1810 and 1820, he gave them five such solemn promises, only to break each of them with equal solemnity. Now that the battle was won, he ordered even the name of the "War for Freedom"—*Freiheitskrieg*—changed to "War of Liberation"—*Befreiungskrieg*. The very word Freedom was suspect.

The Congress of Vienna had decreed and brought into being a "German Confederation" of thirty-eight states. Prussia, now swollen by the absorption of one half of Saxony, Pomerania, and the Rhine provinces, stood at their head. With indefatigable efficiency and thoroughness all the achievements of the revolutionary and Napoleonic eras were abrogated. The universities, which had been the centers of the patriotic revival, were placed under special surveillance. Student organizations were spied on—and subsequently dissolved. University professors were investigated, and those found "unreliable" were either dismissed or imprisoned. The Carlsbad Resolutions of 1819 reestablished a general censorship and victimized such eminent scholars as Arndt, Schleiermacher, Humboldt, and the Welckers.

As always in times of repression, the Jews suffered most. The economic crisis which followed the "Wars of Liberation" made it particularly easy to turn the discontent of the people against them. The Jews had already lost most of the economic and political rights they had achieved during the Emancipation. In many towns, they were forced to return to their ghettoes. They were expelled from Lübeck and Bremen. In Frankfurt, where they had bought civic rights with a payment of 450,000 gulden, they were told after the Restoration that the agreement was void. But no effort was made to repay the gold. Once more they were locked up in the Judengasse.

Anti-Semitic pogroms took place all over Germany. University professors and scholars provided the learned ammunition against the Jews. The great philosopher J. G. Fichte saw in them an inimical state within a state, and urged that they be packed off to the Promised Land. Hartwig Hundt (sic!) counselled that they be sold to the English as slaves. The chorus of Jew-baiting and anti-Semitism mounted in a terrifying degree. It seemed as if the Middle Ages had returned.

BARRED FROM PRACTICALLY ALL OCCUPATIONS except trading and money-lending, a number of Jews had profited from the economic upsurge brought about by the Napoleonic wars, when their business sense was greatly in demand. It was during this period that a number of prominent Jewish banking dynasties were established—notably those of the Rothschilds and the Foulds. The rigid caste system which prevailed in most of the German states had barred the aristocracy from commerce and money-lending. With the collapse of the feudal restrictions during the Napoleonic era, the way was opened to the Jews as well as to many others to participate in the economic and political life of their country. In 1807, thirty out of fifty-two banks of Berlin were in Jewish hands. It was this fact that the Jew-baiters kept constantly in mind, altogether oblivious of the fact that in Prussia alone ninety-two percent of the Jewish population consisted of petty retail traders, peddlers, and beggars.

Among the most successful of Hamburg Jews was Heine's uncle, Solomon Heine—Samson's brother. He had begun life with practically nothing, but by 1816 he was governor of a bank, and one of the wealthiest men in town. True, as a Jew, he was ineligible to become a citizen of the free city of Hamburg. But he consoled himself for that disqualification when town councillors and even better men doffed their hats to him in the street, and were royally entertained at the luxurious villas he owned.

Betty Heine, whose dreams of a diplomatic and clerical career for Harry had gone down in ruins, now planned to make him a great banker. He was dispatched to a business school, and shortly thereafter he was apprenticed to a banking firm in Frankfurt. What a future his parents foresaw for a nephew of the great Solomon Heine! Hamburg became the magnet of their hopes and prayers. When the uncle beckoned, the nephew came to him, and was installed in a banking house, and not long thereafter provided with his own establishment, "Harry Heine & Co.", dealers in British manufactured goods. The firm did not prosper, and was liquidated in 1819. It became obvious that Heine was not suited for a business career. Perhaps he would be more successful at law. Uncle Solomon was willing to help, and in the summer of that year, Heine left Hamburg for the University of Bonn.

Emotionally he was never to leave Hamburg, no matter how far he was to move from that city. It was to remain forever the "castle of affronts," which held him in its grasp. The proud, dominating uncle, whom he admired, revered, hated, and feared, and against whose rock-ribbed strength of mind and fortune he was pitting his own more sensitive poetic genius and intellect, became almost symbolic of the world the poet wanted to conquer and dominate. Heine wished to be accepted in his own right—but instead, he was merely the needy son of an unsuccessful brother—and a would-be poet, to boot. Like all solid and substantial Philistines of Hamburg, Solomon

Heine too looked down on all artists as impractical dreamers for, like Philistines all over the world, he measured success by the gold standard. Solomon Heine was never able to understand why anyone who was capable of doing other things should ever trouble to write verses.

Solomon Heine had an eighteen-year-old daughter, a proud, spoiled, good-looking girl. Heine fell in love with her, with a violence that was to remain one of the major fixed points—and fixations—of his entire life. Like her father, Amalie was contemptuous of poetry, insensible to the arts, and indifferent to her poor but brilliant cousin, of whom great things might be expected once he settled down to a respectable career. In his eyes, she was the most desirable object in the world—she possessed beauty, wealth, and station—and he was henceforth to love and hate her, as he loved and hated his uncle. Neither father nor daughter accepted him at his own worth, and rejection by them became one of the most crucial psychological factors in his mental history. The bitter injury he suffered at the hands of Amalie he kept carefully concealed from even his best friends. Very rarely did he refer to it in his conversation or letters. He communicated it only in his poetry.

GERMAN UNIVERSITY LIFE AFTER THE NAPOLEONIC WARS was not in a flourishing state. At one time centers of nationalist revival, the universities were, after 1815, special objects of governmental suspicion. Student associations, the so-called Burschenschaften, were animated by strong anti-French and anti-Semitic feelings, and their gaze was fixed on the past, on the one-time "greatness of Germany" which they dreamt of resurrecting once more. Caste distinctions were finely drawn, and duelling and student rowdyism were the fashion.

However, the university at Bonn had preserved some of its earlier distinction. It had a brilliant faculty, especially in the fields in which Heine was interested, philosophy, literature, and history. Here A. W. von Schlegel, who with his brother, Friedrich, was one of the dioscuri of the Romantic movement in Germany, held court. Young Heine was impressed by him. For August Wilhelm Schlegel was not only the prophet of the "religion of art," as the Romantics conceived it, but he was also one of its ablest interpreters. Though no very original poet or dramatist in his own right, he was one of those indispensable stimuli to other poets—a penetrating critic of younger men's efforts and a formidable translator and interpreter of foreign literature. His version of Shakespeare was then already a classic. In addition, he had brought to the Germans a very sympathetic understanding of Italian, Spanish, and Oriental literature. Heine relished the older man's enthusiasms and interests. Schlegel was drawn to the lively and budding talents of the youth. He encouraged his early poetical efforts, called his attention to Byron's works, urged him to translate them, and impressed upon him the importance of form.

But Heine was not happy at Bonn—nor, was he, for that matter, ever to be happy in any of the other universities he attended. He was a Jew, he had little interest in the mystical Pan-Germanism of the fraternities, their offensive snobbery and their loud boastfulness which only concealed their inner poverty of thought and their frustrations. In addition, he was unwell, very much in love, and far from the girl he adored.

From Bonn he went on to Göttingen, and liked it there even less. He found the intellectual life of the university completely arid, the professors mediocre, and the aristocratic students insufferable. What was most depressing was the total absence of interest in German history and letters. In a student body of 1300, there were only nine who possessed sufficient interest to attend courses on the history of the German language. "Oh, Germany," he wrote at that time, "land of oaks and stupidity!" Yet he managed to write a number of poems, and began preparing them for publication. "The sausages and university professors" who, as he was to write later, made Göttingen famous, had not dampened his poetic ambitions. But his days at the university were numbered. He became involved in a silly duel with one of his fellow students, and though the affair was settled amicably, the university authorities, acting in this instance even more stupidly than university authorities have a right to, gave him a *consilium abeundi*—in student slang, his "walking papers."

HIS NEXT STOP WAS BERLIN. Before transferring there, he revisited his family. With them matters had been going from bad to worse. Samson Heine's business affairs had fallen on evil days as a result of the economic crisis following the wars, and the whole family had moved closer to Hamburg and the benefactions of Solomon Heine. The disgraced student found the home atmosphere depressing. "My father is in a bad mood, my mother suffers from a migraine, my sister has a cold, and both my brothers write bad poetry," he wrote in one of his letters. The poet was in none too happy a state himself. There were matters he could not divulge to his family. For example, the shock he had experienced on learning that his cousin Amalie was betrothed to Johann Friedländer. The wound rankled and festered. "The moment I came near Hamburg," he wrote to one of his friends, "it was as if all that I had thought and felt during the intervening years had vanished." He visited the house in which his beloved lived—like Almansor, a character in a play he was composing—and stood under her window. Concerning the other cause of his sorrow he could be even less communicative. It is only too likely that during his stay at Göttingen he had contracted a venereal disease and was already beginning to suffer those tortures which, at a much later date, were to bring him to his "mattress grave."

He was glad to leave. Berlin represented a pleasant change from Hamburg. Though the city itself was unattractive and without character, it was intellectually alive. Hegel was holding forth brilliantly at the university. In the Berlin salons, presided over by witty and charming ladies, mostly Jewish, one could meet the cream of Berlin's literary and artistic life. Mendelssohn's daughter, Henriette Herz, Sarah Levy, Elise von Hohenhausen, translator of Byron, and Rahel Varnhagen von Ense each ruled an intellectual domain. Rahel was then already in her fifties, a brilliant though not good-looking woman. A Jewess by birth, she had, like so many of her contemporaries, become thoroughly assimilated, had married a Christian, and with magnificent gusto and tact had gathered around her men like Alexander von Humboldt, the greatest of contemporary naturalists, Hegel, the mighty architect of philosophical systems, Ranke, the historian, and the poets Chamisso and Fouqué. Heine, already known for his poetry, was drawn into the magic circle, and fell under the sway of the charming *salonnière*.

Until her death she was to remain his guardian angel—an intellectual mother who guided, reproved, corrected, and encouraged the erratic young genius. Perhaps she understood him better than most of the other people he came in contact with. She, in turn, was attracted by this Byronic, wayward, slight and pale poet, dressed like a dandy, blond-haired, retiring, melancholy, and ironical. He was a Jew—already racked by "Judenschmerz"—seeking to understand his relation to his own people. She was a convert to Protestantism who had lost complete touch with Jews. He found the ghetto all around him. She innocently believed—she was to learn better toward the end of her life—that she had broken down the walls of the ghetto by entering the capacious bosom of the German Protestant church. She was not alone in that belief. In the first decade of the nineteenth century no less than one tenth of the German Jewish population had been converted either to Protestantism or to Catholicism—if not converted, at least baptized.

Among the unconverted Jews of Berlin, the desire to bring their coreligionists into the orbit of German culture and thought had produced the Society for Jewish Culture and Science. Founded two years before Heine's arrival in that city, it included the most brilliant of Berlin's Jewish intellectuals—Leopold Zunz, great Jewish historian and savant, Eduard Gans, distinguished legal philosopher and ardent Hegelian, Moses Moser, Ludwig Marcus, and many others. The Society was established to carry forward the liberating work of Moses Mendelssohn, to break down the walls of the ghetto, to raise the intellectual level of the Jewish community, to effect a marriage between traditional Judaism and modern scientific and philosophical systems—to modernize the Jew and to enlighten the Christian concerning the Jew. Its magic wand was the new historical method, which it applied to a reinterpretation of Jewish history and culture. Its goal was the emancipation of a disfranchised minority. It was a movement of intellectuals, with a profound faith in the power of the word. In the hothouses of their quixotic intellectualism they already saw blooming the full flower of the emancipation.

Heine, who was in search of some sort of group identification, joined the Society in 1822, and became its secretary as well as an instructor in its school. Keen as he was, it did not take him long to see the futility of the venture. He observed its isolation from the masses of the Jewish people—he saw how narrow and abstruse were its efforts to approach them. In Berlin, the Society could boast of only fifty members; in Hamburg, of no more than twenty. Rich Jews saw no need to support it—poor Jews knew nothing about it, and even if they could have read the learned dissertations which appeared in its short-lived magazine, they would not have understood them. Having failed to uncover the social and economic roots of discrimination (although the pogroms of 1819 were still vividly before all German Jews), the Society was doomed to failure. The remarkable scholarly achievements of his fellow-members, especially those of Zunz, Heine knew how to honor. But he was under no illusions about the spurious tolerance which seemed to prevail in the literary salons.

Given the proper occasion, that too would evaporate—along with the pipe-dreams of Jewish romantics.

Heine was a very keen observer. In Berlin he saw how the salons, the theaters, and the opera—not to mention the doings at the royal court—served as safety valves for popular feelings and unrest. While Hegel was electrifying crowded university halls with his oratory, and unfolding before astonished eyes the whole panorama of the Progress of Reason—which culminated in the absolutism of the Prussian state—the Berlin police were suppressing political discussions, persecuting Polish students for their anti-Russian agitation, taking careful note of Schleiermacher's lectures, and prohibiting the performance of Goethe's *Egmont* and Schiller's *William Tell*, and the ubiquitous censor was red-pencilling even the most innocent political remarks.

Heine was no orthodox believer. His early education, his eighteenth century reading and the lectures of Hegel had long given his religious faith its *coup de grâce*. But he was not one to accept that spurious substitute and fashionable affectation which then went under the name of "reform" Judaism. At one time a movement of enlightenment and emancipation, it now was nothing but veiled effort on the part of a well-to-do section of the Jewish population—the Jewish bourgeoisie—to merge with bourgeois Christianity through gradual obliteration of differences, such as those of religious service (substitution of German for the Hebrew prayers, introduction of organ-music, etc.), customs and dress. On a brief visit to Prussian Poland, Heine had had the occasion to observe the wretched conditions of both Poles and Jews in the Posen region. But he came away with a healthy respect for both of these national groups because they appeared to have preserved an inner dignity and strength of conviction he found lacking in their German counterparts. He published an essay on Poland which aroused dismay, because he dared to portray Germans faithfully, and because he "raised the Jews to the *tiers état* of Poland." Speaking of middle-class Jews of Berlin and Hamburg he knew so well, he was forced to admit: "We no longer have the strength to wear beards, to fast, to hate, and to suffer hatred."

Yet his contact with the Society for Jewish Culture and Science had very positive consequences for Heine. It deepened and broadened his understanding of Jewish problems and awakened in him a strong desire to become more thoroughly acquainted with Jewish history. It was to be the starting point for that literary preoccupation with Jewish subjects which was soon to find expression in *The Rabbi of Bacherach*. He had discovered that the greatest portion of the Jews were poor, disinherited, and humble. He had once tended to identify the rich Hamburg Jews with all Jews, and had failed to see that the characteristics they manifested were those of the social class to which they had risen—that the new finance aristocracy was the same the world over, that the new Philistinism was international.

THE FIRST PUBLISHED BOOK of Heine's poetry, *Poems by H. Heine*, appeared in Berlin in December 1821. It was a slim volume, containing a number of poems which had already appeared in magazines. It was unquestionably the work of a young man of talent; but certain small sections of it were unmistakably the work of a new genius.

Unknowingly, he was ushering in a new era in literature. Many years later, when he came to evaluate his own place in German letters, he wrote: "With me the old school of lyrical poetry comes to an end; with me the modern German lyric begins."

He was right. For he was, at one and the same time, the last of the great Romantics, and the first of the great moderns.

Romanticism in literature is a protean thing. It varies from place to place, and from time to time. There have been hundreds of attempts to define its character, and they have all failed simply because they regarded it as a single movement and tried to fix its nature outside the context of geography and history. The Romantic Movement in literature is the expression of the bourgeois revolutions of the eighteenth and the nineteenth centuries. It is the translation into the vivid language of poetry, music, and the pictorial arts of the struggle of the modern world for the emancipation of the middle classes, and is the artistic and fervent counterpart of the Declaration of Independence and the Declaration of the Rights of Man. It speaks in the name of humanity—because the liberating class is allied with and assisted by the more inarticulate lower classes and rallies them for the overthrow of feudal and absolutist prerogatives. But the bourgeois revolutions did not break out in all European countries at the same time. England led the way. Then France followed. Germany was far behind.

The character of literary and artistic movements is determined by their historical conditions. Hence it follows that the so-called "Romantic" schools—much as they may have in common—betray marked differences. In England, where the revolutions had already taken place and the bourgeoisie had already come into power, Romanticism was saturated with the spirit of freedom. Burns chanted "A man's a man for a' that," while young Wordsworth spoke of the bliss of being alive in the day of the French Revolution. Young Coleridge, William Hazlitt, and William Blake were similarly inspired. In France, which did not deliver its crushing blows to feudal absolutism until 1789—the struggle between the old and the new schools is much sharper, and the victory of the new school comes at a later date. But the latter, likewise, is filled with the great ideals of liberty and equality though it has its own plentiful crop of dreamers, nostalgics, and restless geniuses. The new voices in France are those of Victor Hugo, Lamartine, Gautier, Vigny, and George Sand. But once the bourgeoisie has triumphed, and through its victories more clearly reveals and even enlarges the fissures and cleavages in society, once the old hopes of "liberty, equality, and fraternity" for all of mankind fall very short of fulfillment, Romanticism enters upon an era of disenchantment and disintegration.

But where was Germany in the era of revolutions? Politically and economically backward, a conglomeration of rival states, feudal or semi-feudal in character, still suffering from the devastations of the Thirty Years' War—Germany was not to experience her bourgeois revolution for years to come. Her middle classes were only beginning to emerge on the historical scene. The fervor which the French Revolution inspired in her writers and thinkers, in men like Friedrich Schiller and the youthful Goethe, was quickly extinguished. The brilliant young men and women—and there were many of them—who sought to find expression in literature and art were hemmed in on all sides by the triviality and pettiness of provincial life; the oppressive hand of the monarchs and the nobility was felt everywhere; the six and thirty ruling fathers supervised all thoughts and activities of their subjects—but left them one great realm of freedom—that of the imagination. In fantasy, in the dream world of unreality, in sickliness, and in death many of the German Romantics found a free field in which to roam. The pathetic strivings and careers of such great talents as Novalis, Hölderlin, and Kleist (German Romanticism is full of early deaths, suicides, and insanity) are clear symptoms of the intensity of frustrations which prevailed. Revolt, instead of turning against the outside world, consumed itself within—and almost always died of passiveness and inertia. Is it an accident that the dream-world of the German Romantics often became the companion of darkness and obscurantism and medieval reaction, or that so many of them eventually became the pillars of either the religious or political *status quo*—like the brothers Schlegel, for example? Is it any wonder that those who advocated action and sought to change the world around them generally found their way into prison or exile?

The German Romantics made their finest contributions to literature in the lyric, the ballad, and the short story. The magnificent ballad collections of Herder and of Arnim and Brentano brought together the greatest treasures of popular poetry. Goethe himself had written simple ballads and lyrics—and men like Eichendorff, Uhland, and Wilhelm Müller followed in his steps.

Heine's first book of poems echoed many traditional strains. Dreams, death, the grave, the supernatural, all the faded paraphernalia of a dying romanticism, are to be found in it. Side by side with these, one suddenly comes upon such miracles as "The Two Grenadiers" and "Belshazzar," and the wonderful quatrains—sharp and gem-like —in which the poet's unhappy love finds an outlet. These are anticipations of the quintessential Heine in their revelation of poetic economy, dramatic and narrative gift, simple and vivid realism, and exquisite music.

The book was well received. Heine's royalties consisted of forty copies, a number of which he dispatched to other poets. Goethe never troubled to acknowledge the receipt of the volume.

By the time his second book appeared, in April 1823, Heine's poetical genius had grown considerably. *Tragedies, and a Lyrical Intermezzo* contains, in addition to two immature poetic plays, *Almansor* and *William Ratcliff*, his first perfect group of lyrics. These reveal the consummate artist. *Lyrical Intermezzo* is a cycle of love poems—a tiny novel in verse—which begins with the ecstatic and laconic "In May, the magic month of May," continues the story through longing and heartbreak—"On wings of song" and "A pine tree towers lonely"—in which dream and waking disenchantment alternate, and concludes with the fervent vow to end this sorrow and to bury "the evil old songs."

Great composers have set these poems to music on innumerable occasions. The world has taken them to its heart, and ever since they have become the folksongs of the people. For in them Heine uttered what many people felt and could understand easily, spoke in their speech, and what he transmuted into music and images became their music and their images. Gone is the ancient panoply of a dreary romanticism. This is the new poetry of lyrical realism, shaped to a perfection that conceals its artistry—the meticulous metrical structure, the fine chiselling of each line and stanza, the rounded completeness of the word. Here and there one experiences that "ironic shock"—the sudden transition from one emotional state to another, the twist which brings one up with a start, as if the poet were mocking his own sorrows, as if he were distrustful of his own feelings . . .

HEINE WAS NOW ALMOST TWENTY-SIX. He had produced a great work of art. He should have felt very happy. Instead, he was depressed, sick in heart and body, and at a loss as to what to do next. The idea of practising law seemed more distasteful than ever. He was haunted by the thought of leaving Germany and going to Paris.

Instead, he went back to Lüneburg, near Hamburg, where his family now lived. He was received without fanfare. "My mother," Heine wrote to his friend Moser, "read my tragedies and songs, but did not like them over-much, my sister can barely stand them, my brothers do not understand them, and my father hasn't even read them." Lüneburg was excruciatingly dull, and in July he went off to Hamburg, irresistibly drawn by the "lovely cradle of his sorrows." Amalie Heine was no longer there. She was married and lived on her husband's estate in Prussia. But the old woe burned afresh. "Hamburg, my Elysium and Tartarus—all in one!" he complained. "Place that I detest and love most of all, where horrible feelings torment me, and yet where I long to stay, and where I shall certainly often return in the future . . ."

He had a special gift for creating Elysium—as well as the less fortunate one of creating Tartarus. Amalie was gone. But Amalie's younger sister, Therese, had blossomed into a beautiful girl. She was now sixteen. It cannot have been merely her remarkable resemblance to her older sister that stirred the sick poet. With that fatal gift of unhappy repetition which is the lot of the sickly, Heine proceeded to "fall in love" once more. This "homecoming" was indeed a thing of bitterness and dread! Was he again to be doomed to love unhappily? Hamburg seemed no better than Lüneburg. The same tasteless humdrum pursuit of gold, the same contempt for the poet. Heine found scant consolation in returning contempt for contempt. He was still dependent on his rich uncle, who had agreed to finance the poet's studies for another period, but had not taken the trouble to conceal his feelings and who pointed to Heine's own fellows, now already successful businessmen, while he was still a mere student.

But neither uncle, nor Hamburg, nor a glum family, nor even a new love-affair kept him from his literary work. His play, *Almansor*, which had been produced in Brunswick, was hissed off the boards in a demonstration provoked by a drunken Jew-baiter. In January 1824, he was back at Göttingen. He immersed himself in the study of Roman law, but he was patently bored, and sought solace in the reading of Jewish history, and writing a story about the Rabbi of Bacherach. He was glad of any chance to break the monotony of his existence, and in the fall he set off on a trip to the Harz mountains. On the way, he stopped at Weimar and paid his respects to Goethe. For days, he had been preparing himself for the great moment, but when he was face to face with the Olympian, he lost his voice, and stammered sheer inanities.

On June 28, 1825 he formally went over to the Protestant faith, and the following month he received his degree. In August he returned to Hamburg with a doctor's diploma, a baptismal certificate, and a very heavy heart. The diploma and the certificate gave him the right to practise law. His heavy heart reproached him for his betrayal of his finest feelings. He despised converts—and himself not least of all. There was some measure of consolation in the knowledge that he had brought back from Göttingen precious manuscripts containing two prose works, *The Journey to the Harz* and the first section of *The Rabbi of Bacherach*, as well as a considerable number of new poems.

THOUGH HE WAS INWARDLY AT WAR WITH HIMSELF, revolted by his own renegacy which he was reluctant to rationalize, his genius matured and his creativeness expanded. Hamburg was no better than before. "I am now hated by both Christians and Jews," he wrote ironically. "I have become a true Christian—I now sponge on rich Jews." "I often get up at night and stand before a mirror and call myself all sorts of names." The greater the hostility of the outside world, the more intensely he felt the need to fulfill himself as an artist.

The publishing firm of Hoffmann and Campe of Hamburg was a most enterprising one. Julius Campe, its head, was a shrewd man who had made it his business to publish the works of authors who were either suspect or banned in the German states and hence in great demand. Among his writers he numbered Ludwig Börne, Gutzkow,

Dingelstedt, and Hoffmann von Fallersleben. To this list he was now to add Heine, in what was destined to be a life-long association.

It was under the imprint of Hoffmann and Campe that Heine's next book—the first volume of the *Travel Pictures*—appeared in May 1826. In addition to his first major prose work, *The Journey to the Harz*, it contained two new series of poems, *The Homecoming* (*Die Heimkehr*) and the first cycle of the *North Sea Poems*. Rarely had a publisher been so well favored by fortune. The book proved immediately successful.

With *The Journey to the Harz*, Heine established himself as a great German prose writer. Prose gave him an opportunity to be discursive, to write by association—to leap from one emotion to another, to be sentimental, reflective, impudent, and satirical at the same time, to combine simplicity with complexity—in short, to ramble mentally, as he was doing physically through the Harz region, and to give free rein to his rich fancy. Heine was thoroughly German—and what German did not relish wandering on foot through the country-side, sadly jubilant, awake and dreaming at the same time, idling in body here and there, while his soul roved freely all through the world? But Heine's was no mere sentimental travel diary. His was a poet's book, thumbing its nose shamelessly at the pedants of Göttingen, at the stupidities and pretentiousness of university life, at Philistinism, at the rowdy student fraternities, and the little youngsters who were already aping the pedantries of their elders. His was a poet's book which looked to the mountains and pastures for inspiration—and to shepherds, miners, and country-folk for companionship. Prose alternates with verse—just as one mood follows another: seriousness and triviality; impudence and humility. But throughout—as in all great humor—there is the undertone of earnestness, for Heine was already, as in the lovely *Mountain Idyll*, proclaiming himself the "Knight of the Holy Ghost" who was battling for the equality and happiness of mankind.

So much for *The Journey to the Harz*. To poetry also, Heine was bringing fresh poetic materials. He had read about the ocean in Byron's works, but he had not fully appreciated its grandeur and power until he came upon the North Sea himself. "The sea is my true element," he wrote to Varnhagen von Ense. He felt like those Greek legionnaires of whom Xenophon tells, who in their retreat from Persia came once more upon the friendly Greek waters, and cried, "Thalatta, thalatta!" To give voice to his exultation, he devised a new poetic form, an unrhymed free verse, which could render the surge and thunder of the ocean and express the riot of his own heart, its laughter, doubts and fear.

In the traditional quatrains of *The Homecoming* he was more subdued, singing again of love's sorrow—was it Therese he was mourning now?—modulating and varying the theme with exquisite mastery. For his sister Charlotte he wrote the delightful reminiscence of their childhood; for his friend Count Breza the jovial poem, "I dreamed: I am the dear Lord God"; for himself and his love, "Beside the fisherman's cottage," and "You lovely fishermaiden"; for an unknown girl, "You're lovely as a flower"; and for the whole world, the most famous of all his poems, "The Loreley."

This was to be a sort of last testament to a lost love. From now on, he proposed to turn to new themes and from his restored heart he promised to write songs glorifying a new spring.

"I HEAR THAT MY *Travel Pictures* ARE THE TALK OF GERMANY," he wrote to one of his friends shortly after the appearance of the book. Spurred on by its enthusiastic reception, he set to work on a sequel, which, he predicted, would be "something remarkable, not because of its idle gossip, but because it treats of world-affairs. . . . Napoleon and the French Revolution are in it—in life size."

Heine was as good as his word. The new book of travel sketches was not a tame replica of *The Journey to the Harz*, as many hoped it would be. No, the new book was to be a challenge to the German people. Poor, dreamy-eyed Germany was to be roused from her sweet slumber, that contented, quiet slumber, which was only disturbed from time to time by the rattling of prisoners' chains, the suppressed rumblings of discontent, and the clatter of the censor's shears. For Heine was about to sing a paean of praise to an idea—a great idea—the very greatest idea, it seemed to him, the world had seen—the idea of Napoleon. He was to embody that idea in the person of a little French drummer, Le Grand. Hence the title of his book, *Ideas—Book Le Grand*. In a day of humiliation and depression, it was to glorify "*les jours de gloire!*"—the heroic glory of France. It was a bold thing to do—to try to rouse anti-French Germans from their dreams of the past into reality by evoking pictures of French heroism. We Germans, Heine says in effect, compose heroic epics; the French live them. We possess a fervent imagination, and the French very little of one. "That is perhaps the reason the good Lord has helped them out in another fashion; all they need to do is to recount faithfully what they have seen and done in the last thirty years and they have a literature of experience such as no other nation and no other age has produced."

In extolling Napoleon, Heine was merely reflecting the general feeling of hundreds of writers of the period. He himself was later to revise and moderate his judgment—always honoring the genius of the man of action, though he was to deplore the despotism of the world-conqueror—but at this time he saw in Napoleon the man who had swung himself aloft by his genius, and through the mighty concurrence of a historical epoch and his own personality had become the conqueror of kings, ruler of half the world, and destroyer of the rotting bastions of a feudal Middle Age.

But there was much more in these new travel pictures than hosannas to Napoleon. There were charming stories of Heine's childhood and youth, his first sight of the French and of Napoleon, and the remarkable French drummer. There were reflections on literature and people, thrown together helter-skelter—an intellectual and sentimental journey in the manner of Sterne, with political and philosophical reflections which would have startled that Englishman. This was a book which would not pass unnoticed. As if in anticipation of the storm he expected would break, Heine sailed for England on the eve of its publication.

His uncle Solomon had generously provided him with a draft for four hundred pounds, part of it for expenses; the whole amount, however, was intended as a letter of introduction for the nephew of the great banker. That nephew proceeded to live like a banker, and in the course of a few months ran through more than half of the money. In addition to taking advantage of the amenities of the land, Heine observed it very closely. He disliked England, he disliked London— he was repelled by the fever of activity, the mercantile spirit which seemed to prevail, the misery and poverty he saw all around him. Here were the fruits of England's commercial and industrial triumphs. He observed the rigorous caste system, which was kept alive there, though without the ostentation and brashness of the continental nobility. And he saw Wellington, the little man who had vanquished Napoleon the Great.

HE RETURNED TO HAMBURG IN SEPTEMBER 1827. His uncle fumed at his extravagance. His second volume of *Travel Pictures* was a *succès de scandale.* Immediately on its appearance it had been prohibited in the Rhineland, Austria, and Hanover. He saw Amalie once more. He learned that Therese was about to be engaged to a Dr. Halle. "The world is stupid and insipid and disagreeable," he wrote to Varnhagen, "and reeks of faded violets." Not even the publication of his collected poems, *The Book of Songs,* could raise his spirits.

He was eager to be gone, and when the publisher Cotta offered him the joint-editorship of the *Political Annals,* which was appearing in Munich, Heine eagerly accepted. Soon, however, he grew weary of his job, the climate of Munich did not agree with him, and the high expectations he had nurtured of obtaining court appointment or a university post had failed to materialize. He had not been too squeamish about the methods he employed. He flattered and compromised—he, the sworn foe of the aristocracy—and in turn, he was plagued by a cabal of "enemies and intriguing priests." He was happy to report that the government thought him "not so bad." But he got nowhere. In the summer of 1828 he left for Italy. Like hundreds of other pilgrims, he set foot on Italian soil with reverence. He visited Milan, Genoa, Florence, Verona, and, of course, Marengo, and he spent considerable time in Lucca. His mind was touched and saddened by the ruins of ancient greatness—they appealed to him because he felt that he too was a ruin. But living people interested him much more, and it was about them that he was to write in his next *Travel Pictures.*

While he was in Venice he received news of his father's grave illness. He hastened home. In Würzburg he learned that Samson Heine had died on December 2.

HE WAS THIRTY-ONE YEARS OLD—and still a bird of passage. The restless wanderer longed for rest—yet he was incapable of achieving it, at least in Germany. He seemed to be a barometer not only of his own internal pressures but of those of Europe as well. He was at work on the third volume of the *Travel Pictures* and looked back with nostalgia on his Italian trip. "Alas," he wrote to Friederike Robert, "I am sick and wretched, and as if in self-mockery, I am now writing about one of the most splendid periods of my life, of a time when, drunk with pride and happy love, I exulted on the mountain-tops of the Apennines and dreamed of wild, great deeds which would resound in every corner of the earth, even to the farthest isles, where the sailor would speak of me in the evening by the fireside. Now you see how tame I've become since my father's death. All I desire now is to be like a little kitten on some far-off island, to sit by a warm hearth and listen to stories of great deeds."

His tensions found release in work. Into his books of Italian and English travel sketches he was writing his political testament—his last words on German soil. They were to be his summing up. He had charted his course, and uncertain and haphazard as it might seem to other eyes, it began to show direction and goal. His understanding of his times had matured profoundly. He was now ready to appraise the European situation with self-assurance. He had stood on the battle-field of Marengo, but he no longer saw Napoleon with the eyes of his youth. Awe-inspiring as the figure might seem, it was that of a despot, the last of world conquerors. History was entering upon a new order of upheavals, and these were the consequences not of national ambitions but of new alignments—of "parties." Two vast armies were massing in Europe—cutting across national lines—those of the old order and of the new. "Every age has its own task," he wrote in the *English Fragments*. "And what is the great task of our day? It is emancipation. Not simply the emancipation of the Irish, the Greeks, the Frankfurt Jews, the West Indian blacks, and all such oppressed peoples, but the emancipation of the whole world, and especially of Europe, which has now come of age and is tearing herself loose from the apron-strings of the privileged classes, the aristocracy." Feudalism had made its valuable contributions to history, he admitted; but today it was an anachronism, "an obstacle which revolts all civilized minds." With unparalleled imaginative sweep he traced the movements of emancipation in the history of the world. Those revolutions for the equality of mankind were begun by Christ—continued during the Reformation by the Peasants' Revolts, and proudly advanced by the glorious French in the eighteenth century. That revolution was still incomplete.

"Freedom," he proclaimed, "is a new religion, the religion of our age. If Christ is no longer the God of this religion, he is, at least, one of its high priests; and his name sheds comforting beams into the hearts of his young disciples. The French are the chosen people of this new religion. In their language are written its first gospels and dogmas. Paris is the New Jerusalem, and the Rhine is the Jordan which divides the land of freedom from the country of the Philistines."

As a farewell, he was also settling accounts with his personal enemies—especially the poet, Count Platen. He had never intended to insert an attack on him in the *Travel Pictures*, where it now seems altogether out of place, but the provocations were such as his self-respect could no longer ignore. Count Platen was a poet of the Munich circle—a man of talent with a penchant for verses modelled on pseudo-Oriental and pseudo-Greek themes. He inclined—to put it mildly—toward paganism, especially in his worship of beautiful boys. In the first volume of the *Travel Pictures* Heine had included some verses by Karl Immermann which poked fun at Platen's Orientalism. Platen savagely retorted in a play, *The Romantic Oedipus*, in which he set himself the task of chastising both Heine and Immermann. Platen's satirical comedy was a vulgar attack on Heine's Jewish ancestry, his baptism, and his "garlic smell." Platen had underestimated his adversary. Heine was provoked, and with all the weapons of invective at his command—and they were devastating weapons—he struck back and annihilated his foolhardy opponent, along with all his Munich coadjutors. Heine's German readers were appalled at this vehemence directed against an aristocrat and a poet of standing. It is hard today to agree with them. Platen had touched Heine where he was most sensitive. He had attacked him as a Jew.

IN JUNE 1830 HE WAS IN HELIGOLAND ON THE NORTH SEA. He was tired and listless, torn by the conflicts within him, by hope and despair, love and hatred, longing for rest and need for action. Where was he to go? Italy lay prostrate under the Austrian heel. England was a huge market-place of traders and hagglers. America was an equalitarian Tartarus, in which, however, millions of Negroes were branded with the mark of Cain. France was languishing under a restored Bourbon tyranny. As if to remove himself from the ugly present, he immersed himself in the history of the French Revolution and in the Bible.

Then suddenly came the glad tidings. In July the people of Paris had risen up against Charles X and driven him from the throne. Heine knew little of the details of the revolution, nor of the events which followed. All he heard was that the citizens of Paris had erected barricades and had fought the Bourbon monarchy and overthrown it. The revolution he had longed for had at last come! Even in far-off Heligoland it seemed as if a new day had dawned. A local fisherman said, "The poor have won." And the poet exclaimed, "Lafayette, the tricolor, the Marseillaise!" Gone was the torpor which had numbed his faculties. Gone was all despair. He knew what to do. "I am the son of the Revolution and I take up the charmed weapons upon which my mother has breathed her magic blessing." He thought that all people in Europe would understand the meaning of the July days. Perhaps the Germans, too, would turn their oak-trees into barricades for the liberation of the human spirit! Perhaps he himself was no Don Quixote, dreaming idle dreams. "The Gallic cock has crowed for a second'time," he cried to his countrymen. It seemed to him as if Germans were beginning to rouse themselves from their metaphysical dreams. Perhaps their philosophical cycle was now completed, and they were ready to embark on their political revolution?

Anxiously he waited. Europe was on fire. In the winter of 1830 the Poles rose up against Czar Nicholas I. Belgium proclaimed her independence of Holland. There were rumblings in Aix, in Cologne. Charles of Brunswick was driven from the throne. In many localities the uprising took curious and disturbing forms. Thus, for example, in Hamburg, the rage of the populace was directed against the Jews.

Paralyzed for a moment, the forces of reaction began bestirring themselves very soon. The Polish uprising was crushed in 1831. The sporadic upsurges in the German states were quickly quelled.

The liberals were again in retreat. Heine could now read the writing on the wall, but he did what he was to do so often in times of great crisis—he wrote a new call to arms. This took the form of a preface to a pamphlet, "Kahldorf on the Nobility." He knew what he was about and what risks he was running. "I am full of evil omens," he confessed to Varnhagen. His days in his homeland were numbered. In April 1831 he left Germany. On the first of May he crossed the Rhine.

"He was a fine man of thirty-five or thirty-six years, with every appearance of robust health; one would have said a German Apollo, to see his high white forehead, pure as a marble table, which was shadowed with great masses of brown hair. His blue eyes sparkled with light and inspiration; his round, full cheeks, graceful in contour, were not of the tottering romantic lividness so fashionable at that date . . . A slight pagan *embonpoint*, which was expiated later on by a truly Christian emaciation, rounded the lines of his form. He wore neither beard, nor moustache, nor whiskers; he did not smoke nor drink beer, and, like Goethe, even had a horror of these things."

That was the way Heine appeared to the poet Théophile Gautier shortly after his arrival in Paris.

The "German Apollo" loved Paris. For Paris was not a city—it was a civilization. It was the nerve center of Europe—the great electric power-house which sent out political and intellectual currents throughout the world. Heine wandered through the streets as if under constant enchantment. "Paris, the singing, the springing," seemed like a new life after the slow death of Hamburg and Lüneburg, and the dry, sand-like pedantry and hair-splitting of Berlin. In its streets had been fought the great political and cultural battles of the world. Every nook and alley was replete with history. But Paris was not a monument to a dead past—Paris was a living, pulsing city, and Parisians were alive, gay, witty,—and so very polite! Paris was one great salon where one could meet the great writers and thinkers of France— Victor Hugo, Alfred de Vigny, Gautier, George Sand, Honoré de Balzac, Alfred de Musset, Daumier, Berlioz and Meyerbeer.

Paris was the political workshop of Europe. In its smithies had been wrought the great liberating words and deeds of revolution. Only recently the French had driven out a Bourbon who had sought to throttle them with a regime of resurrected émigrés and priests, and had tried to stifle all opposition by suppression of the press and a severe modification of the electoral laws. Charles X went, and Louis Philippe of the house of Orléans came in. In place of nobility and clergy, the financial bourgeoisie was now in power, and its symbol, Louis Philippe, the "citizen king", paraded the streets with his citizen hat and umbrella, and shook hands with all other citizens of Paris. The great new day of glory, it was true, had not yet been ushered in; as a matter of fact, the workers of France who had fought and shed their blood in the revolution were not yet allowed to vote, and out of a total French population of thirty millions, only about 200,000 could go to the polls.

The great heart of the French Revolution which was named Paris found a place for many exiles from less fortunate lands, especially Germany, and Heine was welcomed with open arms. Like Ulysses, he became a "part of all that he met." He was caught up in the whirl of Parisian life. He was not merely a German man of letters. He was in Paris precisely because he was also a political thinker. And what better place than Paris to explore all the various manifestations of political thought?

While he was still in Hamburg, meditating departure, he had come across the program of the Saint-Simonians and had been greatly attracted by it. In fact, he had already then fancied himself a prospective member of the cult. Here in Paris, in the Salle Taitbout, he had occasion to participate in the fiery discussions of that group. The master and founder of the new religion, Claude Henri de Rouvroy, Count de Saint-Simon, had been dead for six years. A legendary figure, such as not even the most imaginative novelist could have invented, Saint-Simon had been in turn heir to a princely fortune, pauper, salesman, merchant, adventurer, engineer, scholar, soldier in the American Revolutionary armies—and builder of new worlds. Like his famous contemporaries, Charles Fourier and the English manufacturer, Robert Owen, he was deeply moved by the lot of "the most numerous and poorest class in society"—"*la classe la plus nombreuse et la plus pauvre*"—whose hopes for a better world appeared to have miscarried when the triumphant property-owning middle classes shattered a decaying feudal regime. Those lower classes of society were too weak and too poorly organized to challenge the dominance of the new masters, for capitalist production was still very immature. Undaunted by neglect and poverty, Saint-Simon set about providing correctives for the injustices he saw about him, and produced plan after plan for the amelioration of society. He wished to found what he called a "physico-political science." He identified the moral and physical well-being of man. He combined the passionate faith of the eighteenth century encyclopedists with what was for his time a penetrating understanding of the structure of society. In his eyes, the French Revolution was not merely a struggle that involved the nobility and the bourgeoisie, but the propertyless lower classes as well. The victory of the propertied classes had produced a society in which men were now divided into workers and idlers. "All men should work," Saint-Simon proclaimed. Among the workers he included not only artisans and proletarians, but manufacturers, merchants, and bankers. Science and industry could provide the solution for the distresses of mankind, and leadership should be placed in the hands of scholars, manufacturers, and bankers. Politics was merely the science of production. The "golden age" of mankind was not to be sought in the past but in the future. That future "belongs to us." Religion had the function of helping man to achieve happiness through work and well-being here on earth. The watchwords of the new century were to be the trinity of Love, Wisdom, and Power, or Religion, Science, and Industry.

With that in view, Saint-Simon addressed fervent words to the ruling princes of Europe. "Princes: Harken to the voice of God who speaks to you through me. Be good Christians once more. Cease thinking that your hired armies, your nobles, your heretical clergy and your corrupt judges are your mainstays. United in the name of Christianity, learn to fulfill all the duties which she imposes on the powerful. Recall that she commands you to use all your energies to increase as quickly as possible the social well-being of the poor."

The notion that the princes and rulers of the world—including those newly anointed ones, the manufacturers and bankers—would unite to achieve the well-being of mankind and once and for all remove poverty from the face of the earth was touching. That somehow the benefactions of the dominant powers would rain down on those below was the naive faith of many of the Utopian socialists. Saint-Simon did not live long enough to see the class which was most numerous and most dispossessed of worldly goods grow to sufficient strength to wrest some measure of happiness and well-being through its own efforts.

Inspired by the doctrines of the new religion which proclaimed the unity of flesh and spirit, challenged the despotism of the aristocracy and the clergy, and wished to assure the benefits of work to all mankind, Heine attended the meetings of the Saint-Simonians frequently, and no doubt was struck by the contrast between the ideals debated there—already the mantle of the first prophet was being fought over by his succession—and the world outside. While the Saint-Simonians argued and the Fourierists fulminated—the princes of the stock-exchange who had brought Louis Philippe into power speculated and enriched themselves, at the expense of a poorly industrialized country, consisting in the main of small manufacturers, artisans, shopkeepers and farmers. Louis Philippe steered the ship of state carefully, trimming the sails whenever necessary. "*Jamais une position nette*," Metternich said of him. He was an opportunist, the king of the middle course, of the so-called "*juste-milieu*." (Heine said that he was also the king of the "juste-millionaires.") And his two leading statesmen, Adolphe Thiers and François Guizot, two sides of the same coin— one a "constitutional monarchist," the other a "legitimist"—were both minions of the *status quo*, and kept a watchful eye on the people below. Louis Philippe was certainly worth the eighteen million francs he received each year, not only to the French financiers, but to all the ruling houses of Europe.

These matters did not escape Heine's observant eyes. He rendered a vivid account of them to his German readers in Cotta's *Allgemeine Zeitung*. Prudence and a rigid censorship made for some discreet omissions or toning down—for Metternich's agents were active in Paris and not without influence there. By turns Heine was attracted and ·repelled by Louis Philippe. He saw in the king a tight-rope walker. He watched with keen interest the manipulations on the stock-exchanges, he noted the peculiar responses of their quotations to internal and external affairs, and began to understand where the true masters of France and her King resided. He sensed the rumblings that went on underneath the surface of the *juste-milieu,* which seemed so calm, so tranquil. He attended the meetings not only of the Saint-Simonians, but also of other socialist societies, and he listened very carefully. He met many of their most prominent leaders, men like Blanqui—whose oratory and sincerity impressed him,—Pierre Leroux, Louis Blanc. He was on intimate footing with Prosper Enfantin and Michel Chevalier, leading Saint-Simonians. He described the ominous little upsurges—occasioned now by the cholera, now by the funeral of some important political figure—which were symptomatic of the unrest of the Paris population.

He attended concerts, art exhibitions, and the theatre. He strolled on the boulevards, and observed men and women, especially the latter. He was a welcome visitor in the literary salons, particularly that of the Princess Belgioioso—that attractive and fabulous blue-stocking in whose life the sublime and the ridiculous merged fantastically. A generous patroness, herself an exile from Italy, she interceded with Thiers, and obtained for Heine a government stipend of 4800 francs a year, a fact which came to light only in 1848, not without unpleasant consequences for the poet.

HE NEVER LOST TOUCH WITH GERMANY. He could not have, even if he had wanted to, for there were at that time almost 80,000 Germans in Paris, a great number of them political exiles. Among these were ardent republicans. The most consistently militant of these was Ludwig Börne, who was considerably older than Heine, and like him, a converted Jew and a political rebel. The Germans in exile naturally looked to Heine for support, but he, who rarely failed to compromise himself in his writings, was loath to attach himself to parties. Though he was in sympathy with the Saint-Simonians, he never became one of them. As for the republicans, Heine thought them too radical, prosaic, and impractical. They, on their side, naturally resented what appeared to them to be equivocation. Heine was forever opening himself to this sort of attack. His insights were frequently profounder than his actions—and his actions sometimes lagged behind his thoughts. He was a declared enemy of the *status quo*, in disfavor with the political authorities of the German states, a Saint-Simonian at heart; yet he preferred to adhere to a romantic conception of monarchism. Inconsistencies such as this pervaded his whole life. They gave occasion for gossip, some of it very unsavory, and most of it unjustified. How unjustified, Heine was to prove when the occasion demanded.

The censorship had been harrying him and his publisher, Campe, for a long time. Not even the formidable Cotta was immune from it. In response to a courteous but firm warning from Gentz, a henchman of Metternich's, Heine's journalistic contributions to the *Allgemeine Zeitung* were terminated.

On May 27, 1832, 25,000 men and women gathered at Hambach to celebrate the anniversary of the winning of the Bavarian constitution. The speeches were fiery, though the demands raised were moderate: "one Germany," political reforms, support of Polish independence. Side by side with the black, red and gold, fluttered the banners of France and Poland. Heine and Börne had been invited to participate, but only the latter was present. Fearful of another July revolution, the Federal Diet immediately struck back. On June 18, it announced that in every case its authority superseded that of the individual state members. It imposed an even more rigid censorship, arrested Dr. Wirth and Siebenpfeiffer, who had participated in the Hambach festival, and suppressed their journals.

Though he had openly expressed his opposition to the German republicans, Heine did not leave them in the lurch. His own correspondence had been mutilated by the censorship, and he decided now on publishing an ungarbled version of his preface to the volume of *French Affairs*, in both French and German. It was his *"J'accuse,"* launched against Austria, and even more forcefully against Prussia. His pen dipped in the most corrosive acid of brilliant invective and irony, he laid bare the hypocrisy of Prussia and her King, Frederick William III, who had so often perjured himself before the very subjects who had rescued him from Napoleon and whom he was now generously requiting with the heavy Prussian bludgeon. He excoriated the equanimity of the Germans, who like the "great fool" were only too willing to cringe and cower. "I took no part in their follies," he said, speaking of the republicans, "but I shall always share their misfortunes." He made an irrevocable vow: "I will not go back to my native land so long as a single one of these noble fugitives, who could not listen to reason because enthusiasm carried them away, languishes miserably in a foreign land." Beware, he warns the monarch, beware of the great "German fool." Some day he may rise and crush you. . . .

That was his answer to the autocrats, Junkers, and ignoble kings. That was his answer to critics who had called him a time-server. He urged Campe to publish the preface in its entirety, without mutilations: "Just because the cause of liberalism is in such a bad way these days, everything possible must be done for its sake. I know that the doors of Germany will be closed to me so long as I live, should my preface appear. But it *must* appear."

That was to be the pattern of his life henceforth. Whenever he thought he could "quietly slip back into the realm of poetry," something horrible would occur to rouse him and lash him right back into the arena of conflict and controversy. Now it was the sight of German emigrants on their way to Algeria—good, solid Suabian peasants who had never harmed anyone and yet had been driven from their land by the unsupportable oppressions at home—now it was another story of persecution in Germany.

A group of writers, called "Young Germany," whose program, if program it may be called, professed a mild kind of Saint-Simonianism and an aesthetic which asked for a closer tie between literature and the problems of the day, soon fell foul of the authorities. The leaders of the school were Ludolf Wienbarg, Theodore Mundt, Heinrich Laube, and Karl Gutzkow. Their radicalism was of a very vague kind, more emotional than political. A spiteful enemy of theirs, the critic Wolfgang Menzel—once a friend of theirs and Heine's—launched a vicious attack on them, charging them with being pro-French, pro-Jewish, immoral and indecent. On December 10, 1833, the Federal Diet promulgated its now infamous decree "against the wicked, anti-Christian, blasphemous literature that wantonly treads all morality, modesty, and decency under foot." It explicitly banned the works of the "Young Germans", both past and future, and forbade their publication and their circulation. Heine was included in the proscription. Börne, whose name had been omitted through an oversight, was later added to the list. The authors who were then in Germany were prosecuted; some fled, some were imprisoned, some recanted.

From Paris, Heine wrote a defense of his literary colleagues. In *The Informer*, which he aimed at Menzel, he defended the patriotism and morality of "Young Germany," and contrasted these unfavorably with Menzel's. He himself had been called anti-German and Francophile. The cry had been raised again when he published two of his most important critical prose works, *The Romantic School* and *Religion and Philosophy in Germany*. The edict of the Diet was unquestionably intended to cut him off completely from his German readers. In his own equivocal fashion—perhaps with tongue in cheek —he addressed a humble plea to the Federal Diet, protesting his patriotism and morality.

The Romantic School AND *Religion and Philosophy in Germany* appeared originally in French and were designed to acquaint Frenchmen with the intellectual life of Germany. But the books had an even higher purpose—to recapitulate the achievements of German literature and philosophy and to formulate a program for the future.

Though written in a sprightly vein, they are serious works nonetheless. Read today, in the light of recent historical events, they strike one as amazingly keen appraisals of men and ideas. For Heine was studying these not with the abstracted air of some *Privatdozent*, who writes of literature and philosophy as if they existed in worlds apart from our own, but as manifestations of life within the framework of history, and as reflections of "social" meaning.

His own standpoint was that of Saint-Simon, a believer in progress. "I believe in progress. I believe that mankind is destined for happiness, and I have a better opinion of the deity than those pious souls who imagine that He created man only for suffering. Yes, here on earth I would establish by means of the blessings of free political and industrial institutions that beatific state which according to the opinions of the pious will be realized only on the Day of Judgment— and in Heaven."

He pleads for a "rehabilitation of the material"—not as something opposed to spirituality, but as the greatest manifestation of spirituality. The schism brought into the world by the Judaeo-Christian ideal— the schism of flesh and spirit—was now to be healed by a third testament, which he calls "the new pantheism." Hence he attacks the glorification of the Middle Ages—Catholic feudalism, with its chivalry, its hierarchies, and its corporations—as a futile attempt to revive a dead corpse. He does not deny the historical contributions of feudalism in its own day. But today, we must "vindicate the delights of this world, this beautiful garden of the Lord—our inalienable patrimony." "Bread," he wrote, paraphrasing a saying of St. Just's, "is the divine right of man."

The German Romantic School was saturated with the spirit of medievalism—the "Christian-Pan-German" outlook. Brilliantly Heine exhibits the historical conditions which made the soil for such views favorable. The country was in the profoundest depths of humiliation. Its kings lay humbled at the feet of Napoleon. The present was ugly. But the past appeared beautiful. Especially the past that revealed a united Germany—a Holy Roman Empire—powerful and whole. That German past was a useful magic formula with which to rouse Germans from their slumber and inspire them to throw off the yoke of the French conqueror. Once that had taken place, the leaders of the Romantic School became the upholders of the restoration, the apostles of reaction, clothing it in the garb of medieval romance, giving the dead corpse the appearance of life. One by one they found their way into the receptive arms of obscurantism. The heaven-stormers who had so vehemently proclaimed the freedom of the heart now spoke the language of submissiveness. Such was the history of Tieck, Werner, Adam Müller, the Schlegels, Arnim, Brentano. Those who did not follow them, men like Jean Paul or Uhland, were silent or in exile. Thus had the Romantic worship of sickness, death, medievalism, and anarchic love run its full cycle.

But the "poetry of life is greater than the poetry of death," Heine insisted. Hence even Goethe, whom the Romantics rejected because of his paganism and his lack of national feeling, is censured because of his Olympian aloofness. Poetry which does not lead to action is sterile.

No different was the course of German philosophy as Heine traces it. That too had run its full gamut—from the time of Luther, through Spinoza, Mendelssohn, and Lessing, "the continuer of Luther," culminating in the Robespierre of philosophy, Immanuel Kant. It spoke the language of freedom and was the ally of reason. But now the great philosophers too had gone over to the camp of reaction. In Berlin Hegel was justifying the Prussian state, in Munich Schelling was preaching the glories of medievalism.

German philosophy was no longer that finely spun web of abstract, aerial arguments which honestly sought to test the basis of knowledge and experience. German philosophy was a serious thing—something for Frenchmen to treat with gravity. Heine warns the French not to minimize its implications, not to rest content with the traditional picture of Germans as idle dreamers who never act. In words pregnant with prophecy he sketches the future, when those indefatigable weavers of philosophical systems would turn from revolutions in thought to revolutions in life, and begin translating ideas into deeds. "Remain on your guard," he adjures the French. "Always be armed!"

"Despite your present Romanticism, you are really classicists at heart, and you know Olympus well. Among the naked gods and goddesses who there rejoice over nectar and ambrosia, you may see one immortal who even amidst all this festive gaiety always wears a coat of mail and bears a helmet on her head and a spear in hand. It is the Goddess of Wisdom."

In 1834, Heine met Mathilde. Her real name was Crescentia Eugénie Mirat. She was nineteen, and he thirty-seven. She had come from the country to work in her aunt's glove and shoe shop in the Passage Choiseul. Bright, gay, light-hearted, temperamental, still excited by the wonders of Paris, she caught the fancy and heart of the world-famous poet, who was at home in the most fashionable and intellectual salons, who associated with the great men and women of politics, literature and finance—the strange German poet, who for some reason had been seeking out his loves in the streets of Paris. She had never heard of Henri Heine, of whom thousands of people spoke with respect and admiration. In her eyes he was a charming young man who wanted her. To him she was the pretty Parisian child, delightful to love and fondle.

"Have you ever seen a real Parisian grisette?" he wrote to a friend. "Frank, sprightly, always cheerful, faithful and true? You must not read your German ideas into my picture, otherwise you will soil it. Mathilde is not a passionate creature; but neither is she sentimental. She is really a good girl. Not an innamorata in the lyrical style, but such a friend as only a Frenchwoman can be."

Gossips of the academic and non-academic variety have made much of this relationship between Germany's greatest lyric poet and an ignorant Paris girl, and their estimates of Mathilde have not always been flattering. They have tended to forget that the marriage—for a marriage it was, though it was not formalized until seven years later—lasted through more than twenty years, until the poet's death—that it survived the trials of temperamental and intellectual differences, the inconstancies of the poet, and the ordeal of the "mattress grave."

He loved her not as one loves a mature woman—completely—but as a child-wife. His emotional insecurities—which could not be totally satisfied by the cursory amours of the Paris boulevards, the real or imagined Hortenses, Clarissas, Kittys and Katharinas—required that he *possess*, but even his possession of Mathilde was incomplete. He was always unsure of her, because he was always unsure of himself. He was still the rejected lover of Amalie, of Therese, perhaps even of the Princess Belgioioso—he was always in dread of being rejected.

She gave him as much as she received. She bore with his moods, his jealousies, his waywardness—he bore with her extravagance and flightiness. In the physical relation they found partial satisfaction for emotional incompleteness. She was his "song of songs"—his "wife and child"—and as she chattered, sang, or scolded, and she did all of these with gusto, he listened with delight and amazement. She lived for the day and the pleasures thereof, and made the most of an imperfect world. She did not read his poems, and she probably did not understand what he meant when he referred to her as the body, and to himself as the soul. If he was the soul, he was always fleeing and returning to the physical frame. Like his own Tannhäuser, he was always the thrall of Venus.

LUDWIG BÖRNE DIED IN 1837.
It is sad to reflect that the staunchest champion of German republicanism, and Heine, the most brilliant of German literary radicals, rarely saw eye to eye on political matters. Together, they would have constituted a formidable expression of German liberal opinion abroad. As it was, their open and concealed feuds constitute an unpleasant chapter in the history of German liberalism. In his relations with Börne, Heine revealed himself as less generous than might have been expected of a professed foe of autocracy.

Three years after Börne's death, Heine published a little book on him which roused a storm of resentment, culminating in a slightly ridiculous affair of honor.

The immediate cause of Heine's bitter attack was the unfavorable reference to him which Börne had made in his *Letters from Paris*. Ludwig Börne's career had paralleled that of Heine in many respects. He was a Jew, who had lived in Frankfurt, and he had gone through all the vicissitudes of the Jews during the period of the Emancipation and the reaction. He had lost a small government post, his pension had been reduced, and he had finally turned Protestant. He was one of the most valiant and clear-sighted of dramatic critics, at a time when neither the theater nor theatrical criticism was held in great esteem. He brought to his judgments a keen social conscience, and one of his most famous reviews had attacked anti-Semitism on the German stage. He fell in love with Jeannette Wohl, a very gifted woman who was then separated from her husband. Under the pressure of reaction at home, and subsequent to the Carlsbad Resolutions, he grew more and more pronouncedly militant, and his visits to France strengthened his liberal convictions. He had been fighting all along for a moderate program of reform—popular representation through annual parliaments, freedom to engage in occupations, equality before the law—all to be achieved within the framework of a constitutional monarchy. The July Revolution made a republican of him, made him, in fact, the most articulate of German republicans abroad. Like Heine, he came to understand the social and economic implications of the struggles which were being waged—that the world was entering upon a war between the rich and the poor—and in his *Letters from Paris*, which, along with Heine's *French Affairs*, constitutes the keenest analysis of the political events of the day by Germans (aside from that of Marx and Engels), he carried on unremitting warfare against the monarchy.

What it was that Heine actually resented in Börne it is hard to tell. Börne was, in Heine's eyes, a "Nazarene," a puritan; Heine was a hedonist, a pagan. Börne was a circumscribed person, narrow and single-minded in the pursuit of his objectives; but he was incorruptible and inflexible. He would take Heine to task for his political indifference, his running after Parisian women, and his preoccupation with "aesthetic" subjects. He called Heine the "Jesuit of liberalism," in whom no one could have faith, because he "had no faith in himself. . . . Now he defies absolutism; now Jacobinism." Heine had expressed himself in no dubious tones about the futile character of German republicanism. Heine regarded political institutions as secondary; the essence was the economic struggle of the lower classes for well-being. But Heine had opened himself, in one way or another, to many of the charges contained in Börne's criticism. Was Heine's avowed monarchism any less futile than Börne's republicanism? And more defensible? It may have been the implication of venality which rankled most bitterly, though even on that score Heine could boast that his hands were clean and that his actions spoke for him.

Whatever our opinion as to the differences between Heine and

Börne, there can be doubt that in making uncomplimentary references to the relationship between Börne and Frau Wohl (now Frau Strauss) Heine's conduct was most reprehensible. Herr Strauss challenged Heine to a duel, in which the latter was slightly wounded. Thus the affair was terminated. Heine himself later expressed genuine regret for his slighting remarks about Jeannette Wohl. But the stain on Heine's reputation could not so easily be erased.

IT WAS AMAZING THAT IN THE MIDST OF ALL THESE TROUBLES he could go on creating. For in addition to the Börne scandal, he was suffering from nearly total blindness. For some time now, he had been writing mostly prose. Now suddenly he returned to poetry. In the next four years he was to compose two of his longest and most important single poems, *Atta Troll* and *Germany—A Winter's Tale*.

He was vacationing in the French Pyrenees during the summer of 1841 when he conceived the idea of writing a strange phantasy, a "swan song" of Romanticism, whose thousand years' reign was now coming to an end. What better setting than the rugged mountains near Cauterets? In the market-place of the town he had watched with interest the performance of dancing bears. That was to be his subject—bears! His imagination took fire. Men have always passed judgment on bears—now let the bears judge man. Atta Troll, princely bear, and his wife Mumma, entertain the populace by dancing. Suddenly, Atta Troll breaks loose and escapes into his mountain cave, where he rejoins his brood. Here he gives himself over to moral reflections. To his son he says: Do not trust men, not even Germans. Once they were good, but now they are all atheists. What a sad lot they are! Just as they once brutally sacrificed their own kind to their ancient gods, they now sacrifice them to the modern god of gold. They speak of the sacredness of property, by which they mean the right to steal,—as if Nature had brought us into the world equipped with pockets! We bears will bring equality into the world—for all—except that we will forbid the Jews to dance. Such are Atta Troll's homilies. In the meantime, his master, Laskaro, has begun the chase, accompanied by the poet. With the aid of Laskaro's mother, a witch, Atta Troll is lured back and killed. Mumma ends up in a Paris zoo, where she is being wooed by a polar bear. And Atta's pelt now graces the bedroom of the poet's little friend, Juliette. Fittingly, the poem is dedicated to Varnhagen von Ense—"my chosen comrade-in-arms, who helped to bury the old times, and was midwife to the new."

FOR MANY YEARS HE HAD DREAMT OF RETURNING TO HAMBURG for a brief stay. He longed to see his mother and his sister, Charlotte, his uncle Solomon, and his publisher Campe. In the fall of 1843 he was in Hamburg again after an absence of twelve years. But he soon returned to Paris, in December, because he had gone without his Mathilde, and could not bear to stay away from her. He was to make another trip the following year—this time accompanied by Mathilde—to see his mother for the last time.

Not long after his return from his first trip, when the idea of writing a long poem on Germany had already taken shape, he met a young man of twenty-six, like himself an exile from Germany. The brilliant journalist had been the editor of a liberal magazine, *Die Rheinische Zeitung*, but after its suppression in the spring of 1843, he came to Paris to continue his studies. Now he was collaborating with Arnold Ruge on a new venture, the *Deutsch-Französische Jahrbücher*, and was about to participate in the publication of a German newspaper in Paris, *Vorwärts*. Naturally he had sought out the most brilliant and witty of German poets in Paris in order to win him for his publications. The young man's name was Karl Marx. The two became fast friends. Marx had been an admirer of Heine's for years, and knew most of his poems by heart. Heine was attracted by the brilliant intellect of the German revolutionary, and the charm and wit of his wife, Jenny von Westphalen.

Marx's sharp analytic mind, his profound knowledge, and clarity of vision stimulated the poet. Heine's poems took on incisive political tones. Under Marx's influence he wrote for the *Jahrbücher* and *Vorwärts* those amazing and devastating satires in which he exposed to ridicule the rulers of Germany, the impotent new King of Prussia, Frederick William IV, and King Ludwig of Bavaria. It was in the *Vorwärts* that Heine read of the uprising of the Silesian weavers in June 1844. Deeply moved, he wrote Germany's greatest social lyric, "The Silesian Weavers." It was in the *Vorwärts* that a portion of his most provocative satirical poem, *Germany*, was published.

For the shorter *Poems for the Times* were merely preliminary skirmishes. Heine was drawing his long-bow for a master-shot. The complete poem, *Germany—A Winter's Tale*, appeared in the fall of 1844.

Heine knew what to expect. In his preface, he anticipates the obloquy and denigration which his new work would encounter. Of course, he would be called "a contemner of his fatherland," and "a friend of the French." It was the same old story. Yes, he contends, "I am a friend of the French, as I am the friend of all men who are sensible and good. . . . Do not fear. I will not yield the Rhine to the French for the simple reason that the Rhine belongs to me. Yes, it is mine by the inalienable right of birth. I am the free Rhine's even freer son; my cradle is on its banks. When we complete the work left unfinished by the French, when we destroy slavishness in its very last hiding place, i.e., heaven, when we liberate from abasement God who dwells in human beings on earth, when we become the saviours of God, when we restore dignity to the poor people who are deprived of happiness, and to genius condemned to scorn and to desecrated beauty . . . , then we will inherit not only Alsace and Lorraine, but all of France, and thereafter all of Europe; yes, all the world will become German."

This was not a Pan-German speaking. It was the citizen of the world who wished to erase national boundaries and who saw all of humanity united in a brotherhood of equals.

Then the poem begins. The poet is in Germany once more. When he touches German soil he feels young again. The foolish customs officer examines his bags, overlooking the more dangerous contraband to be found in the poet's head. The gloomy reality of German life contrasts with the vision of a Germany that might be.

> A new song and a better song
> Oh, friends I'll sing for you,
> Here on earth we mean to make
> Our paradise come true.
>
> We mean to be happy here on earth,
> Our days of want are done,
> No more shall the lazy belly waste
> What toiling hands have won.

Legend and contemporary history are fused in the magic of the poet's call for German liberation. The new Aristophanes who could scourge with scorpions could also be tender and loving. The coming of revolution is anticipated in the magnificent figure of the axe-man who accompanies the poet and materializes the latter's thought. I have become no sheep, Heine tells his fellow-Germans. I am still unvanquished. The figure of Barbarossa is invoked, with humor as well as passion, to come and shatter the bastions of stupidity and tyranny.

That is the dream. But what Heine actually sees in Hamburg, when the goddess Hammonia vouchsafes him a vision of the future, is too horrible to tell. The anti-climactic conclusion is perhaps the sole weakness of the poem. After the incomparable preparation, one expects a call to arms—not a warning to the King to respect poets, because their vengeance is mightier than that of Jove. Even Heine must have known that poets do not have that much power!

HE WAS DECIDEDLY UNWELL. He was losing his eyesight. Sometimes he was totally blind. A gradual paralysis of his face was an omen the meaning of which neither he nor his physicians fully understood. He still moved about, was gay and as witty as ever.

In December 1844 Solomon Heine died. He had been assisting his nephew with an annual allowance of 4800 francs which, together with his income as a writer and a grant from the French government, assured him of a comfortable, though by no means luxurious, life. He had expected his uncle would continue to provide for him in his will. What was his shock when he was informed by Solomon's heir, Karl Heine, that the will provided for a legacy of 8000 francs—and no more! Heine was beside himself with rage and disappointment. He had known all along that the Hamburg cabal had been conspiring against him; he knew that his cousin, Karl, hated him; but he had never suspected that his uncle would be so completely influenced by the gossip. Karl Heine offered to continue the annual payments provided Heine agreed to a censorship of all his writings in which the family was mentioned. The squabble which followed the publication of the will, the charges, countercharges, threats, and counterthreats do not make for pleasant reading. It was a mean vengeance on the part of the uncle, a millionaire; and an even meaner one on the part of his heir. After all, Heine was a world-famous poet, and he was a sick man. When reports of his approaching death began to multiply, Karl Heine became alarmed, and in February 1847 settled on him an annual payment to be continued during Mathilde's life.

The poet's health was rapidly deteriorating. His face was now completely paralyzed. He could not eat. He suffered frequent fainting spells. His body had shrunk. "I know I am past saving," he wrote to Campe.

IN 1848 A STORM SWEPT OVER EUROPE. It arose in France, and then blew across the Rhine, into Austria, and beyond. There had been signs and portents which the discerning eye could not fail to understand. An economic crisis had broken out in England. In France, the peasants and workers of Tours rose in protest against the rise in food prices. The social structure of France had changed considerably within twenty years; heavy industry had made notable advances, and the number of workers had increased correspondingly. Industrial capitalism now began to challenge the rule of the financial aristocracy, a corrupt, irresponsible, and venal group which had speculated itself into fortunes on the stock-exchanges of Europe. The economic crisis of 1847 brought matters to a head. Almost two-thirds of the working population of Paris were thrown out of work. Tradesmen and artisans went bankrupt. Despite the iron rule which Louis Philippe and his masters imposed on the country, despite the banning of all meetings, the people of Paris rose up.

On February 22, the workers and artisans of Paris came out into the streets. The next day barricades were erected. Then the National Guard went over to the insurgents. On the 24th, Louis Philippe abdicated, and the cry of "Long live the Republic!" resounded through the streets. A middle-class provisional government was proclaimed, a ten-hour work day was announced, universal suffrage was established, and the first election was set for April 23.

The hearts of the ruling monarchs of Europe were sick with dread. Leopold of Belgium wrote to Frederick William IV of Prussia: "The terrible misfortune in Paris represents a most serious danger not only to European monarchs, but to the very existence of society. . . . Property, family, religion, even our treasured freedom and security are at stake."

On March 13, the people of Vienna rose and drove Metternich from the country. On March 18, the citizens of Berlin forced the surrender of their king. In almost every major city of Europe uprisings took place. In London, the Chartists marched on Parliament bearing a petition with six million signatures.

Unfortunately, once they were in power, the leaders of the Revolution, mostly middle-class representatives, became uncertain of their aims, suspicious of one another and fearful of their working-class allies. Soon they leagued against them with their enemies. Such was the history of the French uprising, where men like Louis Blanc, Lamartine, and Barbès turned against the workers. The Hungarian and Polish revolts were soon crushed through Russian intervention. In Germany, Frederick William IV showed his contempt for his people by scornfully rejecting the imperial crown offered him by the Frankfurt Assembly on May 18, 1848. "Against democrats our only remedy is the army."

The counter-revolution marched swiftly and ruthlessly. The workers of Paris were provoked into an uprising in June 1848, and massacred by an army led by General Cavaignac. Louis Napoleon was elected President of the Second French Republic. By the *coup d'état* of 1852 he succeeded in having himself proclaimed Emperor of France.

There were few men in Europe who fully understood the meaning of the events which had taken place. Thousands of exiles poured through Paris and London. Among the very few of them who looked at the historical struggles with clear and critical eyes were Marx and Engels. They pointed to a new and astonishing phenomenon that had taken place in this revolution—an independent force had emerged which was destined to make history. It was the working class. On the basis of their analysis they had already—on the eve of the Revolution—written the most important political document of the century, the *Communist Manifesto.*

THE STREETS WERE FILLED WITH THE SOUND OF GUNS and shouting, when Heine went out for the last time in May 1848. Thereafter he was confined to the "mattress grave" for eight long years. The German Apollo whom Gautier had greeted seventeen years before, was now a bearded, emaciated skeleton, powerless to move from his couch in the Rue d'Amsterdam. He had to be carried like an infant.

But his mind remained impenetrable to the ravages of sickness. It burned clearly and intensely, and illumined the darkness around him. His wit was no less sharp than before. The visitors who came to see him, sometimes impelled by kindness, often by curiosity, were not always aware of the agonies he was suffering. He was almost completely blind. To see them, he would raise one eyelid with his hand. A quip or jest was always at the tip of his tongue. From the next room would come the chatter or laughter of Mathilde, and Heine would stop, listen, and smile. She tended him faithfully, brought him coffee with rich cream. He jestingly observed that she was growing stout.

His interest in the world outside never abated. Books and newspapers were read to him, and the gossip of the town was brought to him. He who had loved life so much—and who still loved it passionately—was now confined to living it vicariously. For eight years he wrestled with Death. His mother never knew the gravity of his illness.

He was done with politics. Yet the publication by the *Revue Rétrospective* of Louis Philippe's list of pensioners, with Heine's name among them, and the subsequent accusation that he had been a hireling of Guizot's and of France, forced from him a proud self-vindication. The new Napoleon failed to inspire him. "The beautiful ideals of political morality, legality, civic virtue, freedom and equality, the roseate morning dreams of the eighteenth century, for the sake of which our fathers met their death so bravely, and which we, no less eager for the martyr's crown, dreamt together with them—now lie at our feet, broken, scattered potsherds. . . ." He had foreseen and forewarned.

But his poetic genius grew in richness and maturity. It was during those mattress-grave years that he attained the peak of his poetical powers. In *Romancero*, which was published in 1851, and in the 1854 collection of his poems—the last to appear in his lifetime—he stands revealed as one of the great European poets.

His fancy roved far and wide. At night he composed his poems, and in the morning he dictated them to his secretary. In those nocturnal wanderings, as sane and vigorous as those on which any poet ever ventured, he ranged through history and all the lands of the world. *Romancero* is the gem of Heine's balladry, the equal of that composed anywhere. His ballad characters are for the most part historical figures, Charles I of England, Marie Antoinette, King David, the Persian poet Firdusi, the troubadour Geoffrey Rudel, Cortez the Conquistador. Into them he concentrated all of his great dramatic genius —the genius he possessed of simplifying, objectifying and compressing. Where shall we find the equal of "The Battlefield of Hastings," "The Asra," or "Woodland Solitude"? They are modern creations with the subtle psychological overtones which only a great modern poet could give them. This is not the work of a dying poet, but of one who has reached the fullness of poetical vitality. Here too is to be found *Lazarus*, a great litany of suffering—also objectified and transmuted—that litany which is defiance of death and victory over it— ironic, grim, touching, chiding. Was he not Lazarus himself of whom it is written that he "was a certain beggar . . . which was laid at the gate of the rich man, full of sores, and desiring to be fed with the crumbs which fell from the rich man's table. Moreover the dogs came and licked his wounds." The lot of the poet in the world is not a happy one, whether he be the God Apollo or Firdusi.

Here too are *The Hebrew Melodies*, the flower of his Jewish poems, including the magnificent hymn to Princess Sabbath, the symbol and the glory of all ceremonials through which the immortality of a people speaks—and his unforgettable reconstruction of Jehuda Halevy, the epitome of the woeful and heroic history of Israel.

He was the pilgrim of sorrow who had left the Greek Parnassus or Mount Olympus, and reluctantly had returned to the altar of a personal Jehovah. He now told himself and the world that he had foresworn the freethinking of an earlier day, the roseate Hellenism of the German Apollo, and the god of Hegel, and had come back to a personal God, to whom he would now confide his most secret midnight thoughts as well as his personal affairs, whom he could chide and reprove and with whom he could argue.

How hard it was to tear himself from those lovely deities of ancient Greece! Even as late as 1851 he confessed:

"I have abjured nothing, not even my old heathen gods, from whom I did indeed turn away, but the parting was affectionate and friendly. It happened in May 1848, on the day on which I left my house for the last time, that I took leave of those glorious idols whom I had adored in the days of my good fortune. Painfully I dragged myself to the Louvre, and I was near collapse when I entered the lofty hall where the blessed goddess of beauty, Our Lady of Milo, stands on her pedestal. I lay at her feet for a long time, and I wept violently. And the goddess looked down upon me compassionately, and at the same time so disconsolately, as if to say, 'Can you not see that I am without arms and powerless to help you?' "

Upon its publication, *Romancero* at once went into four editions. Julius Campe, who had for over three years refrained from even writing the sick poet, must have been overjoyed.

THE LAST YEARS OF HIS LIFE were spent in the Rue Matignon, close to the Champs Elysées. From near and far friends and relatives came to see him—perhaps for the last time. Therese Heine, a very unhappy woman, and Charlotte; his brothers Gustav and Maximilian, both successful men; the poets Béranger, Gérard de Nerval (who predeceased Heine), Heinrich Laube, and his old friend, Elise von Hohenhausen.

Gautier saw him for the last time in January 1856. "Illness had attenuated, emaciated, dissected him at will, and with the unwearied patience of an artist of the Middle Ages; from the statue of a Greek god it had shaped a Christ gaunt as a skeleton, in which the nerves, the tendons, and the veins were revealed. Thus ravaged, he was still beautiful. When he raised his heavy eyelid a flash shot from his half-blinded pupil. Genius resuscitated this dead face. Lazarus came forth from his grave for a few minutes."

He fell in love again—this time with a mysterious girl who came to him one day in July 1855, and visited him frequently till the day of his death. She had a past—checkered and obscure. She had been the mistress of Heine's friend Meissner before she came to know the poet. After Heine's death, she became the mistress of Taine, and wrote under the name of Camille Selden. Whoever she was, "la Mouche" (the "Fly"), as he called her, lightened his last days. To her he wrote his saddest and most amusing letters; for her he wrote some of his loveliest verses. Both are grotesquely marked by paroxysms of frustration which overcame the poet now condemned to platonic amours.

Catherine Bourlois, his nurse, was the last person to see him alive. On February 17, 1856, four o'clock in the morning, he died. He had asked for and was given the simplest of funerals. Neither a Catholic nor a Protestant clergyman officiated. A hundred people accompanied his last remains to the cemetery in the Montmartre district. Mignet, Dumas and Gautier were among those who paid him a last tribute, and Gautier wrote: "There was neither a long procession, nor lugubrious music, nor muffled drums, nor black cloth starred with orders, nor emphatic discourse, nor tripods crowned with green flames." But the mourners knew that they "were assisting at the funeral of a king of the mind."

THE BATTLE OVER HEINE which was carried on even during his lifetime, continued with unabated fury after his death. During the last years of his life, he had been writing his autobiography and confessions. Soon after his death, the Heine family succeeded in laying its hands on a good portion of his literary remains and probably destroyed them. The "Castle of Affronts" haunted him even in his grave.

Mathilde survived him until 1883. He had provided for her—and she remained faithful to his memory, though, if legend is to be credited, not to his whimsical wishes. He is alleged to have asked her to marry again, so that at least one person might regret his death!

His German fatherland, which found room for innumerable monuments to innumerable German mediocrities, did not deem him worthy of such a memorial, and the column designed by the sculptor Herter finally found a haven in New York. The Nazis officially consecrated the obloquy by consigning him to oblivion and by removing his name from his most famous poems. No greater tribute could have been paid any poet. He had become part of the living poetry of the people, and his poems had become folksongs. The work of desecration still continues, and the legend of a heartless, insincere, Francophile, traitorous Heine persists in many academic halls and is trumpeted abroad by "scholars" who have never ventured beyond the confines of their libraries and many of whom had by their complacency or worse paved the way for the coming of the Third Reich.

"NOT MARBLE NOR THE GILDED MONUMENTS OF PRINCES shall outlive his powerful rhyme." Nor, one might add, the jabbering of geese. He had many faults—he was inconsistent, often frivolous, cynical, if you will, weak and wayward. The gold of his genius was not unalloyed. But he stands revealed today, for all that, as a great poet and humanitarian. He is a modern whose eye pierced the future. What he foresaw has since come to pass.

Within himself he shadowed the conflicts of his times, the struggle between the old and the new. Within him the "Nazarene"—the Judaeo-Christian ideal of renunciation and poverty—struggled with the "Hellene," the life-affirming, the cheerful, the realistic. He had once thought to cut himself loose from the Jewish people. He became the German Apollo with a baptismal certificate. But he only found the terms of the struggle changed—not the struggle itself. For what did such titles as "Nazarene" and "Hellene" mean in a world of ineluctable conflicts for bread and decency?

He came to see history not as a disjointed mass of incoherent facts, but as a process which revealed the struggles of mankind for freedom. All great martyrs of freedom joined hands in that indivisible work. Christ was such a liberator. And Moses too. Martin Luther, and in a greater measure, Thomas Münzer, the peasant leader. And the heroic men of the French Revolution. Heine was not the least—nor the last—of them.

In his day he saw the struggle assuming new forms. Armies of the dispossessed were challenging the divine rights of the possessors. Wherever he looked, he witnessed preparations for war. Was he not among the very few Germans who had correctly appraised the role of the Chartists—that first organized political movement of the working-class in England? Had he not time and again drawn attention to the neglected but potentially mighty forces of socialism in France?

Had he not confidently proclaimed the great task of the nineteenth century to be the liberation not of this or that oppressed minority, but of all oppressed peoples? He had incessantly warred on Junkers, aristocrats, autocrats, political clergy. He hated the moneyed aristocracy with all the virulence of a Balzac—but unlike the latter he looked to the future and not to the past for liberation from them.

"We have measured the earth, weighed the forces of Nature, reckoned the resources of industry, and behold!—we have found that the earth is spacious and wide enough for everyone to build his hut of happiness on it—that the earth can feed us all decently, if only every one of us works, and no one lives at another's expense—that it is no longer necessary to preach the blessedness of heaven to the large masses of the poor."

He wrote that he might be read. He never separated the word from the deed, and the deed from its social consequences. He had consecrated himself to the task of making "the great portion of mankind understand our own times," so they would no longer "allow themselves to be provoked by the hireling scribblers of the aristocracy into hatred and war." He foresaw a "great confederation of peoples—the Holy Alliance of Nations," when "we shall not longer need to sustain standing armies of many hundreds of thousands of murderers because of mutual distrust. We shall use our swords and horses to plow with, and we shall win peace, prosperity and freedom."

Though he was a true citizen of the world—rather, *because* he was a true citizen of the world—he loved his own land, not the land of dreamy-eyed sluggards, of phantasts, of arrogant rulers, but the country of good, simple people, the miners of the Harz, the fisherfolk of Nordeney. He honored all great Germans who had contributed to the emancipation of the human mind—Luther, Lessing, Kant, Goethe and Schiller. He was proud of being a German poet. He wished to bring Germany into the mainstream of European history and culture.

That he did not succeed in doing so is the tragedy of Germany and of the world.

DACHAU, BELSEN, MAJDANEK—are they not objectified fulfillment of Heine's predictions? The nation of professors, *Privatdozenten*, doctors of philosophy, musicians and poets—had it not become one vast army of destruction, such as Heine described in his book on *Religion and Philosophy in Germany?* Have not the invokers of the old pagan gods, the worshippers of Aryanism, the unrelenting hordes of Pan-Germans fulfilled the worst of Heine's fears?

As he had assigned to the Germans the role of liberators of the world, provided they allied themselves with the great forces of freedom and equality, so he came to see the liberation of the Jews as a phase of world freedom. His identification with the Jews—like his identification with Germans—was the fruit of a wisdom which taught him that all wars and warriors for freedom have a common fatherland, that battles of humanity merge into one another, that to fight as a Jew and to fight as a German meant to fight against oppression and tyranny and exploitation.

So he sought in the history and martyrdom of the Jews for a clue to an understanding of them. He who had once thought of them as symbolized by the hagglers and money-changers of Hamburg came to honor them as men, "mighty and unyielding . . . despite eighteen centuries of persecution and misery." He reappraised the Bible, their "portable fatherland" and its giant hero Moses, in whom he saw one of the great emancipators of mankind, a hater of slavery at a time when Hellenes and the whole world surrounding the little land of Palestine was still slave-ridden. *The Rabbi of Bacherach* had reaffirmed Israel's heroism in the character of Sarah, whose words, addressed to a cynical renegade, were written in Heine's own blood: "My noble Lord," she says, "if you would be my knight, you must fight whole nations, and in that battle there are scant thanks to be won, and even less honor. And if you would wear my colors, then you must sew yellow rings on your cloak, or bind a blue-striped scarf around you. For such are the colors, the colors of my house, the House of Israel, the house of misery, which is despised and scorned in the streets by the children of good fortune."

In 1840, the Turks revived in the blood-libel of Damascus the gruesome, ancient accusation that Jews used Christian blood for their Passover ritual. Heine was roused to indignation. He saw more clearly than before the political and social roots of anti-Semitism. He was shocked by the indifference of the rich Jews of France to the plight of their coreligionists; he lashed out at the hypocrisy of French political leaders, who along with the reactionary cliques of French society were using the libel to advance their own political interests in the Near East.

Heine's great essay on Shakespeare's *Merchant of Venice* marks the apex of his understanding of the nature of anti-Semitism. Aside from the fact that it is one of the more remarkable examples of Shakespeare criticism, it is a brilliant analysis of the role of Shylock, the Jew, who is contrasted with his "Christian" victims. Heine's most pregnant words are devoted to the social role of the Jews. They are so far ahead of the general thinking of his day—and even of our own— that they deserve repeated quotation:

"The common people hated in the Jews only the possessors of money; it was always the heaped-up metal which drew the lightning of their wrath down on the Jews. They were glad if religion allowed them to give full sway to this hatred." Today, anti-Semitism "no longer wears the gloomy, fanatical monk's mien, but the flabby, 'enlightened' features of a shopkeeper, who is afraid of being outdone in his business dealings by Jewish business sense." Why did the Jews engage so predominantly in commerce and trade? "The whole world compelled them to be rich" by barring them from all other enterprises, and then "hated them for their riches."

It was natural that Heine should draw the conclusion that Jews would only achieve emancipation when "the emancipation of the Christians was fully won and secured." Hence the Messiah who came to liberate mankind would free not only Israel, "but all of suffering humanity."

YET HIS MIND RECOILED AT ACCEPTING the inexorable consequences of his own thoughts. He who had spoken powerful words on world emancipation was content to remain a professed monarchist! The destroyer of romantic fictions held on to the romantic fiction of a beneficent king who would reconcile the conflicts of society, check and neutralize a parasitic money-aristocracy, and an equally parasitic nobility and clergy, and win bread and happiness for the common man.

He was too honest not to perceive the character of the coming struggles, of what he called the "great duel" between the possessors and the dispossessed. Often he had said, "Bread is the divine right of man." But the romantic poet within him trembled for the future of poetry once the people had set about vindicating the divine right to bread. In the coming revolution, would the world of dreams and poetry and music go down in ruins, and his own *Book of Songs* serve to wrap groceries? Perhaps his faith in man was not so strong as he had claimed. Perhaps his prophetic vision was blurred. His *Book of Songs* was eventually mutilated not by people fighting for equality and happiness, but by a nation bent on domination, fed and abetted by the very moneyed aristocracy he had himself castigated.

But the die was cast, and so he concludes with sorrow:

"A terrible syllogism holds me in its grip, and if I am unable to refute the premise, 'that every man has the right to eat,' then I am forced to submit to all its consequences. From much thinking about it I am on the verge of losing my reason. I see all the demons of truth dancing triumphantly around me, and at length the generosity of despair takes possession of my heart and I cry: 'For long this old society has been judged and condemned. Let justice be done! Let this old world be smashed in which innocence is long since dead, where egoism prospers, and man battens on man! Let these whited sepulchres be destroyed from top to bottom, these caverns of falsehood and iniquity. And blessed be the grocer who shall one day use the pages of my poems as paper bags for the coffee and snuff of poor old women, who in this present world of injustice too often have to go without that solace. *Fiat justitia, pereat mundus!*' "

BUT THE WORLD DOES NOT PERISH WHERE JUSTICE IS DONE. When the world achieves complete justice, of the kind of which Heine wrote, his books will not serve as wrapping paper for grocers. For grocers, along with millions of others, will read Heine and preserve his works and the works of all great masters. It is after all the people who have kept his memory alive; they have sung and recited his poems for generations. They will honor in him not only the poet of love but also the poet of freedom, the greatest wit of the century, the satirist whose place is beside Aristophanes, Cervantes, Rabelais, Swift, Molière, and Anatole France. They will honor in him the great critic and social thinker.

They will echo his own imperishable epitaph:

I have never laid great store by poetic glory, and whether my songs are praised or blamed matters little to me. But lay a sword on my bier, for I have been a good soldier in the wars of human liberation.

Poems and Ballads

BOOK OF SONGS

PROLOGUE   *Das ist der alte Märchenwald!*

It was the forest of fairy-tales!
How fragrant the linden-flower!
The magic lustre of the moon
Had seized me in its power.

I walked along, and as I went
I heard a wild refrain.
It was the nightingale—she sang
Of love, and lovers' pain.

She sang of love, and lovers' pain,
Of laughter and of tears.
So gay her sob, so sad her laugh,
I dreamed of forgotten years.

I walked along, and as I went
I reached an open field,
Where looming upon towering spires,
A castle was revealed.

The gates were barred; a heavy peace
And gloom lay everywhere;
It seemed that silent death had made
Those desolate walls his lair.

There lay a sphinx before the gates,
A hybrid of lust and dread,
With a lion's body, a lion's claws,
But a woman's breast and head.

A beautiful woman! What fierce desire
Blazed in her marble eyes!
Her lips were locked, but they had the smile
Of one who is more than wise.

So sweetly sang the nightingale,
My heart was wholly won—
I kissed that lovely face, and I
Was hopelessly undone.

The marble features came to life;
The stone began to groan.
She drank my kisses' burning flame
With thirst that matched my own.

She nearly drank my breath away—
And, in her passion's greed,
She clasped me with her lion-claws—
Till I began to bleed.

Ravishing torture and blissful pain!
Terror and ecstasy!
The while her kisses thrill my soul
Her claws are wounding me.

The nightingale sang: "O beautiful sphinx!
Listen, o Love, and explain!
Why must your ecstasy be mixed
With such inhuman pain?

"O beautiful sphinx! Explain to me
Your riddle of laughter and tears!
For I have pondered over this
Thousands and thousands of years!"

TRANSLATED BY AARON KRAMER

❧ *Young Sorrows*

DREAM PICTURES

Im nächtgen Traum hab ich mich selbst geschaut

I fell asleep and dreamed at eventide:
I saw myself, as for some festive day,
Decked in silk vest, white shirt, and best array;
And then I saw my love stand by my side:
I bowed and said: "My dear, are you a bride?
Then I'll congratulate you if I may!"
But the cold speech half choked my breath away,
And in my throat the words had almost died.
Then bitter tears began to flow apace
From my love's eyes, and in a mist of tears
Was wellnigh hid from me her gentle face.
—O tender eyes! though you have lied to me,
Both waking and in dreams these many years,
Yet I believe you all too readily.

TRANSLATED BY ALMA STRETTELL

Was treibt und tobt mein tolles Blut?

What is this frenzy in my veins?
Why does my heart go up in flames?
My blood is mad, and fires start
A furious feast upon my heart.

My blood is mad—it foams and steams;
For I have dreamed the worst of dreams.
The Son of Night stood black before me,
And, as I gasped, away he bore me.

The house he brought me to was bright:
With glowing torches, candle-light,
And harps resounding through the din;
I reached the hall, I stumbled in.

A joyous wedding-feast was here:
At every table song and cheer.
But when the bridal pair I spied—
O grief! My sweetheart was the bride.

My sweetheart was the radiant bride;
A stranger gloried at her side;
Behind her seat I stood unknown,
As silent as a thing of stone.

The music rose; I stood quite still—
The noise of gladness made me ill.
The bride appeared so full of bliss:
The bridegroom squeezed her hand in his.

He filled his glass with wine, and tasted;
And then he elegantly placed it
Before the smiling bride—alas!
My own red blood was in the glass.

The groom accepted from his wife
A pretty apple; took a knife
And cut the ruddy fruit apart—
O misery! it was my heart.

They eyed each other; long they eyed;
The bridegroom boldly hugged the bride,
And kissed her cheeks for all to see—
Alas! cold death is kissing me.

My tongue is lead; I try to shout,
But not a single word comes out.
A rustling starts—the dance begins—
In front the spruced-up couple spins.

And while I watch without a sound
The dancers briskly whirl around.
He whispers, and her cheek's aglow;
But no displeasure does she show.
TRANSLATED BY AARON KRAMER

SONGS

Morgens steh ich auf und frage

Rising with the sun I cry,
    "Comes my love to-day?"
To my bed at eve I sigh,
    "Still she stays away!"

All the night long with my sorrow
    Wide awake I weep,
And I dawdle through the morrow
    Dreaming, half asleep.
TRANSLATED BY M. M. BOZMAN

Lieb Liebchen, leg's Händchen aufs Herze mein

Beloved, lay your hand on my heart in its gloom.
Do you hear that! Like tapping inside of a room?
A carpenter lives there. With malice and glee
He's building a coffin, a coffin for me.

He hammers and pounds with such fiendish delight
I never can sleep, neither daytime nor night.
Oh, carpenter, hurry the hours that creep;
Come, finish your labors—and then I can sleep.
TRANSLATED BY LOUIS UNTERMEYER

Schöne Wiege meiner Leiden

> Lovely cradle of my sorrow,
>   Lovely tomb where peace might dwell,
> Smiling town, we part tomorrow.
>   I must leave; and so farewell.
>
> Farewell, threshold, where still slowly
>   Her beloved footstep stirs;
> Farewell to that hushed and holy
>   Spot where first my eyes met hers.
>
> Had you never caught or claimed me,
>   Fairest, heart's elected queen,
> Wretchedness would not have maimed me
>   In its toils, as you have seen.
>
> Never have you found me grieving
>   For your love with anxious prayer;
> All I asked was quiet living,
>   Quietly to breathe your air.
>
> But you drove me forth with scourging,
>   Bitter words and lashing scorn;
> Madness in my soul is surging,
>   And my heart is flayed and torn.
>
> And I take my staff and stumble
>   On a journey, far from brave;
> Till my head droops, and I tumble
>   In some cool and kindly grave.
>
>   TRANSLATED BY LOUIS UNTERMEYER

Anfangs wollt ich fast verzagen

> First I wasted in despair,
> Thought it more than I could bear;
> Yet I've borne, and bear it now—
> Only, never ask me: How?
>   TRANSLATED BY AARON KRAMER

ROMANCES

POOR PETER *Der Hans und die Grete tanzen herum*

I

Hans and Grete whirl around
And shout for sheer delight.
Peter does not make a sound,
His cheeks are chalky-white.

Hans and Grete are bride and groom,
Their wedding-jewels are bright.
Biting his nails in the back of the room
Peter's a sorry sight.

He watches while they sing and sport,
And murmurs with fists clenched tight:
"If I weren't such a rational sort
I'd kill myself tonight."

TRANSLATED BY AARON KRAMER

II

"Within my breast there's such a woe
That I am torn asunder.
It stirs, and though I stay or go
It drives me always yonder.

"It drives me to my love, it cries
As though she still could heal me.
Alas, one look from Gretel's eyes
And I must fly, conceal me.

"I climb the mountain's highest peak:
Man is, at least, alone there;

Where all is still and none may seek
My heart may weep and moan there."
TRANSLATED BY LOUIS UNTERMEYER

III

Poor Peter slowly staggers by;
His face is pale as death, and shy.
The people stop and look aghast
Whenever Peter stumbles past.

The girls are whispering in dread:
"He must have risen from the dead!"
It isn't so, dear girls—alack!
He's going there—not coming back.

Lost is the love he once caressed,
And so the grave will suit him best,
Where he can sleep his grief away
Until the final Judgment Day.
TRANSLATED BY AARON KRAMER

THE TWO GRENADIERS *Nach Frankreich zogen zwei
Grenadier*

Toward France there journeyed two grenadiers:
In Russia they had been bound;
And when they crossed the German frontiers
They bowed their heads to the ground.

For here they heard the tidings of woe:
That the glory of France was drained—
Her great host vanquished and crushed by the foe—
And the emperor, the emperor chained.

The grenadiers together cried
At the sorrowful news of the war.
Said the first: "I'm all one ache inside;
How my wound flares up once more!"

The other said: "The song is done;
I'd die with you today—
But I've a wife and a little one
Who'd starve with me away."

"What matters child, what matters wife?
There's a loftier pulse in my veins;
If they hunger, let them go begging through life—
My emperor, my emperor's in chains!

"There's one thing, brother, you must do:
Promise that when I die
You'll carry my corpse to France with you;
In French earth let me lie.

"The honor-cross on its scarlet band
You must lay upon my breast,
Gird on my sword, and in my hand
Allow my gun to rest.

"So, like a sentry, I'll lie in my tomb
And silently take heed
Till at last I hear a cannon-boom
And the trot of a neighing steed.

"Then will the Emperor ride over my grave,
While sabres flash and rattle:
Then will I rise up armed from the grave—
For the Emperor, the Emperor to battle!"

TRANSLATED BY AARON KRAMER

DON RAMIRO *Donna Clara! Donna Clara!*

"Donna Clara! Donna Clara!
All these years my darling lady!
You've determined on my ruin,
And determined without mercy.

"Donna Clara! Donna Clara!
Sweet to be among the living,
But it's dreadful to be buried
In a gloomy, frosty coffin.

"Donna Clara! Smile: tomorrow
Don Fernando shall salute you
At the altar, as your husband—
Will you ask me to the wedding?"

"Don Ramiro! Don Ramiro!
What you say is sharp and bitter,
Bitter as the stars' prediction
Ridiculing my desire.

"Don Ramiro! Don Ramiro!
Drive away your melancholy;
On this earth are many maidens;
Heaven willed that we be parted.

"Don Ramiro! you whose courage
Conquered Moors without a number,
It's yourself you now must conquer—
Come tomorrow to my wedding."

"Donna Clara! Donna Clara!
Yes, I'll be there; yes, I swear it!
I will lead you in the dances.
Now, good night. I'll come tomorrow."

"Good night!"—And the window clattered.
Sighing, Don Ramiro stood there,
Stood a long time like a statue,
Then he vanished in the shadows.

And at last the night surrenders,
After a long fight, to morning;
Spread out like a multi-colored
Flower-garden lies Toledo.

Palaces and splendid buildings
Glitter brightly in the sunshine;
And the towering domes of churches
Blaze with splendor, as though gilded.

Buzzing loud, like bees in cluster,
Ring the bells of the cathedrals.
Pious songs of prayer rise sweetly
Up from God's religious houses.

But behold, behold the pageant!
From the chapel in the market
Streams the motley crowd of people—
In a wave of gay commotion.

Shining knights, bejewelled ladies,
Court-domestics, gaily gleaming,
And the bright bells burst out laughing,
And the organ murmurs with them.

But respectfully the people
Move aside, and make a pathway
For the fair young bridal couple,
Donna Clara, Don Fernando.

To the palace of the bridegroom
Rolls the crowd of joyous people;
Here begin the rites of marriage:
Solemn, and of age-old custom.

Knightly games and merry feasting
Alternate 'mid loud rejoicing;
Speedily the hours vanish,
Till the light fades into evening,

And the wedding-guests assemble
In the dance-hall, for the waltzes.
In the radiance of the candles
How their splendid garments glitter!

Bride and groom survey the dancers
From their elevated places,
Donna Clara, Don Fernando,
And they bandy loving phrases.

And the jewelled waves of people
Billow brightly in the dance-hall;
And the kettle-drums are rolling,
And the trumpets bray their thunder.

"Tell me why, oh lovely lady,
Tell me why your eyes keep turning
Toward that one deserted corner?"
The astonished knight inquires.

"Don't you see the man who stands there
All in black, my sweet Fernando?"
And he gently smiles and answers:
"Oh, that's nothing but a shadow."

But the shadow slowly nears them,
And a man's in the black mantle.
Recognizing Don Ramiro,
Clara greets him in confusion.

And the dance is set in motion:
Merrily the guests go spinning
In the waltz's frenzied circles,
And the floor resounds and trembles.

"Certainly, dear Don Ramiro,
I will join you in some waltzes;
But you did not have to come here
Covered in a night-black mantle."

Don Ramiro, with his piercing,
Staring eyes, regards the beauty;
Clasping her he answers sadly:
"But you told me I was welcome!"

And the dancing pair is quickly
Sucked into the gay confusion,
And the kettle-drums are rolling,
And the trumpets bray their thunder.

"Snow-white are your cheeks," she murmurs,
And mysteriously shudders;
"But you told me I was welcome!"
Hollowly Ramiro answers.

In the hall the candles glimmer
Through the flowing throng of people;
And the kettle-drums are rolling,
And the trumpets bray their thunder.

"Ice-cold are your hands," she murmurs,
And her very soul is shaken;
"But you told me I was welcome!"
And they plunge into the whirlpool.

"Leave me, leave me, Don Ramiro!
It's a dead man's breath you're breathing!"
Once again the gloomy answer:
"But you told me I was welcome!"

And the dance-floor smokes and blazes,
Gay the violin and viol;
Like a crazy web of magic,
Guests and lights are wildly whirling.

"Leave me, leave me, Don Ramiro!"
Clara whimpers in the whirlpool.
Don Ramiro always answers:
"But you told me I was welcome!"

"Now begone, begone in God's name!"
Clara shrieks with sudden firmness;
And this word is scarcely uttered,
When she sees Ramiro vanish.

Clara stares, her face is deathly,
Cold and night are woven round her;
Faintness draws the radiant woman
Down into its gloomy kingdom.

Finally the slumber leaves her,
Finally she lifts her eye-lids,
But the sight is so astounding
That her eyes can scarce stay open.

For she has not left her bridegroom
All the while the crowd's been dancing,
And she's sitting still beside him,
And the anxious knight inquires:

"Tell me why your cheeks grow pallid?
And your eyes—why do they darken?"
"But Ramiro?—" stutters Clara,
And her tongue is stopped by terror.

Deep and earnest are the furrows
On the forehead of her bridegroom:
"Lady, seek no bloody tidings—
On this noon Ramiro perished."

TRANSLATED BY AARON KRAMER

THE MINNESINGERS *Zu dem Wettgesange schreiten*

Come the minnesingers, raising
Dust and laughter and lament.
Here's a contest that's amazing;
Here's a curious tournament.

Wild and ever restless Fancy
Is the minnesinger's horse,
Art his shield, the Word his lance; he
Bears them lightly round the course.

Many women pleased and pleasant,
Smile and drop a flower down;
But the right one's never present
With the rightful laurel-crown.

Other fighters nimbly canter
To the lists, care-free and whole;
But we minnesingers enter
With a death-wound in our soul.

And the one who wrings the inmost
Song-blood from his burning breast,
He's the victor; he shall win most
Praise and smiles and all the rest.

TRANSLATED BY LOUIS UNTERMEYER

JOURNEY BY WATER *Ich stand gelehnet an den Mast*

Counting the waves as they roll by
I lean against the mast.
Goodbye, my lovely fatherland!
My ship is sailing fast.

I pass my pretty sweetheart's house
And see the windows shine.
I stare until my eyes pop out,
But no one makes a sign.

You blinding teardrops, leave my eyes,
That I may clearly see.
Sick heart of mine, don't break beneath
This giant agony.

TRANSLATED BY AARON KRAMER

SONNETS

TO MY MOTHER, B. HEINE *Ich bins gewohnt, den Kopf*
recht hoch zu tragen

I

It's been my way to walk with head held high;
I've got a pretty tough and stubborn mind;
And if the king himself should pass, he'd find
That I'm a lad who'll look him in the eye.

And yet, dear mother, this I'll frankly say:
No matter how puffed up my pride may be,
When I am near your sweet serenity
My haughtiness begins to melt away.

Is it your soul that strangely holds my flight?
Your towering soul, that bravely pierces all
And soars up flashing toward the heavenly light?
Or am I tortured now when I recall
My many wrongs, that filled your heart with woe?
Your beautiful, big heart that loved me so?

II

I left you once in wild insanity—
To travel through the world from end to end,
To see if love were hiding in some land,
That I might lift and clasp it lovingly.

I looked for love on all the streets; I'd wait
With arms outstretched in front of every door—
For little alms of passion I'd implore—
But, laughing, all they gave me was cold hate.

And ever did I stray toward love; forever
Toward love; and yet I came upon it never—
And turned back home, in sickness and despair.
But here you were—I saw you drawing nigh—
And ah! the thing that swam within your eye—
That sweet, that long-desired love, was there.

TRANSLATED BY AARON KRAMER

≥ *Lyrical Intermezzo*

PROLOGUE   *Es war mal ein Ritter trübselig und stumm*

There once was a knight full of sorrow and doubt,
  With cheeks white as snow; indecision
Would lead him to stumble and stagger about
  As though he were trailing a vision.
And he was so wooden, so awkward and dumb
That flowers and maidens, whene'er he would come,
  Would watch him, and laugh in derision.

And often he'd sit in his gloom-shrouded place
  (From men and their joys he had broken)
Stretching thin arms in a yearning embrace,
  Though never a word would be spoken . . .
But just as the hours to midnight now ran,
A marvelous singing and ringing began,
  With a knock at his door for a token.

And lo, his love enters—a zephyr that blows;
  Of shimmering sea-foam her dress is.
She glows till she grows like the bud of a rose,
  Her veil gleams with gems; and her tresses

Fall to her feet in a golden array;
Her eyes are impassioned. The lovers give way
 And yield to each other's caresses.

He holds her so close that his heart almost breaks.
 The wooden one now is afire;
The pallid one reddens, the dreamer awakes,
 The bashful is bold with desire.
But she, she coquettes and she teases, and then
With her magical veil she must blind him again,
 Who blindly does nought but admire.

In a watery palace of crystalline light
 She has 'witched him, and all that was bitter
Turns golden and fair, all is suddenly bright;
 His eyes are bemused with the glitter.
The nixie still presses him close to her side;
The knight is the bridegroom, the nixie the bride—
 Her maidens keep playing the zither.

Oh, sweetly they sing and sweetly they play;
 Fair feet in the dances are shown there;
The knight in his ardor is swooning away
 And tighter he clasps her, his own there . . .
Then all in an instant is plunged into gloom,
And our hero is sitting once more in his room.
 In his poet's dim garret—alone there!

TRANSLATED BY LOUIS UNTERMEYER

Im wunderschönen Monat Mai

In May, the magic month of May,
When all the buds were breaking,
Oh then within my heart
The fires of love awakened.

In May, the magic month of May,
When birds were merry-making,
Oh then I told my darling
Of how my heart was aching.

TRANSLATED BY AARON KRAMER

Aus meinen Tränen spriessen

> From all my tears of sorrow
> Beautiful flowers arise,
> And nightingales in chorus
> Soar up from my sighs.
>
> And, darling, if you love me
> I'll give all my flowers to you;
> And nightingales at your window
> Shall sing the whole night through.
>
> TRANSLATED BY AARON KRAMER

Die Rose, die Lilie, die Taube, die Sonne

> The rose, the lily, the sun and the dove,
> I loved them all once in the rapture of love.
> I love them no more, for my sole delight
> Is a maiden so slight, so bright and so white,
> Who, being herself the source of love,
> Is rose and lily and sun and dove.
>
> TRANSLATED BY P. G. L. WEBB

Wenn ich in deine Augen seh

> Dear, when I look into thine eyes,
> My deepest sorrow straightway flies;
> But when I kiss thy mouth, ah, then
> No thought remains of bygone pain.
>
> And when I lean upon thy breast,
> No dream of heaven could be more blest;
> But, when thou say'st thou lovest me,
> I fall to weeping bitterly.
>
> TRANSLATED BY ALMA STRETTELL

Lehn deine Wang an meine Wang

> Oh, let your tears with mine bedew
> The cheek you lay your cheek on,
> And let the flames of heart on heart
> Blaze in a single beacon.
>
> And when that fiery signal must
> To tidal tears surrender,
> Oh, then I'll hold you to my heart,
> And die of love's mere wonder.
>
> TRANSLATED BY HUMBERT WOLFE

Es stehen unbeweglich

> The stars, for many ages,
> Have dwelt in heaven above;
> They gaze at one another
> Tormented by their love.
>
> They speak the richest language,
> The loveliest ever heard;
> Yet none of all the linguists
> Can understand a word.
>
> I learned it, though, in lessons
> That nothing can erase;
> The only text I needed
> Was my beloved's face.
>
> TRANSLATED BY AARON KRAMER

Auf Flügeln des Gesanges

> On wings of song, beloved,
> I'll bear you away through the air,
> Away to the Ganges River:
> I know of a valley there.

Deep among rose-red bowers,
Under a tranquil moon,
The sacred lotus-flowers
Await their sister bloom.

The violets kiss, and titter,
And up at the stars they peer;
What tales the roses twitter
In one another's ear!

The wise gazelles forever
Leap by, and listen, and play;
And the waves of the holy river
Are murmuring far away.

There, among the flowers,
In the shade of a palm we'll rest;
And peace and love will be ours,
And we'll dream the dream of the blest.

TRANSLATED BY AARON KRAMER

Die Lotosblume ängstigt

The lotus-flower is harassed
By the sun's majestic light,
And with her face turned downward
She dreamily waits for the night.

The moon is her adorer,
He wakens her with his rays,
And sweetly she uncovers
Her gentle flower-face.

She blooms and glows and blazes,
And looks at her light above;
She pants and weeps and trembles
With love and the pain of love.

TRANSLATED BY AARON KRAMER

Du liebst mich nicht, du liebst mich nicht

> You do not love me, sweet one? Why,
>   That is a trifling thing;
> Let me but see your face, and I
>   Am happy as a king.
>
> "I hate you, hate you!" even this
>   The little mouth has said;
> Yet give me but that mouth to kiss,
>   Child, and I'm comforted.
>
>> TRANSLATED BY ALMA STRETTELL

Ich grolle nicht, und wenn das Herz auch bricht

> I shall not mourn, although my heart is torn;
> Forever vanished love! I shall not mourn.
> Bediamonded in splendor though you gleam,
> Within your heart's black night there falls no beam.
>
> I've known it long. In dreams I saw you plain,
> And saw the night within your heart's domain,
> And saw the snake that feasts upon your heart—
> I saw, my love, how miserable you are.
>
>> TRANSLATED BY AARON KRAMER

Die Linde blühte, die Nachtigall sang

> The nightingale sang; the linden flowered;
> The sun laughed kindly; and then you showered
> Kisses upon me, and clasped me, and pressed
> My breast against your heaving breast.
>
> The leaves came down, the raven's cry
> Was hollow, the face of the sun turned wry;
> And then we frostily said: "Good night!"
> And the curtsy you curtsied was most polite.
>
>> TRANSLATED BY AARON KRAMER

Sie haben dir viel erzählet

They have told you many stories
And made a great to-do;
But why my spirit worries
Has not been told to you.

They made a stir and pother,
Complaining and shaking the head,
"A devil!" they said to each other;
And you believed all they said.

And yet the very worst thing
They never have even guessed;
For the worst and most accurst thing,
I carry hid in my breast.

TRANSLATED BY LOUIS UNTERMEYER

Ein Fichtenbaum steht einsam

A pine tree towers lonely
In the north, on a barren height.
He's drowsy; ice and snowdrift
Quilt him in covers of white.

He dreams about a palm tree
That, far in the East alone,
Looks down in silent sorrow
From her cliff of blazing stone.

TRANSLATED BY AARON KRAMER

Aus meinen grossen Schmerzen

Out of my great woes
A little ballad springs;
It raises tinkling wings
And away to her heart it goes.

It finds the heart of my fair,
But comes back in distress;
Comes back, and won't confess
What it discovered there.

TRANSLATED BY AARON KRAMER

Und als ich so lange, so lange gesäumt

And thus, as I wasted many a day
In wandering and dreaming the hours away,
My love found the waiting too long a recess,
She started to sew on her wedding-dress;
And caught in her arms (oh, deluded and dupèd)
As husband, the stupidest one of the stupid.

My loved one is so mild and fair
Her likeness haunts me everywhere;
The rose-cheeks and the violet-eyes
Year in, year out, their ghosts arise.
And that I should lose a love so dear,
Was the stupidest act of my stupid career.

TRANSLATED BY LOUIS UNTERMEYER

Manch Bild vergessener Zeiten

From graves of times forgotten
    Old visions come to me
Revealing what, when near you,
    My life once used to be.

By day I wandered dreaming
    Through streets and alleys until
The people looked at me wondering;
    I was so gloomy and still.

By night it was somewhat better—
    The streets were an empty rout;
And I and my shadow together
    Went staggering blindly about.

With ever-echoing footsteps
I crossed the bridge by chance;
The moon broke through the darkness
And shot me an earnest glance.

I stood there, before your dwelling,
And gazed into the night;
Gazing up at your window
My heart was torn at the sight . . .

I know that, from the window,
Those lonely streets you scanned,
And saw me in the moonbeams,
Like some white pillar stand.

TRANSLATED BY LOUIS UNTERMEYER

Hör ich das Liedchen klingen

Whenever I hear the song
My love sang long ago,
I feel that my heart is wrung
By a wild, a savage woe.

I'm driven to the crown
Of a lofty forest-height.
And as the tears stream down
My giant grief grows light.

TRANSLATED BY AARON KRAMER

Ich hab dich geliebet und liebe dich noch!

I've loved you, and love you this very hour!
And though the whole world crashes,
Still the flames of my love will tower
Over the cities' ashes.

TRANSLATED BY AARON KRAMER

Sie haben mich gequälet

> They have tormented me
> Early and late
> Some with their love,
> Some with their hate.
>
> The wine I drank,
> The bread I ate,
> Some poisoned with love
> Some poisoned with hate.
>
> Yet she who has grieved me
> Most of all,
> She never hated
> Nor loved me at all.

TRANSLATED BY MONICA TURNBULL

Wenn zwei von einander scheiden

> The last farewell of lovers
> Is whispered as they stand
> With tears they cannot conquer,
> And hand in trembling hand.
>
> But when we two were parted
> We did not sigh nor moan.
> We had all life before us
> In which to weep alone.

TRANSLATED BY HUMBERT WOLFE

Vergiftet sind meine Lieder

> My songs are poisoned, say you—
> How should they wholesome be
> When my young blood is tainted
> With a poison poured by thee?

My songs are poisoned, say you—
How should they wholesome prove
When my heart is full of serpents—
And of thee, my Lilith-love?

TRANSLATED BY M. M. BOZMAN

Ich hab im Traum geweinet

In a dream my tears were falling;
You were borne to your burial-place.
I woke, and still the teardrops
Were streaming down my face.

In a dream my tears were falling;
I dreamed you were false to me.
I woke, and for many hours
Kept weeping bitterly.

In a dream my tears were falling;
I dreamed you were true to your vow.
I woke, and my torrent of sorrow
Is pouring even now.

TRANSLATED BY AARON KRAMER

Der Traumgott bracht mich in ein Riesenschloss

The Dream-God led me to a castle grim
    Full of strange lights, strange scents and stranger glamor;
And through great labyrinths there seemed to swim
    Wild multitudes whom nothing could enamor.
Onward they swept, through halls and portals dim,
    Wringing pale hands with an incessant clamor.
Maidens and knights I saw among the throng,
And, with the torrent, I was borne along.

When suddenly I am alone—and lo,
    I cannot find a single face whatever.
Through frowning aisles and winding rooms I go;
    Fiercely impelled by one intense endeavor.

But oh, my feet are lead, my footsteps slow . . .
   To find the gate, and leave this place forever!
At last, I gain the portals with a prayer,
Fling wide the door and leap . . . *O God, who's there!*

My love! Beside that door I saw her stand,
   Pain on her lips and sorrow's crown above her.
Then back she turned me with a waving hand,
   Threatening or warning, I could not discover . . .
Yet, from her eyes, sprang, like a sweet command,
   A fire that made me once again her lover.
Tender and strong, her very glances spoke
The flaming speech of love—and I awoke.

TRANSLATED BY LOUIS UNTERMEYER

Am Kreuzweg wird begraben

> Their graves are at the crossroads
> Whose own hand wrought their doom;
> A sad blue flower grows there,
> The lone Poor-Sinner's Bloom.
>
> I stood and sighed at the crossroads,
> All was silence and gloom.
> Slowly swayed in the moonlight
> The lone Poor-Sinner's Bloom.

TRANSLATED BY AARON KRAMER

❧ Homecoming

THE LORELEY   *Ich weiss nicht wa, soll es bedeuten*

> I cannot explain the sadness
> That's fallen on my breast.
> An old, old fable haunts me,
> And will not let me rest.

The air grows cool in the twilight,
And softly the Rhine flows on;
The peak of a mountain sparkles
Beneath the setting sun.

More lovely than a vision,
A girl sits high up there;
Her golden jewelry glistens,
She combs her golden hair.

With a comb of gold she combs it,
And sings an evensong;
The wonderful melody reaches
A boat, as it sails along.

The boatman hears, with an anguish
More wild than was ever known;
He's blind to the rocks around him;
His eyes are for her alone.

—At last the waves devoured
The boat, and the boatman's cry;
And this she did with her singing,
The golden Loreley.

TRANSLATED BY AARON KRAMER

Als ich, auf der Reise, zufällig

I happened to meet, while travelling,
My sweetheart's family—
Sister, father and mother;
And gladly they greeted me.

They asked how I was feeling,
And hastened then to say
That I hadn't really changed much,
Except that my face was gray.

I asked about aunts and cousins,
And many a bore we knew;
And I didn't forget to mention
Their gentle puppy, too.

And I asked about my sweetheart
Whom someone else had wed;
And with a smile they told me
That she'd been brought to bed.

I smiled felicitations,
And whispered lovingly
That they should remember to greet her
A thousand times for me.

Then spoke the little sister:
"That gentle pup of mine
Became so big and crazy,
He had to be drowned in the Rhine."

The little one's like my sweetheart;
I hear that laughter again;
Her eyes are like those others
That filled my heart with pain.

TRANSLATED BY AARON KRAMER

Wir sassen am Fischerhause

Beside the fisherman's cottage
We sat with sea-ward eyes.
The clouds of evening gathered
And climbed up to the skies.

The lanterns in the lighthouse
One by one were lighted,
And far-off in the distance
Another ship was sighted.

We spoke of storm and shipwreck,
And of the sailor's years
Between the skies and the waters,
Between delights and fears.

We spoke of the north and the tropics,
Of many a distant land,
Where strangers live, whose customs
Are hard to understand.

The trees along the Ganges
Like blossoming giants loom,
And comely folk kneel softly
Before the lotus-bloom.

The Lapland folk are filthy,
Flat-headed, broad-mouthed, small;
They squat around the fire,
Bake fish, and croak, and squall.

The maidens listened gravely,
And soon we spoke no more—
The ship was lost in the darkness
That covered sea and shore.

TRANSLATED BY AARON KRAMER

Du schönes Fischermädchen

You lovely fishermaiden,
Steer your boat to the land!
Come here and sit beside me:
We'll whisper, hand in hand.

Rest your dear head against me,
And do not draw away.
You trust yourself, untroubled,
To the savage sea each day.

My heart is like those waters:
It has its storms and tides;
And deep within its caverns
Many a jewel hides.

TRANSLATED BY AARON KRAMER

Der Wind zieht seine Hosen an

The wind pulls up his water-spouts
His white and foaming breeches;
He whips the waves; he storms and shouts.
The whole sea heaves and pitches!

From the black skies, a furious might
Impels the rain's commotion;
It seems as though the ancient night
Had come to drown the ocean.

To the mast a vagrant sea-gull clings
With a hoarse shrilling and crying.
As though in despair she flaps her wings;
An evil prophesying.

TRANSLATED BY LOUIS UNTERMEYER

Wenn ich an deinem Hause

When early in the morning
I pass your dwelling-place
I'm glad to see the window
Made brighter by your face.

You look at me in wonder,
With eyes so deeply brown:
Who are you, strange, sick fellow?
What sorrow weighs you down?

"I am a German poet,
In German lands I'm famed;
When the proudest names are mentioned
Then mine is also named.

"And, child, the thing that hurts me
Hurts many a German breast;
When the worst of griefs are mentioned,
Mine are among the rest."

TRANSLATED BY AARON KRAMER

Das Meer erglänzte weit hinaus

Far off, in evening's final blaze
The ocean faintly shone;
We sat at the lonely fisherman's place,
We sat there mute and alone.

A gull flew by, the water swelled,
The mist began to rise;
Out of your eyes the teardrops welled,
Out of your love-filled eyes.

I saw them falling on your hand,
And sank upon my knee;
The bitter tears on your white hand
Were sweet as wine to me.

Since then my flesh has been consumed,
My love-racked soul is dying—
The miserable woman doomed
And poisoned me with her crying.

TRANSLATED BY AARON KRAMER

Still ist die Nacht, es ruhen die Gassen

The night is calm; the streets quiet down;
Here lived a lass who was dear to me.
Long years ago she left the town,
But here is her house, as it used to be.

And here is a creature who stares into space
And wrings his hands in a storm of pain.
I shudder when I see his face:
It is my own self the moon shows plain.

You double! You comrade ghostly white!
Why have you come to ape the woe
That tortured me, night after night,
Under these windows—long ago?

TRANSLATED BY AARON KRAMER

Ich stand in dunkeln Träumen

> I stood in the gloom, half-dreaming,
> And gazed at a picture of her,
> And those beloved features
> Strangely began to stir.
>
> Around her lips there trembled
> A most miraculous smile,
> And her eyes, as though with teardrops,
> Were gleaming all the while.
>
> And down my cheeks a torrent
> Of tears began to pour—
> And oh! I cannot believe it:
> That you'll be mine no more!
>
> TRANSLATED BY AARON KRAMER

Sie liebten sich beide, doch keiner

> They were in love, but neither
> Would let the other know;
> And while they were dying of passion,
> Hatred was all they'd show.
>
> They parted at last, and only
> In dream did their love live on.
> Long ago they perished,
> And scarcely knew they were gone.
>
> TRANSLATED BY AARON KRAMER

Mensch, verspotte nicht den Teufel

> Mortal, do not mock the devil,
> Soon the road of life is run,
> And perdition's no mere story
> That an idle brain has spun.

Creature, pay your obligations,
Life's long road is just begun;
Many times you'll have to borrow,
As you have so often done.

TRANSLATED BY AARON KRAMER

Herz, mein Herz, sei nicht beklommen

Let no trouble overcome you,
Heart, my heart—but bear your pain.
Spring shall come, and bring again
All that Winter's taken from you.

And how great is still your treasure!
And the world, how fair a place!
And, my heart, you may embrace
All on earth that gives you pleasure.

TRANSLATED BY AARON KRAMER

Ich wollt, meine Schmerzen ergössen

Oh, could I capture my sadness
    And pour it all into one word;
The glad-hearted breezes would lift it
    And carry it off, like a bird.

They'd bear it to you, oh, belovéd,
    That word of passionate care;
And every hour you'd hear it,
    'Twould follow you everywhere.

Yes, when you have scarce closed your eyelids,
    And slumber over them streams,
That word will arise and pursue you—
    Even into your dreams.

TRANSLATED BY LOUIS UNTERMEYER

Mein Kind, wir waren Kinder

My child, we two were children,
Two children, small and gay;
We used to creep to the hen-house
And hide beneath the hay.

We tried to chirp like chickens,
And hoped the passers-by
Would hear us there and fancy
They heard a chicken cry.

We built a lordly castle
With boxes, in the court,
And set up house together,
Quite grandly as we thought.

The old cat paid us visits
As often as she could;
We used to bow and curtsy
And "hoped her health was good."

We made her pretty speeches,
And spoke of this and that—
Things we have since repeated
To many a grave old cat.

We sat and talked as wisely
As grown-up people may;
Complaining things had altered
Most sadly since our day.

"Love, faith, and truth no longer
Existed anywhere:
But coffee had grown dearer
And money very rare!"

Those days are past, and all things
Are passing by, in sooth:
Money, the world, the ages,
And love and faith and truth.

TRANSLATED BY ALMA STRETTELL

Du bist wie eine Blume

You're lovely as a flower,
So pure and fair to see;
I look at you, and sadness
Comes stealing over me.

I feel, my hands should gently
Cover your head in prayer—
That God may always keep you
So lovely, pure, and fair.

TRANSLATED BY AARON KRAMER

Du hast Diamanten und Perlen

My sweet, you have the jewels,
   And all that men go wrong for—
And the eyes beneath your eyelids—
   What else have you to long for?

And I, my sweet, have written
   Song after deathless song for
The eyes beneath your eyelids—
   What else have you to long for?

The eyes beneath your eyelids,
   My sweet, proved far too strong for
This broken heart—and therefore,
   What else have you to long for?

TRANSLATED BY HUMBERT WOLFE

Wie dunkle Träume stehen

Like gloomy dreams the houses
Stand in an endless row;
Enveloped in my mantle
Past them I silently go.

The church-tower announces midnight;
With kisses and with charms
My lady-love is waiting
To hold me in her arms.

The moon is my companion:
Kindly he lights my way;
Here at last is her dwelling,
And joyously I say:

Thank you, dear old brother,
That made my path so bright;
No longer shall I need you—
Give other lads your light.

And if you find a lover
Lamenting his grief alone,
Console him; shine for him now
As once for me you shone.

TRANSLATED BY AARON KRAMER

Doch die Kastraten klagten

And still the eunuchs grumbled,
    Whene'er my voice arose;
They grumbled as they mumbled
    My songs were far too gross.

And, oh, how sweetly thrilling
    Their little voices were;
Their light and limpid trilling
    Made such a pretty stir.

They sang of love, the leaping
    Flood that engulfs the heart . . .
The ladies all were weeping
    At such a feast of art!

TRANSLATED BY LOUIS UNTERMEYER

Der Tod das ist die kühle Nacht

> Death—it is still, cold night;
> Life—it is sultry day.
> Dusk falls, mine eyes grow heavy,
> Weary am I of the light.
>
> O'er my bed a tree leans near;
> A nightingale sings on the bough.
> She singeth only of love,
> And even in dreams I hear.
>
> TRANSLATED BY M. M. BOZMAN

Sag, wo ist dein schönes Liebchen

> "Tell me, where's your pretty girl-friend,
> Who once had your prettiest praise,
> When the magic fire seized you,
> Setting all your heart ablaze?"
>
> Ah, my heart is cold and gloomy,
> No more does that fire burn—
> Look! my love has turned to ashes,
> And this booklet is its urn.
>
> TRANSLATED BY AARON KRAMER

Mir träumt': ich bin der liebe Gott

> I dreamed: I am the dear Lord God
> Enthroned in Heaven's palace:
> The angels sit surrounding me
> And sweetly praise my ballads.
>
> I ask for costly cakes and sweets,
> And nibble them all day,
> And drink them down with rare old wine,
> And have no debts to pay.

But boredom plagues me terribly;
I have an urge to revel;
And were I not the dear Lord God
I'd go and join the Devil.

You, lanky angel Gabriel,
Put on your boots, begone!
Go find my dear old friend Eugene
And bring him to my throne!

Don't look for him in lecture-halls,
Behind a wine-glass search;
At Mamsell Meyer's look for him,
But not in Hedwig's church.

The angel swiftly spreads his wings
And flutters from the sky,
And picks him up, and brings him here,
My friend, the dear old guy.

Yes, lad, I am the dear Lord God,
And I am Lord of earth!
Haven't I always promised you
Some day I'd prove my worth?

I'll work new wonders every day:
They'll make your senses spin;
And for your sport this day I'll bless
The city of Berlin.

The paving-stones along the street
Shall suddenly be splitting.
And, fresh and clear, in every stone
You'll see an oyster sitting.

A rain of lemon juice shall fall
And sprinkle them like dew,
And gutters take the best Rhine wine
Through every avenue.

How happy the Berliners are!
They quickly run to eat.
The Judges of the district court
Are guzzling from the street.

How happy all the poets are
At such a godly scene!
The ensigns and lieutenant-lads,
They lick the gutters clean.

The ensigns and lieutenant-lads
Are really very clever;
They know: this kind of miracle
Can hardly last forever.

TRANSLATED BY AARON KRAMER

THE PILGRIMAGE TO KEVLAAR   *Am Fenster stand die Mutter*

I

The mother stood at the window,
The son was lying abed.
"Won't you get up, William,
To see the procession?" she said.

"I am so ill, o mother,
That I cannot hear or see.
I think of my dead Gretchen,
And it drains the heart in me."

"Get up, we'll start for Kevlaar;
Bring the book and the beads.
The Mother of God will see you
And heal your heart that bleeds."

The church-flags are aflutter.
The chant has a holy tone;
This is the great procession
That surges through Cologne.

The mother follows the people;
She keeps her son at her side.
Both of them sing in chorus:
"Mary, be glorified!"

II

This day God's Mother in Kevlaar
Puts on her finest gown;
This day she has much to accomplish:
—So many sick are in town.

Limbs that of wax are fashioned
The ailing pilgrims bring;
Wax feet and hands they carry
To serve as offering.

Whoever offers a wax hand,
His hand is healed of its sore;
And whoever offers a wax foot,
His foot is whole once more.

Many came here on crutches
Who dance on the tightrope today,
And many whose fingers were ailing
Now take up the viol and play.

The mother took a wax-candle
And shaped it into a heart.
"Bring this to Mother Mary,
And she will soothe your smart."

Sighing, he took the wax heart,
Went sighing to the saint.
Out of his eyes rained the teardrops,
Out of his heart the words rained:

"Thou holiest of the holy,
God's Maiden, without stain,
Empress of earth and Heaven,
To Thee I tell my pain.

"Once I lived with my mother
In Cologne, the city of prayer;
Many hundreds of chapels
And churches are standing there.

"And close by us lived Gretchen;
But now she lies entombed.
Mary, I bring Thee a wax heart;
Rid Thou my heart of its wound.

"Rid Thou my heart of its torment:
From dawn to eventide
I'll pray and sing with fervor:
Mary, be glorified!"

III

The ailing son and his mother
In their little chamber slept.
Up to his bed so softly
The Holy Mother stepped.

She bent above the sick one,
And softly seemed to lay
Her hand upon his bosom,
And smiled, and vanished away.

The mother saw all in a vision,
And more she was given to know.
She woke up out of her slumber:
The dogs were barking so.

There lay stretched out before her
Her son, and he was dead.
On his pale cheeks was playing
The morning's brilliant red.

The mother's hands were folded;
She felt so strange inside.
She sang devoutly, softly:
"*Mary, be glorified!*"

TRANSLATED BY AARON KRAMER

✍ *The Journey to the Harz*

PROLOGUE *Schwarze Röcke, seidne Strümpfe*

Black dress-coats and silken stockings,
   Cuffs of snowy white—beshrew them!
Soft embraces, oily speeches.
   Ah, if but a heart beat through them!

If a storm could stir your shirt-fronts,
   Ruffle them in any fashion!
Oh, you kill me with your maudlin
   Bursts of imitation passion.

I will go and climb the mountains,
   Where the simple huts are standing,
Where the winds blow fresh and freely,
   And a chest may try expanding.

I will go and climb the mountains,
   Where the mighty pine-trees tower,
Where the birds and brooks are singing,
   And the heavens grow in power.

Fare ye well, ye polished Salons,
   Polished folk and polished chaffing—
I will climb the rugged mountains,
   And look down upon you, laughing.
       TRANSLATED BY LOUIS UNTERMEYER

MOUNTAIN IDYLL (II) *Tannenbaum, mit grünen Fingern*

Low against the little window
Beats the fir with fingers green;
And the moon, the silent listener,
Fills the room with golden sheen.

Softly snoring in the bedroom
Lie her father and her mother;
But we two, with blissful babbling,
We keep sleep from one another.

"When you say you've prayed too often
I'm afraid you're fooling, dear;
Surely it was not by praying
That you learned so well to sneer.

"Every time I see you sneering
I get shivers down my spine,
Though your eyes dispel my terror
By the tender way they shine.

"And I doubt that you're religious
In the pious way of most—
You've no faith in God the Father,
In the Son and Holy Ghost?"

When I was a lad, my darling,
And at mother's knee I stood,
I believed in God the Father,
He who rules us, great and good.

He who made this lovely planet
And its lovely human race;
Gave the sun and moon their highways,
Kept each flaming star in place.

Then, my child, as I grew older,
Greater truths could be perceived;
I perceived, and grew in wisdom:
In the Son I now believed;

The Beloved Son who, loving,
Manifested Love to us,
While, as usual, the people
Nailed His body to the cross.

Now that I've matured, and studied
Many a book and far-off coast,
All my heart, my swelling heart, is
Bowed before the Holy Ghost.

He has worked amazing wonders,
And the best are yet to be—
He has smashed the forts of tyrants;
He has set the bondsman free.

He shall heal the ancient death-wounds,
Let the old law be renewed:
All men, equal-born, shall prosper
In a noble brotherhood.

He shall chase the clouds of evil,
Sweep the gloomy fraud away
That destroys our love and pleasure:
Sneering at us night and day.

He has named a thousand champions,
Armoured well, and armed with steel;
Chosen to fulfill his wishes—
And he's flamed their hearts with zeal.

Their beloved swords are flashing;
Their crusading banners fly!
Ah, you'd like to see, my darling,
Such proud knights go riding by?

Well, then look at me, my darling;
Kiss me—do not be afraid!
I myself am such a champion
In the Holy Ghost's crusade.

TRANSLATED BY AARON KRAMER

⟡ The North Sea

CORONATION *Ihr Lieder! Ihr meine guten Lieder!*

Ye songs! Ye valiant songs of mine
Up, up, and arm yourselves!
Let all the trumpets echo,

And lift this blossoming girl
Upon my shield.
For now my restless heart
Longs for her rule, proclaims her Queen.

Hail to thee, hail—oh, youthful Queen!

From the fierce sun at noon
I'll tear the red and gleaming gold,
And it shall be a diadem
For thy belovéd head.
From the great, waving, blue silk tent of heaven,
Where all the diamonds of the night are flashing,
I'll cut a mighty piece;
And hang it, like a royal mantle,
About thy royal shoulders.
I'll give thee a kingly dower
Of starched and polished sonnets,
Haughty tercets, proud and courtly stanzas.
For Pages I shall give thee my wit;
For Court-fool, my wild imagination;
For Herald, with laughing tears in his escutcheon,
My Humor shall serve thee . . .
But I, myself, dear Queen,
I humbly kneel before thee,
And present to thee, from the velvet cushion,
With deepest homage,
The little reason
That mercifully has been left me
By thy predecessor in the realm.

TRANSLATED BY LOUIS UNTERMEYER

TWILIGHT   *Am blassen Meeresstrande*

I sat on the pale sea-sand
Grieved by my thoughts and lonely.
The sun sank ever lower, and threw
Red hot streaks upon the water,
And the white, the far-away billows,

Urged on by the flood,
Sparkled and murmured nearer and nearer—
A singular noise, a whispering and piping,
A laughing and murmuring, sighing and whistling,
Through all a mysterious cradle-song humming—
I thought I was hearing forgotten legends,
Ancient, lovely fables,
That I once, as a boy,
Learned from the neighbors' children,
When on a summer's evening,
On the steps before the street-door,
We squatted down to the quiet telling,
With little, hearkening hearts
And curious-clever eyes;—
While, opposite us at the window,
By fragrant flower-pots,
The grown-up girls were sitting,
Rosy-faced,
Smiling and lit by the moon.

TRANSLATED BY AARON KRAMER

SEA GREETING *Thalatta! Thalatta!*

Thalatta! Thalatta! [1]
Hail to thee, O Sea, ageless and eternal!
Hail to thee, from a jubilant heart—
Ten thousand times hail!
Hail, as you were hailed by
Ten thousand Grecian hearts;
Calamity-conquering, homeward-hungering,
Immortal Grecian hearts.

The billows rolled higher,
Heaving and howling;
The sun poured eagerly downward
A rain of rosy lights;
The startled sea-gulls
Flew off with loud cries;
And there were sounds of horses stamping,

And the clashing of shields,
And echoes ringing, like a battle-shout:
"Thalatta! Thalatta!"

Hail to thee, Sea, ageless and eternal!
The whisper of your waters is as the speech of my own land;
The shimmer and surge of your billowy wastes
Is as the dreams of my childhood;
And old memory reveals in new colors
All of those lovely, wonderful playthings,
All of those glittering Christmas presents,
All of those rosy branches of coral,
Goldfish and pearls and shining sea-shells,—
All that you cherish and guard
Down in your clear and crystal depths.
Oh, how I have suffered in strange places!
My heart lay in my breast
Like a fading flower
In the tin box of a botanist.
It seems as though I had sat through the whole Winter,
A sick man in a dismal room,—
And now I leave it!
And suddenly there streams upon me
The emerald Spring, the sun-awakened;
And white branches rustle
And the young flowers look at me
With bright and odorous eyes,
And there's perfume and humming and laughter in all that breathes,
And in the blue heavens the very birds are singing:
"Thalatta! Thalatta!"

Oh, dauntless, home-returning heart,
How often, oh, how often,
The barbarian girls of the North have assailed you!
How often have they shot burning arrows
With their great, conquering eyes;
How often have they threatened to cleave the breast
With curved, two-edged words;
How often their chiseled, hieroglyphic letters
Have beaten on my poor, bewildered brain.
I raised my shield against them vainly.

The arrows whistled, the blows came crashing,
And the barbarian girls of the North
Drove me to the sea—
And now, with a great breath, I greet it,
The long-loved, rescuing sea,
"Thalatta! Thalatta!"

TRANSLATED BY LOUIS UNTERMEYER

NEW POEMS

ಳು *New Spring*

PROLOGUE   *In Gemäldegalerieen*

> Often, in museum-shows,
> There's a warrior revealed
> In a brave and martial pose:
> Flourishing his sword and shield.
>
> But the amoretti tease him,
> Rob him of his shield and sword;
> And, against his will, they seize him,
> Tie him up in flower-cord.
>
> So I chain myself with charms,
> Lost in sorrow and delight—
> While my fellows take up arms
> In this day's tremendous fight.

TRANSLATED BY AARON KRAMER

Ich lieb eine Blume, doch weiss ich nicht welche

> I love a flower, but which can it be?
> I do not know.
> I search the flower-cups, to see
> Where a heart may grow.
>
> The flowers smell sweet in the light of the moon;
> A nightingale's heard.
> I seek a heart as deep as my own,
> As deeply stirred.
>
> A nightingale's heard, and its sweet refrain
> Rings in my ear;
> Both of us know such fear and pain,
> Such pain and fear.
>
> TRANSLATED BY AARON KRAMER

Leise zieht durch mein Gemüt

> Over me a melody
> Softly steals; oh, ring!
> Ring out, sing out far and free!
> Little song of Spring.
>
> Ring out till you reach the place
> Where the flowers grow.
> Should a rose turn up her face,
> Say I said Hello!
>
> TRANSLATED BY AARON KRAMER

Gekommen ist der Maie

> Here's May, with all its lifting
> Of leaves and voices high;
> And rosy clouds are drifting
> Across an azure sky.

A nightingale is singing
In every bower and croft;
And little lambs are springing
Where fields are clover-soft.

But I am not singing or springing;
I lie on a grassy plot,
Hearing a distant ringing,
And dreaming of God knows what.

TRANSLATED BY LOUIS UNTERMEYER

Der Schmetterling ist in die Rose verliebt

The butterfly is in love with the rose
And flutters about her all day,
While he, in turn, is pursued by a bright
Sunbeam that follows his way.

But wait—with whom is the rose in love?
For whom does she tremble and pale?
Is it the silent evening star?
The passionate nightingale?

I do not know whom the red rose loves;
But I love you all, for I
Sing nightingale, sunbeam, and evening star,
The rose and the butterfly!

TRANSLATED BY LOUIS UNTERMEYER

Was treibt dich umher, in der Frühlingsnacht?

What whirls you about in the Spring-filled night?
You've driven the flowers mad with fright:
The violets are aquiver!
The modest roses are turning red,
The lilies are as pale as the dead,
They wail, and they quail, and they shiver.

O, dear moon, what a modest crew
The flowers are! Their charge is true,
I have offended grossly!
Yet while I spoke with the stars above,
Intoxicated by blazing love,
Could I know they attended so closely?

TRANSLATED BY AARON KRAMER

Die schlanke Wasserlilie

The slender water-lily
    Stares at the heavens above,
And sees the moon who gazes
    With the luminous eyes of love.

Blushing, she bends and lowers
    Her head in a shamed retreat—
And there is the poor, pale lover,
    Languishing at her feet!

TRANSLATED BY LOUIS UNTERMEYER

Sag mir, wer einst die Uhren erfund

Tell me by whom the clock was planned:
The second hand, and the minute hand?
That was a sad man, cold as stone.
He sat on a Winter's night, alone,
And counted the secret squeaks of the mouse,
The woodworm's peckings upon the house.

Tell me who first invented the kiss?
That was a mouth on fire with bliss.
He kissed, unthinking, all through the day.
It was in the lovely month of May.
Up from the earth the blossoms sprang,
The sun laughed, and the birds all sang.

TRANSLATED BY AARON KRAMER

Mit deinen blauen Augen

> You gaze upon me sweetly
> With your eyes of blue,
> And my brain becomes so dreamy,
> That I've no words for you.
>
> I think about your blue eyes
> Wherever I may be—
> Over my heart are rolling
> Blue thoughts like a sea.
>
> TRANSLATED BY AARON KRAMER

Ich wandle unter Blumen

> I walk in a crowd of flowers,
> And bloom amid their May.
> I walk as though in a vision,
> And at every step I sway.
>
> Oh, hold me tight, beloved!
> For, love-drunk, otherwise
> I'll fall at your feet this instant,
> And the garden is full of eyes.
>
> TRANSLATED BY AARON KRAMER

Wie die Nelken duftig atmen!

> What a fragrance of carnations!
> With what glitter of alarm
> In the violet-blue heaven
> Stars, like bees of fire, swarm!
>
> Through the darkness of the chestnuts
> I can see the villa's glow,
> And I hear the glass-door clatter,
> And my loved one speaking low.

Precious quivering, sweet trembling,
Timidly together clinging—
And the warm young roses listen,
And the nightingales are singing.

TRANSLATED BY AARON KRAMER

Es war ein alter König

There was an aged monarch,
His heart was sad, his hair was grey;
Alas, poor fool, he took him
A wife that was young and gay!

There was a handsome page-boy,
Light was his heart and gold his hair;
The silken train he carried
Of that queen so young and fair.

Dost thou not know my story,
So sweet, so sad to tell?
Death was the lovers' portion
Because they loved too well.

TRANSLATED BY KATE F. KROEKER

Der Brief, den du geschrieben

Your letter does not move me
Although the words are strong;
You say you will not love me—
But ah, the letter's long . . .

Twelve pages, neat and double.
A little essay! Why,
One never takes such trouble
To write a mere good-by.

TRANSLATED BY LOUIS UNTERMEYER

In meiner Erinnrung erblühen

Memories suddenly blossom,
That faded long ago—
What is there in your speaking
That rocks my being so?

Don't tell me that you love me!
I know, each exquisite thing
Must finally fall into ruin—
Love, and the time of Spring.

Don't tell me that you love me!
But kiss, and let nothing be said;
And smile if in the morning
I show you the roses—dead.

TRANSLATED BY AARON KRAMER

Die holden Wünsche blühen

The tender wishes blossom,
   And wither at a breath,
And bloom again, and wither—
   Until they cease in death.

'Tis knowing this that saddens
   For me the love most blest:
My heart has learned such wisdom
   That it bleeds within my breast.

TRANSLATED BY MARGARET ARMOUR

Sterne mit den goldnen Füsschen

Stars with golden feet are walking
   Through the skies with footsteps light,
Lest they wake the earth below them,
   Sleeping in the lap of night.

All the silent forests listen;
  Every leaf's a small, green ear;
And the dreaming mountain stretches
  Shadowy arms that reach me here.

Hush, who called there? My heart trembles
  As the dying echoes fail.
Was it my beloved, or was it
  Just a lonely nightingale?

                    TRANSLATED BY LOUIS UNTERMEYER

Spätherbstnebel, kalte Träume

          Autumn fog, cold fantasies,
          Over hill and valley brood,
          And a windstorm strips the trees,
          And they tremble: ghostly nude.

          Only one lone, silent sad
          Lonely tree, unshorn of leaf,
          Stands and tosses his green head
          Moist, as if from tears of grief.

          Ah, my heart's this savage place,
          And the tree I look on there,
          Summer-green, that is your face:
          So beloved, and so fair!

                    TRANSLATED BY AARON KRAMER

❧ *Miscellaneous*

SERAPHINE

An dem stillen Meeresstrande

> Night has come with silent footsteps,
>   On the beaches by the ocean;
> And the waves, with curious whispers,
>   Ask the moon, "Have you a notion
>
> "Who that man is? Is he foolish,
>   Or with love is he demented?
> For he seems so sad and cheerful,
>   So cast down yet so contented."
>
> And the moon, with shining laughter,
>   Answers them, "If you must know it,
> He is both in love *and* foolish;
>   And, besides that, he's a poet!"
>
>   TRANSLATED BY LOUIS UNTERMEYER

Dass du mich liebst, das wusst ich

> I'd long ago discovered
> How much you really care;
> And yet, when you confessed it,
> It gave me quite a scare.
>
> I sang atop the mountains,
> And capered like a clown;
> I wept beside the ocean
> To see the sun go down.

My heart can blaze as brightly
As any sun above,
And, beautiful and noble,
Sinks in a sea of love.

TRANSLATED BY AARON KRAMER

Wie neubegierig die Möwe

How this too anxious sea-gull
Follows us even here,
Because your lips come closer
And closer to my ear.

Need I confess I'm filled with
More wonder than the bird's;
Anxious if I'm to be thrilled with
Your kisses or your words.

If I were only certain
What shakes my pulse like this!
Tauntingly intermingled
Are promise and the kiss.

TRANSLATED BY LOUIS UNTERMEYER

Sie floh vor mir wie'n Reh so scheu

She fled me timid as a doe—
No doe more swift than she;
From crag to crag she climbed, against
The wind her hair blew free.

I reached her where the rocky cliff
Sinks down into the sea.
With gentle word I gently turned
Her timid heart to me.

So heaven-high, so heaven-blessed,
We sat here; while below

Slowly into the darkening sea
Went down the sunset-glow.

Below us in the darkening sea
Went down the lovely light;
The waves rushed over it with fierce,
Impetuous delight.

O shed no tear, within those floods
The sun did not expire;
He hid himself inside my heart
With all his seething fire.

TRANSLATED BY AARON KRAMER

Das Fräulein stand am Meere

The young miss stood by the ocean
And sighed an anxious sigh;
She felt such deep emotion
Seeing the sunlight die.

My dear, it's an age-old number,
Don't let it weigh on your mind;
Here in front it goes under,
And wheels right back from behind.

TRANSLATED BY AARON KRAMER

Auf diesem Felsen bauen wir

Upon these rocks we'll build a church
To celebrate the splendid,
The Third and Final Testament;
Our sufferings are ended.

Destroyed is the duality
That long has bound us fast;
The stupid torment of the flesh
Is flung aside at last.

Do you hear God's word in the darkened sea?
Thousand-voiced He exclaims.
And can't you see above our heads
The thousand God-lit flames?

The holy Lord is in the light
And in the night's abysses;
And God is everything that is:
He throbs in our kisses.

TRANSLATED BY AARON KRAMER

ANGELIQUE

Ich halte ihr die Augen zu

I close her eyes, and keep them tight
    Whene'er we come to kiss;
Her laughter, curious and bright,
    Asks me the cause of this.

From early morn till late at night
    She questions why it is
I close her eyes and keep them tight
    Whene'er we come to kiss.

I do not even know—not quite,
    What my own reason is—
I close her eyes, and keep them tight
    Whene'er we come to kiss.

TRANSLATED BY LOUIS UNTERMEYER

Wenn ich, beseligt von schönen Küssen

When in your arms and in our kisses
    I find love's sweet and happiest season,
My Germany you must never mention—
    I cannot bear it: there is a reason.

Oh, silence your chatter on anything German;
You must not plague me or ask me to share it.
Be still when you think of my home or my kindred—
There is a reason: I cannot bear it.

The oaks are green, and the German women
Have smiling eyes that know no treason;
They speak of Love and Faith and Honor!
I cannot bear it: there is a reason.

TRANSLATED BY LOUIS UNTERMEYER

Während ich nach andrer Leute

While I gaze at other people's
Cherished ones, and to and fro,
Sick with longing, past the doorway
Of another's love I go,

Then, perhaps, those other people
Pass before another place,
And beneath my very windows
Smile up at my darling's face.

That is human! God in Heaven,
Shelter us on all our ways!
Grant us all, oh God in Heaven,
Benedictions and bright days!

TRANSLATED BY AARON KRAMER

Schaff mich nicht ab, wenn auch den Durst

Don't drop me, though our lovely drink
Has quenched the thirst in you;
Keep me for just a season more,
Then I'll be sated, too.

If you can no longer be my love,
Then treat me as a friend;
The time for friendship just begins
When love has reached its end.

TRANSLATED BY AARON KRAMER

HORTENSE

Wir standen an der Strasseneck

We stood upon the corner, where,
For upwards of an hour,
We spoke with soulful tenderness
Of love's transcending power.

Our fervors grew; a hundred times
Impassioned oaths we made there.
We stood upon the corner—and,
Alas, my love, we stayed there!

The goddess Opportunity,
A maid, alert and sprightly,
Came by, observed us standing there,
And passed on, laughing lightly.

TRANSLATED BY LOUIS UNTERMEYER

CLARISSA

Überall wo du auch wandelst

Every hour, everywhere
You may wander, I'll be there,
And the greater wrongs you do,
Greater grows my bond to you.

Sweet ill-will has always held me,
Just as kindness has repelled me;
If you hope to be set free
You must fall in love with me.

TRANSLATED BY AARON KRAMER

FRIEDRIKE

Verlass Berlin, mit seinem dicken Sande

Escape Berlin, with all its muddy sand,
And too-too clever folk, and feeble tea:
Now with Hegelian logic they can see
How God, the world, and they themselves were planned.
Let's sail for India, for the sunrise-land,
Where fragrance showers from the Ambra-tree,
And, marching toward the Ganges, solemnly
Advances many a white-robed pilgrim-band.

There, where the palm trees blow, and billows gleam,
Upwards to Indra's castle, ever blue,
Rise lotus-blooms along the holy stream;
There shall I worshipfully kneel to you
And press your feet, and piously declare:
"Madame! In all the world there's none so fair!"

TRANSLATED BY AARON KRAMER

KATHARINA

Gesanglos war ich und beklommen

Songless I was, immersed in mourning,
    Now song, at last, the gloom disperses;
Like tears that come with never a warning
    So, without warning, come the verses.

Once more melodic strains are starting
    To sing of great love, greater anguish,
Of hearts that have to break at parting,
    And hearts that only live to languish.

Sometimes I feel mysterious fleetings
    And German oaks about me glimmer;

They hint of home and early meetings—
But they are dreams, and they grow dimmer.

Sometimes it seems I hear them singing,
Remembered German nightingales!
In jets of song the notes are springing—
But they are dreams; the music fails.

Where are the roses, those bright vagrants,
In German fields? They rise and haunt me
Though they are withered, ghostly fragrance.
In dreams they bloom, in dreams they taunt me.

TRANSLATED BY LOUIS UNTERMEYER

Ich liebe solche weisse Glieder

I love this white and slender body,
These limbs that answer love's caresses,
Passionate eyes, and forehead covered
With a wave of thick, black tresses.

You are the very one I've searched for
In many lands, in every weather.
You are my sort; you understand me;
As equals we can talk together.

In me you've found the man you care for.
And, for a while, you'll richly pay me
With kindness, kisses, and endearments—
And then, as usual, you'll betray me.

TRANSLATED BY LOUIS UNTERMEYER

Jüngstens träumte mir: spazieren

Recently I had a dream:
I was strolling up in Heaven,
I—and you, because without you
Heaven would be turned to Hell.

There my eyes beheld the chosen:
The religious and the righteous,
Who, on earth, to save their souls,
Penalized their flesh with torment.

Fathers of the Church, apostles,
Capuchins, ascetic hermits,
Old Odd Fellows, and some young ones,
—And the young ones looked the worst!

Long and holy countenances,
Beards of gray, expansive baldpates,
(Also many Jews among them)—
Passed us rigorously by,

Never glanced in your direction,
Although you, my lovely sweetheart,
Toying hung upon my arm:
Toying, smiling, and coquetting!

Only one would look upon you,
And he was the only handsome,
Handsome man in all this troop;
More than splendid was his face.

Human goodness round the lips,
In his eyes a godly quiet,
That man, as he once regarded
Magdalen, smiled down at you.

Ah! I know, He's well-intentioned—
No one is so pure and noble—
But in spite of this, my heart
Stirred as though with jealousy.

And, I must confess, my sojourn
In the sky became unpleasant.
God forgive me! I was troubled
By our Saviour, Jesus Christ.

TRANSLATED BY AARON KRAMER

TRAGEDY   *Es fiel ein Reif in der Frühlingsnacht*

> A hoarfrost fell on a night in Spring;
> It fell on the frail blue flowerets,
> They faded away, they withered.
>
> A boy was once in love with a girl,
> They fled in secret from the house,
> Nor father nor mother knew it.
>
> They wandered and wandered to and fro;
> Neither good fortune nor star did they have,
> They pined away, they perished.
>   TRANSLATED BY AARON KRAMER

TANNHÄUSER: A Legend   *Ihr guten Christen, lasst Euch nicht*

I

> Good Christians all, be not entrapped
>   In Satan's cunning snare.
> I sing the lay of Tannhäuser,
>   To bid your souls beware.
>
> Brave Tannhäuser, a noble knight,
>   Would love and pleasure win.
> These lured him to the Venusberg.
>   Seven years he bode therein.
>
> "Dame Venus, loveliest of dames,
>   Farewell, my life, my bride.
> Oh give me leave to part from thee,
>   No longer may I bide."
>
> "My noble knight, my Tannhäuser,
>   Thou'st kissed me not to-day.
> Come, kiss me quick, and tell me now,
>   What lack'st thou here, I pray?

"Have I not poured the sweetest wine
Daily for thee, my spouse?
And have I not with roses, dear,
Each day enwreathed thy brows?"

"Dame Venus, loveliest of dames,
My soul is sick, I swear,
Of kisses, roses and sweet wine,
And craveth bitter fare.

"We laughed and jested far too much,
And I yearn for tears this morn.
Would that my head no rose-wreath wore,
But a crown of sharpest thorn."

"My noble knight, my Tannhäuser,
To vex me thou art fain.
Hast thou not sworn a thousand times
To leave me never again?

"Come! to my chamber let us go;
Our love shall be secret there.
And thy gloomy thoughts shall vanish at sight
Of my lily-white body fair."

"Dame Venus, loveliest of dames,
Immortal thy charms remain.
As many have loved thee ere to-day,
So many shall love again.

"But when I think of the heroes and gods,
Who feasted long ago,
Upon thy lily-white body fair,
Then sad at heart I grow.

"Thy lily-white body filleth me
With loathing, for I see
How many more in years to come
Shall enjoy thee, after me."

"My noble knight, my Tannhäuser,
Such words thou should'st not say.
Far liefer had I thou dealt'st me a blow,
As often ere this day.

"Far liefer had I thou should'st strike me low,
  Than such an insult speak;
Cold, thankless Christian that thou art,
  Thus the pride of my heart to break.

"Because I have loved thee far too well,
  To hear such words is my fate,
Farewell! I give thee free leave to go.
  Myself, I open the gate!"

TRANSLATED BY EMMA LAZARUS

II

In Rome, in Rome, in the holy town,
  To the music of chimes and of song,
A stately procession moves,—the Pope
  Strides in the midst of the throng.

This is the pious Pope Urbain;
  The triple crown he wears,
The crimson robe,—and many a lord
  The train of his garment bears.

"Oh, holy Father, Pope Urbain,
  I have a tale to tell;
I stir not hence, till thou shrivest me,
  And savest me from hell."

The people stand in a circle near,
  And the priestly anthems cease;
Who is the pilgrim wan and wild,
  Who falleth upon his knees?

"Oh, holy Father, Pope Urbain,
  Who canst bind and loose as well,
Now save me from the evil one,
  And from the pains of hell.

"I am the noble Tannhäuser,
  Who love and lust would win,
These lured me to the Venusberg,
  Seven years I bode therein.

"Dame Venus is a beauteous dame,
    Her charms have a subtle glow.
Like sunshine with fragrance of flowers blent
    Is her voice so soft and low.

"As the butterfly flutters anigh a flower,
    From its delicate chalice sips,
In such wise ever fluttered my soul
    Anigh to her rosy lips.

"Her rich black ringlets floating loose,
    Her noble face enwreath.
When once her large eyes rest on thee,
    Thou canst not stir nor breathe.

"When once her large eyes rest on thee,
    With chains thou art bounden fast;
'Twas only in sorest need I chanced
    To flee from her hill at last.

"From her hill at last I have escaped,
    But through all the livelong day,
Those beautiful eyes still follow me.
    'Come back!' they seem to say.

"A lifeless ghost all day I pine,
    But at night I dream of my bride,
And then my spirit awakes in me.
    She laughs and sits by my side.

"How hearty, how happy, how reckless her laugh!
    How the pearly white teeth outpeep!
Ah! when I remember that laugh of hers,
    Then sudden tears must I weep.

"I love her, I love her with all my might,
    And nothing my love can stay,
'Tis like to a rushing cataract,
    Whose force no man can sway.

"For it dashes on from cliff to cliff,
    And roareth and foameth still.
Though it break its neck a thousand times,
    Its course it would yet fulfill.

"Were all of the boundless heavens mine,
  I would give them all to her,
I would give her the sun, I would give her the moon
  And each star in its shining sphere.

"I love her, I love her with all my might,
  With a flame that devoureth me,
Can these be already the fires of hell,
  That shall glow eternally?

"Oh, holy Father, Pope Urbain,
  Who canst bind and loose as well,
Now save me from the evil one,
  And from the pains of hell!"

Sadly the Pope upraised his hand
  And sadly began to speak:
"Tannhäuser, most wretched of all men,
  This spell thou canst not break.

"The devil called Venus is the worst
  Amongst all we name as such.
And nevermore canst thou be redeemed
  From the beautiful witch's clutch.

"Thou with thy spirit must atone
  For the joys thou hast loved so well;
Accursed art thou! thou art condemned
  Unto everlasting hell!"

          TRANSLATED BY EMMA LAZARUS

III

The knight Tannhäuser traveled so fast,
  His feet were bloody and sore;
It was well around midnight when he reached
  The Venusberg once more.

Lady Venus awoke from sleep,
  And sprang from her bed in haste:
She clasped the knight in her lily-white arms,
  And they tenderly embraced.

Blood ran down from her nose, and tears
Fell from her eyes in a flood!
She drenched the face of her darling spouse
With a stream of tears and blood.

The knight spoke not a single word,
But lay down on the bed.
Into the kitchen Venus went
To fix him soup and bread.

She gave him soup, she gave him bread,
She washed his wounded feet.
She combed his bristly hair, and laughed
In a voice that was honey-sweet.

"Tannhäuser, noble knight of mine,
How long you've been away!
Where've you been roving all this time?
In what far lands did you stay?"

"Lady Venus, my beautiful wife,
I had some business in Rome;
But just as soon as my work was done,
I left, and hurried home.

"Rome is built on seven hills;
You can see the Tiber flow.
I also saw the Pope in Rome,
He sends you a warm 'Hello!'

"I passed through Florence, coming back,
And skirted Milan, too,
And then climbed over Switzerland
So fast I fairly flew.

"And as I moved across the Alps,
The snow began to fall:
Blue lakes laughed up at me, I heard
The eagles croak and call.

"And, standing on St. Gotthard Peak,
I heard old Germany snore;
In the gentle guard of thirty-six kings
It was sleeping just as before.

"I saw the Suabian poets' school,[2]
Those darling little fools!
With caps upon their heads, they sat
On little toilet-stools.

"I got to Frankfurt on Saturday,
Ate sholet and dumplings there;
Not only is their religion best;
Their giblets, too, are rare.

"In Dresden I saw a poor old dog[3]
Who'd made quite a stir in his youth;
But now he can only bark and piss,
Having lost his one last tooth.

"In Weimar, home of the widowed muse,
The moans were loud and long.
The people lamented: 'Goethe is dead,
But Eckermann's going strong!'

"In Potsdam I heard a noisy yell,
And cried: 'What can it be?'
'It's Dr. Gans in Berlin; he speaks
On the Eighteenth Century.'

"Science blooms in Göttingen,
But every branch is bare;
I hurried through in pitch-black night—
Not a light shone anywhere.

"Hanoverians fill the Celle jail;
O Germans—hear my call:
We need a *national* house of reform,
And one great whip for us all!

"In Hamburg I asked: 'How come the streets
Stink so? Is something dead?'
But Jews and Christians gently smiled:
'It's from the sewers,' they said.

"In Hamburg, in that worthy town,
Some evil creatures dwell.
And when I came along the Bourse
I thought I was still in Celle.

"In Hamburg I visited Altona,
—Now *that's* a place to see!
Some other time I'll let you know
What happened there to me."

TRANSLATED BY AARON KRAMER

ε❧ *Romances*

THE ADJURATION   *Der junge Franziskaner sitzt*

The young Franciscan friar sits
Alone in his cloister cell.
He reads from a book of magic, called
"The Mastery of Hell."

And when the midnight hour strikes,
Nothing can hold him still—
He calls on the chiefs of the underworld:
"Come, Spirits! work my will!

"Fetch me the fairest of all the dead
  And let her life return;
  And let her spend this night with me,
That I may hear and learn!"

He dares to speak the conjuring-word,
And lo! his wish is done.
In shrouds of white there comes to him
The poor dead beautiful one.

Her face is sad. From her frosty breast
A broken sigh is heard.
The corpse sits down beside the monk;
They stare—without a word.

TRANSLATED BY AARON KRAMER

THE UNKNOWN *Meiner goldgelockten Schönen*

My adored and golden-haired one,
Every day I'm sure to meet her,
When beneath the chestnut branches
In the Tuileries she wanders.

Every day she comes and walks there
With two old and awful ladies.
Are they aunts? Or are they dragons?
Or dragoons in skirts and flounces?

No one even seems to know her.
I have asked friends and relations;
But I ask in vain. I question,
While I almost die of longing.

Yes, I'm frightened by the grimness
Of her two mustached companions;
And I'm even more upset by
This, my heart's unusual beating.

I have scarcely breathed a whisper
Or a sigh whene'er I passed her;
I have never dared a burning
Glance to tell her of my longing.

But today I have discovered
What her name is. It is Laura;
Like the sweet, Provençal maiden
Worshiped by the famous poet.

She is Laura! I'm as great now
As was Petrarch when he chanted
And extolled his lovely lady
In those canzonets and sonnets.

She is Laura! Yes, like Petrarch,
I can hold Platonic riots
On this name, and clasp its beauty—
He himself did nothing more.

TRANSLATED BY LOUIS UNTERMEYER

KING HARALD HARFAGAR *Der König Harald Harfagar*

King Harald Harfagar reclines
Beside his lovely fay
Down at the bottom of the sea;
Years come, and flow away.

Bound and charmed by the fairy's spell
He neither lives nor dies:
Two centuries have passed, and still
In blissful ruin he lies.

His head is resting on her lap,
And full of fierce desire
He gazes up into her eyes
With eyes that never tire.

His cheek-bones spectrally protrude,
His golden hair's turned gray;
His miserable form is crushed
By ruin and decay.

Sometimes out of his passion-dream
He suddenly awakes,
For overhead the waters rage,
And the crystalline castle quakes.

At times he seems to hear in the wind
The sound of the Normans' call;
He lifts his arms with joyful haste,
Then sadly lets them fall.

At times above him he even seems
To hear the boatmen sing,
And in a hero-song give praise
To Harfagar, the king.

At this he sobs from the depths of his heart,
And groans, and his eyes grow dim.
Quickly the fay, with laughing mouth,
Bends down and kisses him.

TRANSLATED BY AARON KRAMER

CHILDE HAROLD * *Eine starke, schwarze Barke*

Strong and dark, there sails a bark
Sorrowful upon the wave.
Watchers bowed above the shroud
Bear his body to its grave.

Poet dead, uncovered head,
Quiet as a stone he lies;
Yet the sight of heaven's light
Holds his blue, unresting eyes.

As if cried a merman's bride
Sounds an echo from the deep,
And the lashing billows crash,
And it seems as if they weep.

TRANSLATED BY AARON KRAMER

SIR OLAF *Vor dem Dome stehn zwei Männer*

I

Two men, cloaked in red, are standing
At the door of the cathedral;
One of them's the mighty ruler,
And the other is his headsman.

And the ruler tells his headsman:
"By the monkish chant I gather
That the wedding-rites are over—
Keep your axe, your good axe, ready!"

Chimes of bells and organ-murmur,
And the church pours out its people;
Gay procession, and among them
Come the spruced-up newly-wedded.

Death-pale is the lovely princess,
And her face is sad and frightened;
But Sir Olaf's gay and saucy,
And his ruby mouth is smiling.

And with smiling mouth of ruby
He addresses the dark ruler:
"Father of my bride, good morning!
On this day my head is forfeit.

"I must die today—oh, let me
Live until the midnight hour!
Let me celebrate my wedding
With a banquet, and a torch-dance!

"Let me live! hold off your vengeance
Till the final cup is emptied,
Till the final dance is finished—
Let me live until the midnight!"

And the ruler tells his headsman:
"Let our son-in-law be granted
Respite till the midnight hour.
Keep your axe, your good axe, ready!"

II

At his marriage feast the knight takes up
And slowly drains his final cup.
Against his shoulder quails
His wife, and wails—
The headsman stands at the door.

The dance begins, and he grips by the waist
His pale young wife, and with frantic haste
They take, while the torches burn,
Their final turn—
The headsman stands at the door.

What a happy tune the fiddles play!
The flutes sigh in the saddest way!
Whoever sees them spin

Trembles within—
The headsman stands at the door.

And while they dance in the echoing house
Sir Olaf whispers to his spouse:
"I love you more than you know—
It's so cold below—"
The headsman stands at the door.

III

Sir Olaf, the midnight hour is here,
Your time of life is done!
With lust that would not be restrained
A prince's child you won.

The friars murmur the funeral prayer,
The man in a red cloak stands
Before his black beheading-stone,
—A shiny axe in his hands.

Down to the court Sir Olaf comes,
To the glitter of swords and flares.
A smile's on the ruby mouth of the knight;
With smiling mouth he declares:

"I bless the sun, I bless the moon,
And the stars that roam on high.
I also bless the little birds
A-piping in the sky.

"I bless the sea, I bless the land,
And the flowers upon the green.
I bless the violets that are soft
As the eyes of my darling queen.

"Violet eyes of my queen, my wife,
It is through you I lose my life.
I also bless the elder tree,
Where first you gave yourself to me."

TRANSLATED BY AARON KRAMER

❧ *To Ollea*

WANDER!   *Wenn dich ein Weib verraten hat*

When a woman's false, make haste
And give another your heart;
Or, better still, be rid of the place—
Pack up your bags and depart!

Soon you'll find a sea of blue
Circled by weeping willows;
You'll empty your heart of its little rue,
Among the soothing billows.

You'll climb the arduous hill, and drop
An avalanche of sighs;
But when you've reached the rocky top
You'll hear the eagle-cries.

Then, almost an eagle, you'll startle the air:
Newly-born and free—
You'll feel: what happened to you down there
Was no catastrophe.

TRANSLATED BY AARON KRAMER

OLD FIREPLACE PIECE   *Draussen ziehen weisse Flocken*

Outside flakes of snow go by
Through the darkness, loud's the storm;
Here inside the room it's dry,
Lonely, intimate and warm.

Thoughtful in my chair I settle
By the crackling fire-side;

While the boiling water-kettle
Murmurs tunes that long since died.

And a kitten, sitting near it,
Warms her paws before the blaze;
And some magic moves my spirit
While the fire weaves and sways.

Duskily before me rises
Many a long-forgotten time,
Trains of colorful disguises,
Ghosts of what were once sublime.

Lovely ladies nod, inviting,
Sweet-mysterious and deep,
And among them, mad-delighting,
Harlequins exult and leap.

Marble-gods, from far away,
Greet me; near them, like a dream,
Leaves of legend-flowers sway
In the moon's enchanting beam.

Waddling past my vision swim
Magic palaces' remains;
Galloping in back of them
Come the knights, in splendid trains.

Shadow-swift, the spectres hover,
Hurry past before my eyes—
But alas! the pot boils over,
And the scalded kitten cries.

TRANSLATED BY AARON KRAMER

৯ঌ *Poems for the Times*

NIGHT THOUGHTS   *Denk ich an Deutschland in der Nacht*

At night I think of Germany,
And then there is no sleep for me:
I cannot shut my eyes at all,
And down my cheeks the hot tears fall.

The seasons come and pass away!
Twelve years have vanished since the day
I told my mother I must go;
My yearnings and desires grow.

My yearnings and desires swell.
I'm under the old lady's spell;
My mother's always in my mind—
May God be close to her, and kind!

My dear old lady loves me so!
And all her tender letters show
How dreadfully her hand was shaking;
And how her mother-heart is aching.

I think of her both night and day.
Full twelve long years have flown away,
Full twelve long years have drifted past
Since I embraced my mother last.

The German nation will not fail—
It is a sturdy land, and hale,
And with its towering oak and lime
Will prosper till the end of time.

I would not give it half a care
If mother weren't living there;
The homeland never will decay;
My mother, though, might pass away.

Since my departure, many fell
Of those I knew and loved so well—
When I begin to count the toll
The blood is driven from my soul.

Yet I must count—and with the count
I feel my pangs begin to mount.
My breast is crushed, as though the dead
Roll over it. Thank God! they've fled.

Thank God! at last the morning light
Bursts through my windows: French and bright.
My wife is coming—fair as day—
And smiles my German cares away.

TRANSLATED BY AARON KRAMER

ROMANCERO

THE BATTLEFIELD OF HASTINGS   *Der Abt von Waltham seufzte tief*

The abbot of Waltham turned away
And bitterly he sighed
When tidings came from Hastings field
That Harold the king had died.

He ordered Asgod and Ailric forth
To Hastings battle-ground;
They were to search among the dead
Till Harold had been found.

The monks went mournfully away,
And mournfully came back:
"Reverend father, our luck's run out,
The world is cold and black.

"Defeated is the better man;
 Triumphant is the knave;
 Now thieves in mail carve up the land
 And the freeman's turned to a slave.

"Now they are lords on the British isle—
 Those lousy Norman curs;
 I saw a Bayeux tailor come
 A-riding with golden spurs.

"Woe to him who's a Saxon now!
 You saints of the Saxon race,
 Up there in Heaven—watch your step!
 You, too, are in disgrace.

"Now, alas, we understand
 What the huge red comet meant
 That rode this year on a broom of flame
 Across the firmament.

"That star's black omen was fulfilled
 Upon the Hastings plain;
 We visited the battle-grounds
 And searched among the slain.

"Here we searched, and there we searched,
 Until all hope took wing—
 We could not find among the dead
 The body of our king."

Such words did Asgod and Ailric speak;
 The abbot woefully cried—
 He wrung his hands, sunk deep in thought,
 And finally replied:

"In the heart of the forest of Grendelfield
 Beside the Poet's Stone,
 There stands a humble little hut:
 It's Edith Swanthroat's home.

"Because her throat was like a swan's
 They gave her such a name;
 This beautiful young girl once set
 King Harold's heart aflame.

"He'd loved, and kissed, and fondled her,
And given her up at last.
Time flies; and since the day he left
Full sixteen years have passed.

"Go, brothers, to this woman now
And take her where he lies;
King Harold's body will be found
By Edith Swanthroat's eyes.

"You'll bring back to the Abbey then
The body of the king,
That we may properly bury him,
And for his spirit sing."

The messengers reached her hut in the woods
At midnight, and they cried:
"Edith Swanthroat, awake! awake!
Hurry, and come outside!

"Normandy's duke has placed the crown
Of triumph on his head,
And somewhere on Hastings battle-field
Harold the king lies dead.

"Let's go to Hastings; there we'll seek
His corpse among the killed,
And carry it home to Waltham, as
Our holy abbot willed."

Edith Swanthroat did not speak:
She dressed, and hurried out—
In the fierce night-wind her graying hair
Was wildly blown about.

Barefoot she followed, through swamp and brush;
When dawn began to rise
The chalky cliffs of Hastings field
Stood clear before their eyes.

The fog that quilted the battle-ground
Slowly lifted and broke;
They saw the jackdaws flutter up
And heard their horrible croak.

Many thousands of corpses lay
Upon the bloody ground:
Stripped naked, mutilated, torn;
Dead horses strewn around.

With bare feet Edith Swanthroat came
Wading in blood and mire;
And from her searching eyes the light
Shot out like bolts of fire.

Here she searched, there she searched,
And halted more than once
To scare the hungry corbies away;
Behind her panted the monks.

She'd searched and searched the whole day through;
Once more the darkness fell—
Suddenly from the woman's breast
There burst a dreadful yell.

Edith Swanthroat had found the place
Where Harold's body lay.
She did not speak, she did not cry,
She kissed his face, so gray.

She kissed his brow, she kissed his mouth,
She clasped the lifeless man;
She kissed the wound upon his breast
From which the blood still ran.

She saw on his shoulder, and covered with
A kiss and another kiss:
Three little scars she'd left there once:
Three monuments to her bliss.

The friars fastened trunks of trees,
And soon the bier was made;
And on this wooden funeral-frame
The perished king was laid.

To Waltham Abbey they carried him
That he might be buried there.
Edith Swanthroat slowly came
Behind her lover's bier.

She sang the litany of the dead
In a childlike, pious way;
It sounded so frightening in the night—
The monks began to pray.

TRANSLATED BY AARON KRAMER

THE GOD APOLLO *Das Kloster ist hoch auf Felsen gebaut*

I

The cloister towers atop the rocks;
The Rhine flows by and glistens;
Down from her lattice-window looks
The youthful nun, and listens.

A little boat goes sailing by
In the red of the sunset-hours;
Around it streamers of taffeta fly;
It's crowned with laurel and flowers.

There stands in the vessel, fair to behold,
A gallant with curly blonde hair;
His purple garment, embroidered in gold,
Is fashioned of ancient wear.

And at this godlike creature's feet
Nine lovely women lie;
Their slender bodies hide, discreet,
In tunics tucked up high.

Sweetly the golden-headed one
Sings, and plays the lyre;
And in the heart of the wretched nun
His ballad burns like fire.

She crosses herself again and again,
But nothing can suppress
Her luscious agony of pain,
Her bitter happiness.

II

I am the God of harmonies,
Revered in every land;
On Mount Parnassus' peak in Greece
My temple used to stand.

On Mount Parnassus' peak in Greece
I'd often find repose
Within the shade of cypress-trees
Where bright Castalia flows.

The daughters sat around my knees,
And sang: La-la, la-la!
Their chatter and their revelries
Resounded near and far.

At times we'd hear among the trees
A bugle tooting loud;
The hunting-call of Artemis,
My sister, swift and proud.

I never learned the cause of this—
I needed but to sip
Castalia's water—melodies
Would burn upon my lip.

I sang—with more than mortal ease
My spellbound lyre stirred;
As though behind those laurel-trees
The peeping Daphne heard.

I sang—and at the melodies
Ambrosial fragrance poured;
The whole world lay in ecstasies
Beneath a Glory-chord.

Long, long have I been gone from Greece:
Been driven out, expelled—
And yet, through all the centuries
In Greece my heart has dwelled.

III

Soon the young nun wraps herself
In the habit of Beguines,
Hides her face behind her mantle
With its cape of coarse black serge.

Breathlessly the maiden hurries
Up the road that leads to Holland,
And she hurriedly questions
Everyone who comes along:

"Have you seen the God Apollo?
It's a scarlet cloak he wears;
Sweetly sings and plays the lyre—
And he is my lovely idol."

No one offers her an answer;
Many turn their backs in silence;
Many stare in cold amusement;
Many sigh: Unhappy child!

But a slovenly old fellow
Slowly trudges down the road;
In the air his fingers reckon;
Nasally he hums a tune.

On his back's a sloppy wallet,
On his head a little tricorne;
And his clever eyes keep laughing
As he listens to her story:

"Have you seen the God Apollo?
It's a scarlet cloak he wears;
Sweetly sings and plays the lyre—
And he is my lovely idol."

But the tattered fellow answers,
While he wags his little head
To and fro, and comically
Tugs his pointed little beard:

"If I've seen him? Sure I've seen him!
Not just once, but many times:
Back home up in Amsterdam,
At the German synagogue.

"For he was the cantor there,
And his name was Rabbi Faibish,[5]
In High-German that means Phoebus—
But *my* idol he is not.

"Scarlet cloak? I know that also;
It's a genuine piece of scarlet;
Every yard is worth eight florins,
And it hasn't all been paid for.

"And I'm rather well acquainted
With his father, Moses Yitscher:
Circumcises Portuguese.
He has also clipped some sovereigns.[6]

"And his mother is a cousin
Of my brother-in-law; she sells
Sour pickles in the market,
And decrepit trousers, too.

"They've no pleasure in their son.
He's a first-rate lyre-player,
Yet, alas, he's even better
When he plays *taroc* and *l'ombre*.

"He has even turned free-thinker,
Eaten swine, and lost his job;
Now he roams around the country
With a troupe of painted comics.

"In the stalls, in market-places,
He performs as Merry Andrew,
Holofernes and King David;
In this last he's cheered the most.

"For he sings the Songs of David
In that king's own mother-tongue,
And he makes the music quaver
In the old style of the Nigen.

"Recently he lured some wenches
From the *Amsterdam Casino*,
And he's touring with these 'Muses'
In the role of an Apollo.

"There's a fat one, who surpasses
All the rest in squeaking, grunting;
For her giant laurel head-dress
She's been nicknamed the Green Sow."

TRANSLATED BY AARON KRAMER

CHARLES I   *Im Wald, in der Köhlerhutte, sitzt*

In the woods, in a charcoal-burner's hut,
The king sits sad and alone;
He rocks the charcoal-burner's child,
And sings in a monotone:

Lullaby-lulla, what stirs in the straw?
I hear the bleat of the sheep—
You bear an omen upon your brow
And dreadfully smile in your sleep.

Lullaby-lulla, the pussycat's dead—
An omen's upon your brow—
You'll be a man and swing the axe;
The oaks are shuddering now!

The charcoal-burner's faith is gone;
No more do his children cling,—
Lullaby-lulla—to trust in God,
And even less in the king.

The pussycat's dead, the mice rejoice—
What shall our names be worth—
Lullaby-lulla—great God on high,
And I, the lord of earth?

My courage dies, my heart is sick,
Each day I've deeper pain—
Lullaby-lulla—I know it, child,
At your hands I'll be slain.

My death-song is your cradle-song—
Lullaby-lulla—the old
Locks of my hair you'll cut off first;
At my throat the iron rings cold.

Lullaby-lulla, what stirs in the straw?
You shall not be denied.
You'll take the empire, and cut off my head—
The pussycat has died.

Lullaby-lulla, what stirs in the straw?
I hear the bleat of the sheep.
The pussycat's dead, the mice rejoice—
Sleep, little slayer, sleep!

TRANSLATED BY AARON KRAMER

THE ASRA *Täglich ging die wunderschöne*

Every night the lovely daughter
Of the Sultan slowly wandered
Up and down before the fountain
Where the crystal water plashes.

Every night the youthful captive
Would be standing by the fountain
Where the crystal water plashes;
Every night his face was paler.

Then one night the noble princess
Came right up to him, and murmured:
"I must know what people call you,
Where you come from, what your tribe is!"

And the captive said: "They call me
Mahomet; I come from Yemen;
And my tribesmen are the Asra—
They who perish when they love."

TRANSLATED BY AARON KRAMER

GEOFFREY RUDEL AND MELISANDE OF TRIPOLI *In dem Schlosse Blay erblickt man*

Even now the tapestries
Can be seen in Castle Blay,
Just as Tripoli's great countess
Wove them in a bygone day.

She embroidered all her soul
Into them, and with her tears
Charmed the silken imagery
Where that spectacle appears:

How the countess saw Rudel
Perishing upon the shore,
And perceived in his pale features
All that she had hungered for.

And the lady who had charmed him
In his dreams, Rudel could see
For the first and final moment
In her actual majesty.

Over him the countess bent,
Lovingly she clasped Rudel,
And she kissed the deathpale lips
That had sung her praise so well!

But alas! their kiss of welcome
Turned into a parting-kiss;
So they drained the cup of deepest
Suffering and highest bliss.

Nightly in the Castle Blay
Something seems to rustle, shake;
Suddenly the ancient figures
Of the tapestry awake.

First the troubadour and lady
Shake their slumbering limbs of shade,
Then, descending from the wall,
Through the rooms they promenade.

Tender whispering, sweet secrets,
Lovers' playful pantomimes,
And a posthumous gallantry
From the minnesingers' times.

"Geoffrey! When I hear your voice
There's a warmth in my dead heart;
In the coals that long were lifeless
I can feel new fires start."

"Melisande! My joy and blossom!
Seeing you, I live again;
For the only things that perished
Were my earthly grief and pain."

"Geoffrey! Once we loved in dreams;
Now instead our hearts can meet
In the very tryst of death—
It was Love who wrought this feat!"

"Melisande! And what are dreams?
What is death? But words in air.
Only love lives, and I love you,
You who are forever fair."

"Geoffrey! It's so nice and quiet
In these moonlit halls of mine!
Let's not ever walk outside
Where the lights of morning shine."

"Melisande! My silly dearest!
You yourself are morning-sun!
Where you walk the Springtime blossoms,
Love sprouts up, and Winter's gone!"

So those tender ghosts embrace,
So they wander to and fro,
While the moon, through vaulted windows,
Sends a soft, eavesdropping glow.

But at last the dawnlight enters,
And the lovely ghosts must flee—
Timidly they scuttle back
To the wall, the tapestry.

TRANSLATED BY AARON KRAMER

❧ Lamentations

WOODLAND SOLITUDE *Ich hab in meinen Jugendtagen*

In boyhood days I used to wear
A garland wreathed around my hair:
Miraculously glowed the flowers,
The garland carried magic powers.

Everyone had a liking for it,
But evil fell on him who wore it.
I fled the grudging human race,
I fled to the woodland's lonely peace.

To the woods! to the forest! Here at least
I could live as free as the sprite and beast.
Fairies and haughty-antlered deer
Came up to me and showed no fear.

All unafraid they approached the stranger,
They knew here was no dreadful danger;
That I was no hunter, the roe could see;
That I was no thinker, the fay would agree.

Fools will rave about favors from fairies,
But the rest of the woodland dignitaries
Were so concerned for my every need,
I must publish the facts for all to read.

How sweetly around me the elf-people fluttered!
An aerial nation! They gossipped and muttered!
Their glances were too sharp and bright,
Promising sweet, but deadly delight.

They honored me with Maytime sport,
And told me many tales from the court,
Including one that was quite obscene,
About Titania, the fairy-queen.

The water-bacchantes, the nymph-troop fair
With long silver veils and fluttering hair
Would plunge through the waves, and rise once more,
Whenever I sat on the rivulet shore.

They'd play upon fiddles, their zithers would sound:
This was the water-fairies' round,
A first-rate dance; the posture, the tune,
Was ringing, springing, mad with moon.

But once in a while the beautiful sprites
Were worn out by these taxing rites;
Then at my feet they'd make their bed,
My knees a prop for each tiny head.

Strange ballads they trilled and quavered to me,
For instance, the song of the oranges three.
They also chanted a poem of praise
For me and my noble human face.

Sometimes they stopped their quaverings,
And asked me many embarrassing things;
For instance, "Tell us what God had in mind,
When he created humankind.

"Does an immortal soul reside
In each of you? Is it made of hide
Or a stiff piece of linen? Why should it be
That mortals act so stupidly?"

What I replied I won't disclose,
But to my soul that immortally glows,
You can be assured, it scarcely mattered
What a little water-fairy chattered.

Nymphs and fairies have mischief and grace;
But not the earth-sprites, who serve our race
With loyalty. And those whom they call
Goblins, I loved most of all.

Padded long red cloaks they wear;
They have an honest, but frightened air.
I never let them see that I knew
Why their feet were so carefully hidden from view.

For their feet were webbed, and they really believed
That all of the neighbors were deceived.
It's a wound they bury deep in their breasts
At which I would never hurl my jests.

Ah heavens! we're all like those little creatures;
We all conceal some singular features,
Assuming that not one Christian knows
Where we have hidden our duck-like toes.

I befriended no salamander folk,
And other wood-sprites rarely spoke
About their habits. At night they were shy,
Like phosphorous shadows scurrying by.

They're the length of children, and dry as bone,
Their breeches and jackets are long outgrown:
Embroidered in gold, of scarlet hue;
They're yellowed, and harassed; a sick-faced crew.

Every headlet is weighted down
By a ruby-studded golden crown;
And everyone in imagination
Is absolute king of all creation.

It's surely a work of art, I own,
That flame won't burn them through to the bone;
And yet the uninflammable wight
Is not a genuine fire-sprite.

Mandrakes are the cleverest sort
Of woodland-spirits; their legs are short,
And their beards flow down; a finger-sized clan;
It's not been determined whence they began.

When they somersault under the moon, you'd swear
A meadow of piss-weeds is blooming there;
But since they were noble-hearted toward me
I don't care *how* they came to be.

They taught me little sorcerer-games,
Like conjuring birds, conjuring flames,
And gathering at Midsummernight
The herb that keeps you hidden from sight.

They taught me the stars and the auguries,
To ride without saddle upon a breeze,
And runic sayings, by which the dead
Are called up out of their coffin-bed.

And I was also thoroughly schooled
In a trick by which the woodpecker's fooled,
And his main-root, leading to buried riches,
Is nosed out by these little witches.

I learned what to mumble when digging for gold.
And my teachers patiently tried to unfold
The complete operation—but all in vain!
The gold-digging art is too much for my brain.

I did without gold in my young day;
I wanted for little, and always could pay;
Owned many a Spanish castle of air,
Whose revenues brought me enough and to spare.

O beautiful time! when heaven would sway
With fiddles, when elfin roundelay,
And fairy-dance, and goblin-jest,
Deluded my fable-drunken breast!

O beautiful time! when the trees of the wood,
Arched in their greenness, so grandly stood—
Like Victory-gates—I entered the shrine,
Crowned, as though the triumph were mine!

That beautiful time was bound to pass.
Since then it's all been changed, and alas!
The magic crown has been stolen away
That I wore so proudly upon that day!

The lovely crown was taken from me,
I don't know how it came to be,
But since the crown is off my head
It seems that the soul of my soul has fled.

The masks of the world—how they stupidly glare!
Desolate is the sky, and bare:
De-godded and mute, a churchyard blue;
I go through the forest, stooped in rue.

The elves were quick to disappear—
Bugles, yelping of hounds I hear;
Alone in a thicket, hidden by leaves,
The roebuck licks his wounds and grieves.

Where are the mandrakes? I think they hide
Among the cleft rocks, terrified.
My little friends, I come once more,
But luckless, and lacking the crown I wore.

Where is the fay with the long golden hair,
The first lovely thing that was kind to me there?
The oak she lived in mournfully stands
Dishevelled by wind, with leafless hands.

The brook, like Styx, goes by with a moan;
A water-nymph sits on the shore alone,
Mute as a statue, and paler than snow,
She seems to be sunken deep in woe.

I turn to greet her tenderly—
When up she starts, and looks at me,
And, horror-stricken, runs to escape
As though she had seen a spectral shape.

TRANSLATED BY AARON KRAMER

OLD SONG *Du bist gestorben und weisst es nicht*

You've passed away, but do not know.
Your eyes have lost their living glow.
Your little mouth no more is red,
My perished child, and you are dead.

Upon a gloomy summer eve
I brought your body to the grave.
The nightingales sang a funeral song,
The stars came mournfully along.

We passed the woods, and all the trees
Were shaken by our litanies.
A black hood draped each fir-tree's head;
They murmured requiems for the dead.

We passed a lake of weeping willows;
The elves were dancing on the billows;
Suddenly they stopped their dance
And turned to us with a pitying glance.

And when at last we reached your tomb,
Down from the heavens came the moon.
She made a speech. A sobbing and groaning—
And far away the bells were intoning.

TRANSLATED BY AARON KRAMER

TO THE ANGELS *Das ist der böse Thanatos*

This is the wicked Thanatos,[1]
Upon a fallow steed he goes;
I hear the trot, the beating hoof,
The shadow-horseman bears me off—
He drags me from Mathild; we're torn apart.
And oh, this thought is too much for my heart.

She was both wife and child to me,
And, when I journey down, she'll be
A widow and an orphan-girl!
Alone I leave her in this world,
The wife, the child who, filled with loving trust,
Carefree and faithful slumbered on my breast.

You angels in the lofty skies,
Receive my sobs and pleading cries:
Protect, when I shall lie below,
The wife whom I have cherished so;
Be, to your likeness, guardian and shield;
Defend my poor, unsheltered child Mathild!

By all your tears that ever ran
For the unhappiness of Man,
And by the sacred word that's known
To those of priestly caste alone,
Who name it shuddering; by your grace and beauty,
I charge you, make Mathild's care your duty!

TRANSLATED BY AARON KRAMER

THE LIGHT GOES OUT   *Der Vorhang fällt, das Stück ist aus*

The curtain falls upon the play,
And lords and ladies drive away.
But did they seem to like the show?
I think I heard: *"Bravissimo!"*
A prominent assembly cheered
Its poet to the highest rafter.
But now the house has hushed its laughter,
And all the lights have disappeared.

But wait! What could that sound have been?
Close by the empty stage?—perhaps
It is a feeble string that snaps—
The string of an old violin.
Some peevish rats morosely flit
Backward and forward through the pit.
The whole place smells of rancid oil.
The final lamp goes pale, and sighs,
And hisses bitterly, and dies.
The wretched fire—it was my soul.

TRANSLATED BY AARON KRAMER

AN EVIL DREAM   *Im Traume war ich wieder jung und munter*

I dreamed that I was young and gay again—
High on the mountain stood the country-place;
And down the stony path I ran a race,
Hand in hand with Ottilie I ran.

How well the little thing was formed! How sweet
Her sea-green eyes were, with their e'fin light!
Vigor and grace seemed strangely to unite:
So firm she stood there on her little feet!

Her voice had such a true and fervent ring;
Her soul appeared to sparkle through her eyes;
And every word she spoke was bright and wise;
Her mouth was like a rose in early Spring.

It wasn't pain of love that stole on me;
I still could think, my brain was not ablaze;—
But strangely I was softened by her ways,
And kissed her fingers, quaking inwardly.

I think, at last I broke a lily, gave her
The flower, and at that I loudly cried:
"Marry me, Ottilie, and be my bride,
That I may share your piety and favor!"

The answer that she gave I'll never know,
For suddenly I woke—and I became
Once more an ailing man, who keeps the same
Dark sickroom, while the seasons come and go.

TRANSLATED BY AARON KRAMER

ENFANT PERDU *Verlorner Posten in dem Freiheitskriege*

For thirty years I've clung without retreat
To hopeless posts on Freedom's battleground;
I fought within the shadows of defeat;
I knew I'd never come home safe and sound.

Day and night I waked—I could not sleep
Like all my bands of comrades in their tents;
(And when I tried to doze, these braves would keep
Me wakeful—snoring with such violence.)

Boredom would seize me often in those nights,
And fear—(for only fools are spared that curse);
To banish these and set myself to rights,
I'd pipe a satire's saucy little verse.

Yes, gun on arm I watched, and when some clown
Suspiciously approached, I'd send a shot,
A well-aimed little bullet, hurtling down
Into his evil belly—scalding-hot.

Sometimes, of course, it may have come to pass
That such an evil clown was just about
As good a shot as I—it's true, alas—
My wounds are open—and my blood runs out.

A post is vacant—all my wounds are open—
One soldier falls; another fills his part—
But unsubdued I fall: my sword's not broken.
The only thing that's broken is my heart.

TRANSLATED BY AARON KRAMER

ANNUAL MOURNING   *Keine Messe wird man singen*

There will be no whispered masses,
    There will be no songs nor crying,
None will rise to say a *Kaddish* [7]
    On the day that I lay dying.

But the day may be a fair one.
    Then (the thought is most consoling)
With Pauline upon Montmartre
    My Mathilda will go strolling.

And perhaps she'll carry flowers,
    Immortelles, dead-white and yellow;
And her pretty eyes will moisten,
    And she'll say (in French), "Poor fellow."

I'll be living far too high
    Up in heaven (how it rankles!)
To invite her to sit down
    And relieve her tired ankles.

Oh, my plump and breathless pigeon,
    Walking's quite unnecessary.
See—the carriages are standing
    Just outside the cemetery.

TRANSLATED BY LOUIS UNTERMEYER

POEMS 1853-1854

BABYLONIAN SORROWS   *Mich ruft der Tod—Ich wollt,*
                       o Süsse

Death calls me—Sweet, it might be good
If I could leave you in some wood,
Some forest where the firs are high,
Where vultures nest, and wild wolves cry,
And the savage sow, with dreadful roar,
Calls to her mate, the great blonde boar.

Death calls—still better would it be
To leave you on the open sea,
My wife—my child—it would be kind,
Although the maniac Northpole wind
Lashes the waves there, and out of the deep
The monstrous things that lay asleep,

The shark and crocodile, arise
With open jaws and murderous eyes—
Believe me, Mathild, my wife, my child,
Not half so fearful is the wild,
Avenging sea, or the sulking wood,
As this our present neighborhood!
Fierce though the wolf and the vulture be,
The shark, and other beasts of the sea:
There are monsters of far less virtue and pity
In Paris, the world's bright capital-city,
City of loveliness, laughter and revels,
The Hell of angels, Paradise of devils—
To think that you'll be left behind
In Paris, is driving me out of my mind!
Black flies are buzzing around my bed;
They seat themselves on top of my head,
On my nose and brow. That pesky race—
There's more than one with a human face,
But some of them are especially odd:
They've elephant-trunks like the Hindu god . . .
Inside my brain there's a tumult and cracking;
I think it is a box they're packing,
And my reason journeys off—ah woe!—
Before it is time for me to go.

TRANSLATED BY AARON KRAMER

TO LAZARUS

Wie langsam kriechet sie dahin

How slowly Time, the frightful snail,
   Crawls to the corner that I lie in;
While I, who cannot move at all,
   Watch from the place that I must die in.

Here in my darkened cell no hope
   Enters and breaks the gloom asunder;
I know I shall not leave this room
   Except for one that's six feet under.

Perhaps I have been dead some time;
  Perhaps my bright and whirling fancies
Are only ghosts that, in my head,
  Keep up their wild, nocturnal dances.

They well might be a pack of ghosts,
  Some sort of pagan gods or devils;
And a dead poet's skull is just
  The place they'd choose to have their revels!

Those orgies, furious and sweet,
  Come suddenly, without a warning . . .
And then the poet's cold, dead hand
  Attempts to write them down next morning.

TRANSLATED BY LOUIS UNTERMEYER

Mich locken nicht die Himmelsauen

I'm not allured by a lofty field
In Paradise, on holy ground.
No ladies there could be revealed
More fair than I've already found.

No angel with the daintiest wing
Could compensate me for my wife;
And on the clouds to sit and sing
The psalms, is not my way of life.

O Lord! it would be best to leave me
In *this* world; but I beg of you,
Heal the infirmities that grieve me,
And let me have some money, too.

I know what sinning and deceit
Are in the world; but many years
Upon this pavement trained my feet
To saunter through the vale of tears.

The world's events won't get me down,
For seldom do I leave the house;
In slippers and in dressing-gown
I like to stay here with my spouse.

Leave me with her! My soul rejoices
To hear her chattering. Like wine
I drink that loveliest of voices!
—Her eyes so truly answer mine.

Money and health are all I ask,
Oh Master! Let me live my life
In *statu quo*, and gaily bask
Here in the sunlight, with my wife!

TRANSLATED BY AARON KRAMER

POSTHUMOUS VERSE

⁖ *Love Poems*

Wenn junge Herzen brechen

When young hearts break with passion
   The stars break into laughter,
They laugh and, in their fashion,
   Gossip a long time after:

"Poor souls, those mortals languish
   With Love; 'tis all they cherish.
It pays them back with anguish
   And pain until they perish.

"We never can discover
   This Love, so brief and breathless,
So fatal to each lover—
   And hence we stars are deathless."

TRANSLATED BY LOUIS UNTERMEYER

IN THE MORNING *Meine gute liebe Frau*

My devoted, darling wife,
My own kind, devoted darling
Has prepared my little breakfast:
Rich white cream, and steaming coffee.

And she brings it in herself,
Jesting, fondling, sweetly smiling.
In the whole of Christendom
There's no mouth that smiles so sweetly!

And her voice's flute-like sound
Has no likeness but the angels',
Or perhaps on earth it's equalled
By the noblest nightingales.

Hands how lily-white! The hair,
How it dreamily goes curling
Round her rosy countenance!
Free of blemish is her beauty.

Yet today it seems to me
—Don't know why—a bit more narrow
My beloved's waist could be,
Just a tiny bit more narrow.

                    TRANSLATED BY AARON KRAMER

TO JENNY *Ich bin nun fünfunddreissig Jahr alt*

My years now number five-and-thirty
    And you are scarce fifteen, you sigh . . .
Yet, Jenny, when I look upon you,
    The old dream wakes that will not die.

In eighteen-seventeen a maiden
    Became my sweetheart, fond and true;
Strangely like yours her form and features,
    She even wore her hair like you.

That year, before I left for college,
  I said, "My own, it will not be
Long till I come back home. Be faithful!"
  "You are my world," she answered me.

Three years I toiled; three years I studied;
  And then—it was the first of May—
In Göttingen the tidings reached me:
  My love had married and gone away.

It was the first of May! With laughter
  The Spring came dancing through the world.
Birds sang, and in the quickening sunshine
  Worms stretched themselves and buds uncurled.

And only I grew pale and sickly,
  Dead to all beauties and delights;
And only God knows how I suffered
  And lived throughout those wretched nights.

But still I lived. And now my health is
  Strong as an oak that seeks the sky.
Yet, Jenny, when I look upon you,
  The old dream wakes that will not die.

                TRANSLATED BY LOUIS UNTERMEYER

THE SONG OF SONGS   *Des Weibes Leib ist ein Gedicht*

  Woman's white body is a song,
    And God Himself's the author;
  In the eternal book of life
    He put the lines together.

  It was a thrilling hour; the Lord
    Felt suddenly inspired;
  Within his brain the stubborn stuff
    Was mastered, fused, and fired.

  Truly, the Song of Songs is this,
    The greatest of his trophies:
  This living poem where soft limbs
    Are a rare pair of strophes.

Oh, what a heavenly masterpiece
 That neck and its relation
To the fair head, like an idea
 Crowned with imagination.

In pointed epigrams, the breasts
 Rise under teasing rallies;
And a caesura lies between,
 The loveliest of valleys.

He published the sweet parallel
 Of thighs—what joy to be there!
The fig-leaf grotto joining them
 Is not a bad place either.

It is no cold, conceptual verse,
 No patterned abstract study!
This poem sings with rhyming lips,
 With sweet bones and warm body.

Here breathes the deepest poetry!
 Beauty in every motion!
Upon its brow it bears the stamp
 Of His complete devotion.

Here in the dust, I praise Thee, Lord.
 We are—and well I know it—
Rank amateurs, compared to Thee:
 Heaven's first major poet!

I'll dedicate myself to learn
 This song, the lyric body;
With ardor and with energy
 All day—and night—I'll study!

Yes, day and night, I'll never lack
 For constant application;
And though the task may break my back
 I'll ask for no vacation!

TRANSLATED BY LOUIS UNTERMEYER

❧ *Miscellaneous*

TESTAMENT   *Ich mache jetzt mein Testament*

It's time I wrote my testament;
My final hour will soon be spent.
I'm only amazed that fear and woe
Have not destroyed me long ago.

You jewel and grace of womankind,
Luise, to you I leave behind
Twelve ancient shirts and a hundred fleas,
And three hundred thousand maladies.

And you, dear friend, who'd always bring
Advice, yet never did a thing;
Here's some advice I leave you now:
Get mooncalves on a fertile cow.

Who needs my religion most?
My faith in Father, Son, and Ghost?
Let the Rabbi of Posen, the king of China
Cast lots for the piety of Heine!

The German "free and equal" hope,
Those finest-foaming bubbles of soap,
Krähwinkel's censor may have when I die;
—More nourishing is a loaf of rye.

The undone deeds which I once planned
To liberate my fatherland,
With a hangover recipe, I award
To the heroes of the Baden board.[9]

And I leave a nightcap, white as chalk,
To a cousin of mine, who used to talk [10]
So bravely of Freedom and Brotherhood—
Now he keeps still—as a Roman should.

To Stuttgart's punisher of lust [11]
And guard of religion, I entrust
A pair of pistols (minus lead);
They can scare the bugs from his lady's bed.

A faithful portrait of my rear
Can go to the Suabian school; I hear
You didn't care to have my face;
I hope you'll relish the opposite place.

Twelve jugs of Seidlitz water can pass
To the precious poet-soul who, alas! [12]
Has lately suffered from song-constipation;
Faith, Love and Hope are his consolation.

And here I add a codicil:
Should none accept the terms of this will,
Let the Roman Catholic Church receive
All of the legacies I leave.

TRANSLATED BY AARON KRAMER

WARNING *Verletze nicht durch kalten Ton*

Do not with frosty answer scorn
The youth who, alien and in need,
Approaches you this day to plead
For help; he may be godly-born.

When next you meet him, 'round his hair
You'll see the brilliant halo blaze;
His rigorous, condemning gaze
Will then be more than you can bear.

TRANSLATED BY AARON KRAMER

WHERE? *Wo wird einst des Wandermüden*

Who knows where, fatigued with straying,
Where my final rest will be?
In the South, where palms are swaying?
Underneath a linden tree?

Shall a desert be my host,
Buried by a stranger's hand?
Or along some ocean coast
Shall I slumber in the sand?

Still, God's sky will be my cover
There as here; and every night
Overhead the stars will hover:
Lamps to give the dead their light.

TRANSLATED BY AARON KRAMER

The Mattress Grave

THE DYING MAN   *Erstorben ist in meiner Brust*

Within my breast desire is done
For vain delight beneath the sun.
I hate no longer what is bad:
Hate too is dead. I am not sad
For others' sorrow or my own—
'Tis death that lives in me alone.
The curtain falls upon the play
And, yawning on its homeward way,
My worthy German public hies.
The honest folk are very wise,
They're dining now in ease and pleasure,
They sing and laugh and drink their measure.

'Twas truth the noble hero told
Who spoke in Homer's book of old:
The Philistine of least renown
Alive to-day in Stukkert town
Beside the Neckar—ah, he still is
More blest than I, the great Achilles,
Dead hero who, the king of ghosts,
In Hades rule my shadowy hosts.

TRANSLATED BY MARGARET ARMOUR

Mein Tag war heiter, glücklich meine Nacht

I had a bright day, and a blissful night.
My land exulted when I struck the lyre
Of poetry. My song was joy and fire;
It woke some flames that shot up brave and bright.

Still flourishes the summer of my year,
But I've already gathered all the crop
Into my shed—and must I now give up
What made the world so sweet, so sweet and dear!

My fingers fail the string. The glass I've pressed
So gaily to my wanton lips, is lying
In shiny pieces, shattered where it fell.
Oh God! how ugly bitter is our dying!
Oh God! how sweet and snug it is to dwell
Upon the earth, here in this sweet, snug nest!

TRANSLATED BY AARON KRAMER

Den Strauss, den mir Mathilde band

With pleading hand I wave away
Mathilde's freshly-picked bouquet—
I cannot look at the flowers in bloom
Without a shudder for my own doom.

They tell me I'm alive no more,
But have one foot behind Death's door:
A poor, unburied corpse, who lies
And waits for Death to shut his eyes.

When I smell flowers, I have to cry—
Of all earth's treasures, piled up high,
The beauty and sunlight, the love and the glee,
Nothing but tears are left for me.

How fortunate I was that day
When I saw the opera-rats' ballet!

Now I can hear the shuffling sound
Of rats and moles in the churchyard ground.

O scent of blossoms! you inspire
A whole ballet, a brilliant choir
Of fragrant memories—they spring
Suddenly forward, with a ring

Of castanets, and cymbal-notes,
In naughty, tinsel petticoats—
Yet all their laughter and giggling and play
Can only add to my dismay.

Away with the flowers! Unbearable smells—
Maliciously each fragrance tells
A merry tale of days gone by—
When I remember them, I cry.

TRANSLATED BY AARON KRAMER

Ich seh im Stundenglase schon

The hour-glass' stingy sand
Is running out, I see.
Mathilde, angel-sweet! The hand
Of Death is seizing me.

He's tearing me from your embrace;
It's more than we can fight;
He tears my Soul from her dwelling-place;
She's almost dead of fright.

He drives her from her ancient home
Where she was so glad to live.
She shudders and flutters—where shall I roam?
She feels like a flea in a sieve.

Though I twist and turn, do all I can,
I shall not change this fate.
The body and soul, the woman and man,
Must finally separate.

TRANSLATED BY AARON KRAMER

HALLELUJAH   *Am Himmel Sonn und Mond und Stern'*

The sun and moon and stars on high
To God's great power testify,
And should the pious man but gaze
Skyward, he'll sing the Maker's praise.

I need not marvel at the sky.
God's masterpieces meet the eye
Right here on earth—most anywhere.
With them no planet can compare.

Ah yes, dear people, modestly
I gaze on earth, and here I see
The greatest masterpiece of art
He ever made: our human heart.

Magnificent as is the sight
Of sun, sweet as in silent night
The lustre of stars, the moonlight pale,
Dazzling as is the comet's tail—

Together all the lights on high
Are penny lamps, no more, when I
Compare them with the human flame—
A man's heart puts them all to shame.

This is the world in pygmy size:
Here meadows bloom, and mountains rise;
And deserts, where the wild beasts nest
That often tear the helpless breast.

Here the rock-strewn valley yawns;
Motley gardens, grassy lawns,
Where little lambs or donkeys feed;
Here brooks tumble, rivers speed.

Here are fountains, madly springing
While wretched nightingales are singing
Until consumption wastes their throats,
Hoping a rose may heed the notes.

There's also change aplenty here;
Today the weather's warm and clear,
But autumn's frost is on its way;
By morning, fields and woods are grey.

Denuded waits the fragile flower;
The winds assault with savage power,
And down at last there flutter flakes
Of snow, on frozen streams and lakes.

But now the Winter sports begin;
The masked emotions wander in,
Surrender to the drunken reel,
The masquerade, and madly wheel.

But in the midst of all this gladness
There often steals a secret sadness;
Despite the mask and dance, they sigh
For pleasures that have passed them by.

A sudden thundering—Hold fast!
It is the ice, that breaks at last;
The polished crust now comes apart,
The frost that long enclosed our heart.

Whatever's mournful must surrender;
It's coming back again—oh splendor!—
The Spring, whose beauty has no match,
Awakened by love's potent touch.

Great is the Lord's undying glow,
Great in the sky, and great below.
Kyrie Eleison I will sing,
A Hallelujah to the King!

'Twas he who shaped the human heart,
Who made it such a work of art,
And into it blew life-winds of
His own great breath, the breath called **Love**.

Away with Greece's lyre! Away
The sloven Muses' roundelay!
I'll sing in more religious ways
The Lord of all creation's praise.

Away with pagan tunes! Let ring
Once more the soul of David's string
To join my psalm, my glory-prayer!
Till Hallelujah shakes the air!

TRANSLATED BY AARON KRAMER

FOR THE MOUCHE *Es träumte mir von einer Sommernacht*

I had a vision of a summer night,
Where faded, broken in the moon's cold light
Renaissance ruins, ancient buildings lay:
The remnant splendor of a bygone day.

But here and there a solitary column
Arises from the rubbish with a solemn
Dorian head, and gazes toward the sky
As though she mocks his thrashing thunder-cry.

Shattered portals sprawl upon the ground,
And many sculptured gables lie around:
Those man-beast figures from a fabled era:
The sphinx and centaur, satyr and chimera.

Among these ancient ruins, all unbroken,
A marble, white sarcophagus stands open;
And, unimpaired, there lies inside the case
A dead man, with a mild and suffering face.

The caryatides, their necks astrain,
Appear to hold him up with utmost pain.
On either side the eye is struck by swarms
Of bas-relief, of finely-chiselled forms.

The splendors of Olympus here unfold,
Its pagan godheads lusting uncontrolled.
Beside them Eve and Adam are revealed:
Their sex by fig-leaves modestly concealed.

The fall and firing of Troy appear;
Paris and Helen, Hector, too, are here;
Haman and Esther in their ancient poses,
And Judith, Holofernes, Aaron, Moses.

Beside them can be seen the God of Wine,
With Vulcan, Pluto and his Proserpine,
Apollo, Mercury, and Lady Venus,
The God Amor, Priapus and Silenus.

The ass of Balaam stands not far away,
—So finely wrought, one almost hears him bray—
Here revels Lot who, with his daughters, swam
In wine—and here's the test of Abraham.

The dance of Salome is here portrayed;
Upon a dish the Baptist's head is laid;
The Hell of Satan blazes vividly,
And Peter stands with Heaven's enormous key.

The mischief of lewd Jove is recreated,
His brutal lust that never could be sated:
How Leda by the swan was overpowered,
And down on Danaë the ducats showered.

Here can be seen Diana's frenzied chase:
Dogs, and high-bodiced nymphs, behind her race;
With hand upon the spinning-wheel, one sees
A womanly-attired Hercules.

Close by is Sinai; Israel with his ox
Stands at the mountain; here the orthodox
Are pictured in the temple, turning wild
When challenged by the wisdom of the Child.

Here the contrasts glaringly entwine:
The lust of Greece, Judea's thought divine!
And, in an arabesque design, around
The two of them are ivy tendrils wound.

But marvelous! while, dreaming, I behold
Such sculpture fashioned from the myths of old,
I'm suddenly aware of my own face:
Lifeless within the lovely marble case.

But at my coffin's head a flower grows,
That quivers, and mysteriously glows;
The leaves are sulphur-gold, but a wild power
Of love is holding sway within the flower.

Passion-flower is its common name;
On Golgotha it sprouted, people claim,
When Christ was crucified, and from his wound
The world-redeeming blood poured to the ground.

They say the Martyr fed this flower's seed,
And every tool that served the hangman's need
Upon the martyrdom, was taken up
And reproduced within the flower's cup.

Yes, all the Passion-requisites appear;
That whole vile torture-chamber blossoms here:
The rope, the crown of thorn, the savage flail,
The cross, the cup, the hammer and the nail.

Such flower was my sepulchre's adorning;
And, bending toward me like a woman mourning,
It kissed my hand, my eyes, my frosty brow:
Silent, inconsolably silent now.

But, magic of the vision! Strange! How strange
To see the sulphur passion-flower change!
It turned into a woman—and I knew,
I knew at once, my love, that it was you.

You were that flower of sorrow and of grace—
I knew you by your kiss upon my face.
No lips of flowers learn such tender ways,
No flower-tears so passionately blaze.

My eyes were shut, and yet my soul could see
With what an ecstasy you looked at me:
And bending sweetly in the moon's pale beam,
Your face was lighted by a spectral gleam.

We did not speak, and yet my heart could find
The thoughts that stirred, unuttered, in your mind;
No modesty is in the spoken word;
Silence is love's pure flower—it blooms unheard.

Mute dialogue! you'd scarce believe how fast,
With soundless, tender talk, the time flies past
In lovely visions of a summer night
Woven of horror and of sweet delight.

Never ask of what we spoke, alas!
Ask what the glow-worm glimmers to the grass;
Ask what the billow murmurs to the stream;
Ask of the westwind what his moanings mean.

The bright carbuncle—ask him why he glows;
Ask what they breathe, night-violet and rose—
But never ask of what the martyr-bloom
Whispers with her dead beneath the moon.

I do not know how long a time I lay
Before the lovely vision fled away.
Alas! my mind was not allowed to keep
The rapture of its calm, untroubled sleep.

O Death! with coffin-silence, you alone
Can give us greater joys than all we've known;
Wild fits of passion, cravings day and night,
Are all that life can give us as "delight."

But woe is me! the blessedness departed,
As outside all at once a tumult started;
It was a wild, reviling, stamping fight;
Alas, my flower shrank away in fright.

Yes, outside, with a savage fury, rose
A quarreling, a clash of bitter foes.
Some voices I distinguished from the rest—
Those of the bas-relief upon my chest.

Does superstition haunt the stone once more?
And are these marble phantoms locked in war?
Pan, the savage god of forest, throws his
Terror-cry against the curse of Moses.

O there will never be an end to this;
Beauty and truth can reach no armistice;
The legion of humanity must sever:
Barbarians and Greeks, opposed forever.

They cursed, reviled! No end appeared in sight
To finish off this repetitious fight;
Loudest was Balaam's ass, whose braying drowned
Both gods and saints out, with its raucous sound.

And with this sobbing, nauseating neigh,
This he-haw, he-haw, this revolting bray,
He nearly drove me mad—at last I broke
My silence with an anguished scream—and woke.

TRANSLATED BY AARON KRAMER

Es kommt der Tod—jetzt will ich sagen

Now death draws near, and what unknown,
  Pride counselled, should for ever be,
  I will declare: for thee, for thee,
My heart has beat for thee alone.

My coffin's made, and to my bed
  They lower me, that I may sleep.
  But thou, Maria, thou wilt weep,
And think on me when I am dead.

Thy pretty hands thou'lt even wring.
  Oh, grieve not—'tis the human lot:
  At last defiled in death must rot
Each good and great and lovely thing.

TRANSLATED BY MARGARET ARMOUR

Germany

DEPARTURE FROM PARIS *Ade, Paris, du teure Stadt*

Farewell, beloved town, farewell!
I'm leaving you today;
From all your pleasures and delights
I turn, and go away.

My German heart has suddenly
Been overcome by pain;
There's only one doctor—up in the north—
Can make it well again.

He'll make it well without delay—
His cures are world-renowned;
Yet, I confess, I quake before
The mixtures he'll compound.

Farewell, you gay French brothers of mine!
It is a foolish yearning
That drives me from your land today—
But soon I'll be returning.

Just think! I miss that smell of peat
I've lived so long without—
And the dear little sheep of Lüneburg,
And carrots and sauerkraut.

I miss the watchmen and councillors,
The coarse, uncultured creatures;
I miss brown bread, tobacco-smoke,
And blonde-haired daughters of preachers.

I'd like to see my mother, too—
This fact I won't deny;
Since last I saw her, thirteen years
Have somehow frittered by.

Farewell, my wife, my beautiful wife!
You can't know how I grieve.
I press you so firmly to my heart,
And yet I've got to leave.

How torment drives me from my joys!
Just once, once more, the breath
Of German air must fill my lungs,
Or I will choke to death.

The torment, the pain, the impetuous urge—
How madly they pound and pound!
My feet are shaking—they cannot wait
To stamp on German ground.

By the end of the year I'll be home again,
Better in body and mind,
And then I'll buy you some New Year's gifts—
The loveliest I can find.

                    TRANSLATED BY AARON KRAMER

GERMANY: A Winter's Tale   *Im traurigen Monat November*
                                           wars

I

It was in November, that dreary month;
The days were growing shorter;
The winds ripped all the leaves from the trees;
And I came to the German border.

And as I reached the borderline
A stronger pulse began
To throb within me; down my cheeks
I think some teardrops ran.

And when I heard the German tongue
Strange feelings thrilled my spirit;
It almost seemed as though my heart
Would burst with joy to hear it.

A little harp-girl sang. Her voice
Was strong, though out of key;
And I was deeply stirred to hear
A German melody.

She sang of love and the pain of love,
Of sacrifice on earth,
And meetings in that better world
Where sorrows change to mirth.

She sang of this earthly vale of tears,
Of pleasures that soon run dry;
How the soul will feast on eternal joys
—Transfigured in the sky.

She sang a heavenly lullaby,
The song of renunciation
By which the people, that giant clown,
Is lulled from its lamentation.

I know the authors, I know the tune,
I know it line for line—
In public, water is all they preach;
While in secret they guzzle wine.

A new song, and a better song,
Oh friends, I'll sing for you.
Here on earth we mean to make
Our Paradise come true.

We mean to be happy here on earth—
Our days of want are done.
No more shall the lazy belly waste
What toiling hands have won.

Wheat enough for all mankind
Is planted here below;
Roses and myrtle, beauty and joy,
And green peas, row upon row.

Yes, green peas enough for every man,
As soon as they break their pods.
We gladly leave to the angels and birds
The dainties of the Gods.

And, after our death, if wings should sprout
We'll visit you up there,
And eat the holiest tarts and cakes
That angel-cooks prepare.

A new song, and a better song!
It rings like fiddle and flute.
The *miserere* sounds no more;
The bells of death are mute.

Young Europe's betrothed to Liberty,
That genius of beauty and grace.
They lie in each other's passionate arms,
They feast on their first embrace.

And although they lack the blessing of priests,
Theirs is a proper wedding.
Long live the bridegroom and his bride
And the children of their begetting!

An epithalamium is my song;
A new, a better creation!
Within my soul arise the stars
Of highest consecration.

Inspired stars! they blaze out wild;
In torrents of flame they spill;
I feel that my powers have wondrously grown;
I could shatter an oak at will.

Through my veins, since treading on German soil,
Magical juices flow—
The giant has touched his mother again,
And his power begins to grow.

II

While the young harp-girl was trilling her song
Of heaven's eternal pleasures,
Prussian customs-officials searched
My trunk for its hoard of treasures.

They sniffed at everything, rummaged around
To see if jewels were hidden;
They dug through breeches, handkerchiefs, shirts,
For lace, or a book that's forbidden.

You fools, that search inside my trunk!
Here's nothing that you can find.
The contraband that journeys with me
I've stuck away in my mind.

I've lace that the laces of Mecklenburg
And Brussels can hardly match.
Just wait till my needle-points are unpacked;
You'll feel them prick and scratch.

The future's bright crown-diamonds
Are glittering in me:
The temple-gems of the great unknown,
The God that is to be.

And I carry many books in my head—
Solemnly I state it:
My head is a bird-nest twittering
With books to be confiscated.

Believe me, there can be nothing worse
On the bookshelves of the Devil—
Even von Fallersleben's books [1]
Are on a safer level.

A passenger who stood nearby
Paused kindly to explain
That this was the Prussian *Zollverein*,[2]
The mighty customs-chain.

"The *Zollverein*"—the gentleman said,
"Will be our true foundation,
And bind the dismembered Fatherland
Into one great nation.

"It will bring us material unity:
An outwardly welded state;
While union of soul, on the other hand,
Our censors will create.

"They'll bring internal unity:
No room for minds that doubt.
We need a united Germany:
United Within and Without."

III

Carolus Magnus [3] lies entombed
In Aachen's ancient Dome.
Don't get him mixed with Karl Mayer, who
Makes Suabia his home.

I'd hate being Emperor under that Dome,
Too dead and buried to know it;
I'd much rather live where the Neckar flows,
As Stukkert's puniest poet.

Milling around on Aachen's streets
The dogs were humbly imploring:
"Oh stranger, give us a little kick!
Life has become so boring."

An hour or so in this dull nest
I aimlessly wandered around;
Saw Prussian military again:
They'd changed but little, I found.

Grey cloak, with collar high and red,
Is still the dress of these henchmen.
Körner [4] sang in earlier days:
"Red's for the blood of Frenchmen."

Still the same wooden, pedantic folk:
With stiff right angles they move;
And frozen plainly on every face
The same, undimmed self-love.

They stalk around so stiltedly,
So sprucely bolt upright,
As though they've swallowed the whipping-rod
That bloodied their backs last night.

The whip has never quite disappeared;
They keep it within them now;
One still remembers the "He" of old
When hearing the intimate "Thou."

In truth, the long moustache is just
The pig-tail's newer phase;
The pig-tail that formerly hung behind
Hangs under the nose these days.

The new costume of the cavalry
Is fine—I was quite impressed,
Especially by the bright spiked helm,
With its point of steel at the crest.

This is chivalric, recalling the past:
So far-off and romantic;
The Chatelaine Jeanne de Montfaucon,
The barons Fouqué, Uhland, Tieck. [5]

It calls to mind the squires and knights
Of those lovely feudal years
Who carried loyalty high in their hearts
And a coat of arms on their rears.

It reminds me of tourneys and crusades,
When men were noble-hearted;
When faith was more than a printed word—
Before the first journal was started.

It springs from the very highest wit;
Yes, yes, this helmet I like!
It was a notion befitting a king,
Not lacking a point, a spike!

But should a storm arise, I fear
The sky will be drawn by your spike,
And down upon your romantic head
Most modern lightning will strike.

In Aachen, I saw on the post-office shield
The bird that I despise.[6]
It still sat glaring down at me
With poison-flaming eyes.

Oh hateful bird, if you should fall
Into my hands one day,
I'll pluck each feather from your back
And chop your claws away.

And after this, high in the air
I'll build a perch for you,
And call the huntsmen of the Rhine
To show what they can do.

He who shoots the eagle down
Shall instantly be crowned
And we shall cry: "Long live the King!"
While guns and trumpets sound.

IV

Late in the evening I came to Cologne,
And I heard the Rhine as it moved.
The air that fanned me was German air,
And its influence improved

My appetite. The dish of ham
And omelettes tasted fine.
And since it was salted very well
I washed it down with wine.

Still like gold in the sea-green glass
The Rhinewine brightly glows;
If you drink a couple of pints too much
It climbs up into your nose.

It starts an itching so sweet in your nose,
You are overcome with delight!
It drove me into the echoing streets,
Into the darkening night.

The houses of stone looked down at me
As though they would like to unfold
Tales of Cologne, the holy town,
Forgotten tales of old.

Yes, here the clergy used to go
Upon their pious ways.
Here the black men von Hutten described
Were lords in other days.[7]

Here the nuns and friars danced
The can-can of the Dark Ages.
Here Hochstraaten, the Menzel of Cologne,
Spat out his poisoned pages.

Here the flames of the funeral pyre
Devoured books and people;
Kyrie Eleison accompanied this,
And bells rang out from the steeple.

Here malice and stupidity
Like street-curs used to mate;
The descendants can still be recognized
By their sectarian hate.

But see! clear in the moonlight there
That mighty comrade of stone!
He looms up high, so devilish black:
The Cathedral of Cologne.

It was meant to be the mind's Bastille,
And the Romish plan was clever:
"In this great prison the German mind
Will pine away forever."

Then Luther came upon the scene,
And spoke his mighty "Stay!"
And so Cologne's Cathedral stands
Unfinished to this day.

It never was finished—and that is good.
Its very unfinished condition
Makes it a landmark of German strength
And of the Protestant mission.

Poor wretches of the Cathedral Guild:
You, with your powerless hands,
Hope to revive the halted task
Till the finished stronghold stands.

Oh silly illusion! all in vain
Your alms-bag is hungrily shaken:
Begging of heretics, even of Jews;
It is all so fruitless, mistaken.

Though great Franz Liszt performs for you,
In vain is his contribution;
And in vain a talented king will prove
His power of elocution.[8]

It will never be finished, the spire of Cologne,
Though Suabian fools may send
A ship all loaded up with stones
To bring the job to an end.

It will never be finished, despite the great
Outcry of owl and raven,
Old-fashioned birds, who like to make
A high church-tower their haven.

Yes, instead of being done,
A darker fate approaches:
Its inner crypt will be a stall
For horses and for coaches.

"But if the Cathedral turns to a stall
We'll have a problem to tackle:
What shall be done with the three holy kings
Who rest in the tabernacle?"

Such questions are asked. But need we be
So fretted in our day?
The three holy kings of the East can find
Some other place to stay.

In Münster, high on Saint Lambert's tower,
There hang three cages of iron.
Take my advice, there's no better place
For the three holy kings to lie in.

The king of the tailors sat there once [9]
With his ministerial pair,
But we'll take other majesties
And give them shelter there.

Sir Melchior shall hang at the left,
Sir Balthasar at the right,
Between them Sir Gaspar—when they were alive
God knows where they spent the night!

The holy alliance of the East
That is canonized today
May not have always behaved itself
In a fair and pious way.

Sirs Balthasar and Melchior
May have committed the crime
Of pledging their subjects a better law
At some distressing time—

And later failing to keep their word—
Sir Gaspar may've repaid
His people with a bloody thanks
For trusting the vows he'd made.

V

And when I reached the great Rhine-bridge
Where the forts of the harbor lie,
There in the moonlight I could see
Old Father Rhine flow by.

Greetings, greetings, my Father Rhine!
How has your world been turning?
Many times I've thought of you,
With hunger and with yearning.

I spoke, and I heard in the water's deep
A strangely sullen rumbling;
It sounded like an old man's cough,
A sickly groaning and grumbling.

"Welcome, my son! I'm glad to hear
That I've not been forgotten.
You've been away these thirteen years;
As for me—things have been rotten.

"I swallowed stones at Biberich;
And, son, was that an ordeal! [10]
But the verses of Nicholas Becker made
An even lumpier meal.

He praised me as though I were still a maid
Without a stain upon her
Who won't let anybody lift
Her little crown of honor.

"I feel like plucking out my beard
When his stupid rhymes resound;
I could almost bid the world goodbye
And in myself be drowned.

"That I am not a stainless maid
The Frenchmen long have known.
So often has their victor's reek
Been mingled with my own.

"That stupid song, and that stupid man!
He slandered me with his rot.
And, so to speak, politically,
He put me in a spot.

"For if the French come back again,
My cheeks will blush and burn
I who so often prayed to God
That they might soon return.

"I've always loved the French so well,
These darling little dears!
Are their pants still white? Do they sing and spring
As they did in other years?

"I'd like to see them once again,
But what a ribbing I'i face
Because of that cursed song,
Because of that disgrace!

"That urchin, Alfred de Musset,
Will lead the march, I fear; [11]
He might be the drummer-boy, and drum
His bad jokes into my ear."

Thus poor Father Rhine complained:
Hopelessly sad and frightened.
I offered him many a comforting word,
Hoping his heart would be lightened:

Oh never fear, my Father Rhine,
The mockery of France;
These French are not the French of old,
They even wear different pants.

Their pants are red, instead of white;
New buttons are now in season;
No more do they sing, no more do they spring;
Their heads have grown heavy with Reason.

They're thinkers; now Hegel, *Fischte* and Kant
Are all their conversation.
They smoke tobacco, guzzle beer,
And bowl for recreation.

They're smug philistines, just like us,
And carry it to extremes:
They're beginning to follow Hengstenberg; [12]
Voltaire is through, it seems.

De Musset, it's true, has always been
A rogue, and a rogue he remains.
But have no fear; one of these days
We'll put his tongue in chains.

And if he drums you an evil jest,
We'll whistle an uglier air:
We'll whistle aloud what happened to him
Among his ladies fair.

You can rest untroubled, Father Rhine,
Don't let the bad songs grieve you.
Soon you'll be hearing a better song.
Farewell; for a while I leave you.

VI

With Paganini always came
A "spiritus familiaris,"
Sometimes in the shape of a dog, sometimes
In the form of the late George Harris. [13]

Napoleon saw a scarlet man
Before each grave occasion.
Socrates had his daemon, too;
It was no hallucination.

And at night, while sitting at my desk,
I also used to see
A visitor, in a weird black hood,
Standing in back of me.

Something was hidden under his cloak,
And when I saw, it seemed
An axe—an executioner's axe—
Because of the way it gleamed.

He looked to be of dumpy size;
Each eye was like a star.
He never disturbed me as I wrote,
But quietly waited afar.

For years this singular guest of mine
Had been leaving me alone,
When all at once I found him here
In the moonlit night of Cologne.

I was thoughtfully strolling along the streets,
And back of me he came,
As though my shadow—and every time
I stopped, he did the same.

He halted in his tracks, and stood
With an expectant air;
And when I continued, he followed me
Till we reached Cathedral Square.

I couldn't stand it; I turned and said:
"Now tell me by what right
You follow my footsteps everywhere
Here in the desolate night?

"We always meet when thoughts of the world
Are sprouting in my heart,
When inspiration fires my brain
And flashes of lightning dart.

"You stare with such relentless eyes—
What is it you want of me?
And what have you got there under your cloak,
That glitters so ominously?"

But he replied in a monotone
That was dry, and a bit phlegmatic:
"Don't exorcise me, if you please,
And don't be so emphatic!

"I am no scarecrow, no ghost of the Past
Out of the grave arising;
And I am no friend of rhetoric,
Do little philosophizing.

"I'm of a practical character:
The calm and silent kind.
But know: I carry out, I do
All that you've had in mind.

"And even though the years go by,
I find no satisfaction
Till thought becomes reality;
You think, and I take action.

"You are the judge; the headsman am I,
Who stands and awaits your will;
And whether your judgment be right or wrong,
Obediently I kill.

"The axe of the consul in ancient Rome
Went first, may I remind you.
You've got your 'lictor,' too; but now
The axe is carried behind you.

"I am your 'lictor'; with shiny axe
I follow close behind
On all your travels—I am the deed,
The offspring of your mind."

VII

I wandered home, and slept with songs
Of angels in my head.
In Germany your bed is soft,
For it's a feather-bed.

In the nights of exile, how many times
For these kind pillows I yearned,
When on those hard French mattresses
I sleeplessly tossed and turned!

In German feather-beds you sleep
And dream exceeding well.
Here at last the German soul
Escapes its earthly cell.

The soul escapes, and goes soaring up
To the loftiest realms of the sky.
Oh German soul, in your nightly dreams
How haughtily you fly!

The gods grow pale at your approach!
And everywhere you go
With beating pinions you snuff out
Many a starlet's glow.

The French and the Russians rule the land;
The British rule the sea;
But in the realms of dream we own
Unchallenged mastery.

Here we become one mighty state,
Here, in dreams, we are crowned—
While other peoples build their realms
Upon the level ground . . .

And as I fell asleep, I dreamed
That once again I strolled
In moonlight, on the streets of Cologne,
The echoing streets of old.

And once again behind me came
My comrade, darkly hooded.
Ever on we went, although
I stumbled, weary-footed.

On we went! And in my breast
My heart was torn and bruised.
And from the deep wound of my heart
The drops of scarlet oozed.

Sometimes I plunged my fingers in,
And sometimes I would spread
Over the doorposts, as I passed,
A smear of bloody red.

And every time I marked a house
In such a way, there fell
Moaning sadly and softly afar
The sound of a tolling-bell.

In heaven, though, the moon turned pale:
Soon it was out of sight.
The frenzied clouds came racing past,
Like horses of the night.

And always with his hidden axe
The hooded figure stalked
In back of me—and in this way
For quite a while we walked.

We walked and walked, until we reached
Cathedral Square at last.
The gates were standing open wide,
And through their arms we passed.

Only silence and death and night
Ruled in that giant room;
Hanging-lamps burned here and there
The better to show the gloom.

Along the pillars long I walked,
Only my comrade's pace
Rang in my ears, as step for step
He followed me through the place.

At last we came to a dazzling room
And saw a bright display
Of silver, gold, and precious stones;
Here the Three Kings lay.

But wonder of wonders! the Three Holy Kings
Who'd been content to lie
So still, were sitting upright now
On their sarcophagi.

Three skeletons, in fantastic dress,
With scepters in their hands;
Atop their wretched, yellowed skulls
Were crowns of the eastern lands.

Like jumping-jacks they moved their bones,
That had slept for ages there;
A smell of incense and of mould
Arose and fouled the air.

One of the monarchs moved his mouth
And delivered a long oration,
Explaining why he'd a right to demand
My awe and admiration.

First, because he was a corpse,
Second, because a king,
And third, because he was a saint—
But it didn't mean a thing.

Laughing aloud, I answered him:
Your speech was very clever,
But I can see that you belong
To a time that is gone forever.

Out! out of here! You should have crawled
Down to your graves before.
Life is now coming to confiscate
This chapel's treasure-store.

The future's joyous cavalry
Shall here at last be housed.
And if you're not willing, I'll turn to force:
I'll club you till you're deloused!

So I spoke, and wheeled around;
I saw the terrible glint
Of my silent lictor's terrible axe—
He understood the hint.

He came up close and savagely
Smashed them, scepter and crown;
And with one blow those bones of false
Belief came tumbling down.

Horribly boomed through all the vaults
The echo of that stroke.
Streams of blood shot from my breast,
And suddenly I awoke.

VIII

The fare from Cologne to Hagen is
Five dollars, six Prussian cents.
I had to take the open coach:
—No room in the diligence.

A late Fall morning, damp and gray,
The coach groaned through the mud;
But despite the nasty weather and way
I'd never felt so good.

This is truly my native air!
It touched my cheeks, and they glowed!
And this is the muck of my fatherland:
This mud of the country road!

The horses seemed old friends of mine—
Their tails so cordially swung.
Atalanta's apples were not as fair
As their little cakes of dung.

We drove through Mülheim: a pretty town;
Its people get things done.
I saw them last in the month of May,
In Eighteen Thirty-One.

Everything then was blossom-crowned;
Sunbeams were laughing then;
Full of longing sang the birds;
And there were hopeful men.

"Soon the lean barons will ride away,"
The people used to think,
"And long-necked bottles will be drained
For a departing drink.

"And Freedom will come with song and dance,
With her banner, the white-blue-red;
Perhaps she'll even be able to fetch
Napoleon from the dead."

My God! the barons still are here!
And many who came this way—
Gawky fellows, dry as bone—
Carry big bellies today.

They looked like Love and Faith and Hope,
Those pale invading swine;
Since then their noses have grown red
From too much German wine.

And Freedom has sprained an ankle—no more
Can she leap as in other days.
From the towers of Paris the tricolor droops
With a melancholy gaze.

Since then the Emperor's risen again,[14]
But he had been taught to behave
By the English worms; with his own consent
Once more he's laid in the grave.

I saw his funeral myself,
And the coach that solemnly rolled
With the golden Victory Goddesses
Who carried the coffin of gold.

All along the Champs Elysées,
And through the Triumphal Arch,
Right through the mist, right over the snow,
Advanced the funeral march.

The music was shockingly dissonant;
The musicians numb with frost.
The eagles on the standards seemed
Sorrowful and lost.

And the people were lost in memories,
So ghostly did they seem!
Once again was conjured up
Their old imperial dream.

I couldn't help but weep that day:
My eyes grew dim with tears
When that old cry, "Vive l'Empereur!"
Resounded in my ears.

IX

The following morning I left Cologne;
It was only a quarter of eight.
We came to Hagen almost at three.
In Hagen they always eat late.

Here was the good old German style
Of cooking I knew so well.
Hail to thee, dear sauerkraut!
How goodly is thy smell!

Stuffed chestnuts in green cabbage-leaves,
As if they'd been cooked by mother.
Oh native codfish, my greetings to you!
How smartly you swim in the butter!

To feeling hearts the fatherland
Remains forever precious—
Eggs and herrings stewed dark brown
Are also most delicious.

How the sausages danced in sizzling fat!
The thrushes, those deeply pious
Broiled angels, chirped in the apple-sauce:
"We're glad you've come to try us!"

They twittered: "Welcome, countryman!
It's long since we've seen your face;
You've roved around with foreign birds
So long in a foreign place!"

Upon the table stood a goose:
A quiet, genial thing.
She may have loved me once, when we
Were both still young of wing.

Her gaze was so deeply significant,
So fervent, so pained, so true!
She surely possessed a noble soul;
But she wasn't easy to chew.

In a pewter dish the head of a swine.
Was afterwards brought out.
We still adorn with laurel-leaves
The swine's uplifted snout.

X

As we rode from Hagen darkness fell;
The evening air was raw.
Only at Unna, in the inn,
My bones began to thaw.

I found a pretty maiden there
Who brought me punch, and was friendly.
Her curly hair was like yellow silk;
Her moonlit eyes shone gently.

I heard the lisping Westphalian speech
With pleasure once again.
Sweet memories rose in the steam of the punch;
I thought of those fine young men,

Those dear Westphalians, with whom I drank
Far more than we were able,
In Göttingen, and were so moved
We ended under the table.

Those dear, those good Westphalians
Have always been my friends.
They're all so firm, so sure, so true:
No bragging, no pretence.

How splendidly in the fencing-hall
They stand—those lion-hearts!
So rightly aimed, and so precise
Their tierces and their quartes!

They duel well, they guzzle well,
And when these friendly folk
Shake hands with you, they always cry:
They're sentimental oaks.

Heaven preserve you, valiant race,
Bless your harvest and seed,
Keep you always from war and fame,
From hero and hero-deed!

May God forever grant your sons
Exams that they can pass,
And may He grant a handsome match
To each Westphalian lass!

XI

This is the forest of Teutoburg [15]
Of Tacitus' report.
This is the classical morass
Where Varus was stopped short.

Here he was faced by the Cheruscan chief,
Hermann, of noble blood;
And here the German nation rose
Victorious from the mud.

If Hermann hadn't won the fight
At the head of his fierce blonde hordes.
There'd be no more German liberty—
We'd have bowed to the Roman lords.

Our fatherland would now be ruled
By the Roman tongue and tunic;
Suabians would be Quirites now;
There'd be vestal virgins in Munich.

They'd make a diviner of Hengstenberg;
He'd delve, both day and night,
In the bowels of oxen. Neander would watch [16]
And interpret the swallows' flight.

Birch-Pfeiffer'd be drinking turpentine
Like the Roman ladies of old.
(Because of this their urine smelled
Especially sweet, we're told.)

No German rascal would Raumer be
But a Roman rascalatius.
Freiligrath would use no rhyme,
In the manner of Flaccus Horatius.

The barbarous beggar, Father Jahn,
They'd call Barbarianus.
Massmann'd speak Latin. Me Hercule!
Marcus Tullius Massmannus.

The friends of truth would have to fight
Wild beasts in the arenas—
Not against dogs in the small-time press,
But lions, jackals, hyenas.

Instead of three dozen sovereigns,
One Nero would keep us in chains.
Defying the henchmen of slavery
We would all cut open our veins.

Schelling would be a Seneca; [17]
And he'd be Nero's victim.
To our painter Cornelius we would say:
"*Cacatum non est pictum.*"

Thank God! The Romans were driven away;
The victory was Hermann's.
Varus and all his hordes succumbed,
And we—we still are Germans.

We speak the German we used to speak;
Everything stayed the same.
An ass is an ass—not *asinus*.
The Suabians kept their name.

The Prussian Eagle is Raumer's prize—
He keeps to the German path—
We haven't done away with rhyme:
No Horace is Freiligrath.

Massmann speaks no Latin. Thank God!
Birch-Pfeiffer only writes plays.
She drinks no dreadful turpentine
Like the ladies of Roman days.

Oh Hermann, we give you thanks for this!
And, to honor you and your tribe,
In Detmold they're building a monument.
I was one of the first to subscribe.

XII

The coach bumps on through the darkened woods.
But a wheel has broken away;
And suddenly: Crash! We stop in our tracks.
This isn't very gay.

The coachman dismounts and hurries to town;
And alone in the woods I prowl.
It is the middle of the night;
I hear wild creatures howl.

They are the wolves that howl so wild;
I know their famished cries.
Like candles blazing in the dark
Glimmer their fiery eyes.

They've heard of my coming, I've no doubt;
They set the woods afire
In honor of my visit there—
And greet me with their choir.

It is a serenade they sing—
For me—their celebration!
Deeply moved, I draw myself up
And deliver a grateful oration:

"Fellow-wolves! I'm proud and thrilled
To spend this night among
Such noble souls who howl to me
Their tender welcome-song.

"At this auspicious moment, friends,
My feelings can't be measured;
Believe me, till the day I die
This hour shall be treasured!

"I thank you for the confidence
With which you honor me
And which you've proved in trying times
By acts of loyalty.

"You never doubted me, fellow-wolves,
Never would let them persuade you,
Those villains who called me a renegade,
Who said that I had betrayed you,

"Sold out to the dogs, and soon would be
Chief shepherd-dog in the fold.
It was far beneath me to contradict
The lies that you were told.

"Believe me, though I sometimes wore
A coat of wool, to keep
The cold away, I was never convinced
To fight in the cause of the sheep.

"I am no sheep, no shell-fish, no dog;
I play no Councillor's part;
I've stayed a wolf through all the years,
With wolfish teeth and heart.

"I am a wolf, and with the wolves
I'll howl my whole life through.
Yes, count on me and help yourselves;
Then God will help you too."

That was the speech I made, without
The slightest preparation.
Kolb's *Allgemeine* printed it [18]
With the usual mutilation.

XIII

The sun rose over Paderborn
With a very sullen expression.
Bringing light to the stupid earth—
A wearisome profession!

As soon as he's brightened one corner up
He carries his radiant light
With glittering speed to the other side,
While the first sinks down into night.

The stone rolls back on Sisyphus,[19]
The deep Danaid tun
Is never filled, and the ball of earth
Is lighted in vain by the sun!—

And as the morning mists dissolved
I thought that I could see
An image of the Son of Man
Who bled upon the tree.

Poor cousin of mine, I'm filled with woe
Whenever I see your face.
You hoped to save the world—you fool!
Friend of the human race!

They've given you a dirty deal,
Those lords of high estate.
Who told you to speak so recklessly
Against the church and the state?

Too bad for you, the printing-press
Was a yet-unknown device.
You would have written a book, no doubt,
On the problems of Paradise.

The censor would have stricken out
The most offensive section,
And you'd have not been crucified—
Thanks to his kind protection.

Had you left that Sermon on the Mount
To be preached by later Messiahs,
You'd still have had spirit and talent enough,
And could have spared the pious!

You scourged the bankers, the changers of gold,
You drove them out of the temple.
Luckless crusader, now on the cross
You hang as a warning example.

XIV

Moist wind, dry land; the carriage limps
Through mud; but an old refrain
Keeps singing and ringing in my soul:
"Sun, thou accusing flame!"

It is the refrain of the ancient song
My nurse so often sang—
"Sun, thou accusing flame!" like the call
Of a forest-horn it rang.

There is a murderer in the song:
A carefree, happy fellow;
At last they find him in the woods—
Hanging from a willow.

His death-decree was nailed to the trunk,
That anyone who came
Might see the word of the Vehmic court:
"Sun, thou accusing flame!"

The sun was plaintiff, his voice of doom
Had called the murderer's name;
Dying, Ottilie had screamed:
"Sun, thou accusing flame!"

When I think of the song, I also think
Of my nurse, so dear and old;
I see her brown face once again,
With every wrinkle and fold.

Her birthplace was in Münster-land,
And often I heard her tell
Ghost stories, fables, and fairy-tales—
And she knew the old songs well.

How my heart would throb, when my
        dear old nurse
Told of the princess fair
Who sat alone on the lonely heath
And combed her golden hair!

There she had to tend the geese,
And when, at eventide,
She drove them through the gate once more
She always stopped and cried.

For she could see a horse's head
Nailed where the town-gate stands.
This was the head of the wretched horse
Who'd borne her to distant lands.

The princess sighed, "Oh Fallada,
That you should be hanging so!"
The horse's head cried down, "Alas,
That you ever wished to go!"

The princess sighed, and deeply sighed,
"If my dear mother knew!"
The horse's head cried sadly down,
"Her heart would break for you!"

I used to listen with bated breath
When, gravely whispering,
My dear old nurse began to tell
Of Redbeard, our hidden king.[20]

She'd have me believe the scholars wrong,
She said he was living still
Together with his comrades-in-arms—
Hiding in a hill.

Kyffhäuser is the name of the hill;
A cave's within its walls.
A spectral light of hanging-lamps
Creeps through the gloomy halls.

The first room is a royal stall,
And in this room you see
Thousands of horses in their cribs,
All harnessed brilliantly.

They're saddled well, and bridled well,
But of this fine array
There's none that stirs; as though of steel
They neither stamp nor neigh.

Lying on straw in the second room
Warriors can be seen:
Thousands of soldiers: bearded folk
With warlike, defiant mien.

They're fully armed from head to toe,
But all these men of war
Are motionless; they make no sound;
They lie asleep on the floor.

And in the third room, piled up high,
Weapons and arms are stored:
Armor and helmets of silver and steel,
Battle-axe, spear, and sword.

Very few cannon, yet enough
To form a trophy. Behold!
Above them a banner flutters high:
Its color is black-red-gold.

And in the fourth room lives the king—
For ages he's been there:
His head on his arm, at the table of stone,
Set on the same stone chair.

His flowing beard is red as flame;
At times his old eyes twinkle;
But there are times when worry seems
To make his forehead wrinkle.

Is he asleep, or does he muse?
The answer isn't clear;
But he shall mightily stir himself
When the proper hour is here.

Then shall he seize the worthy flag
And cry: "To war! To war!"
His troops will wake, and leap from the ground
With a tremendous roar.

And each will swing upon his horse
That will neigh, and trample the ground.
They'll ride out into the echoing world
And how their trumpets will sound!

They'll gallop well, they'll battle well;
They'll have slumbered out their time.
The King's tribunal will be severe:
The killers will pay for their crime—

The killers who once thrust their sword
With foul assassin's aim
Through golden-haired young Germany—
"Sun, thou accusing flame!"

There's many a man who thinks himself safe,
And, laughing, sits in his tower,
Who shall not escape the avenging rope
At Redbeard's awakening hour!

How lovely they sound, how sweet they sound,
The tales of that dear old dame!
My superstitious heart exults:
Sun, thou accusing flame!

XV

Like needle-points came prickling down
A fine, an icy rain.
Sadly the horses swished their tails;
I watched them sweat and strain.

I heard the toot of the coachman's horn,
Just as I used to hear it.
"There ride three riders out to the gate!"
Dusk came over my spirit.

I drowsed and fell asleep; and lo!
My dreams went wandering;
They brought me into the magic hill
Before our great old king.

No more did he sit at the table of stone
On his chair of stone—erect.
And he seemed less venerable now
Than one had been led to expect.

He waddled around through the rooms with me
And spoke in an intimate way.
He showed me, with a collector's pride,
The treasures on display.

The art of clubbing he explained
With a few well-chosen words.
He tenderly rubbed, with his ermine fur,
The rust from several swords.

With a peacock-fan he dusted helms
Until they shone like new;
He polished many coats of mail,
And some spiked helmets, too.

He dusted off the flag, and said:
"It makes me feel so good
To think that moths haven't touched the silk,
And there's nary a worm in the wood!"

And as we came upon the room
Where soldiers, armed for the fight,
Were lying fast asleep on the floor,
The old man spoke with delight.

"Here we must softly speak and tread,
To drive no dreams away.
Once more a hundred years have passed,
And they're to be paid today."

And lo! he tiptoed up to them,
Held out a golden ducat
And stuck one quietly away
In every soldier's pocket.

And as I watched him in surprise,
He grinningly began:
"At the close of every century
I pay them one ducat per man."

And in the room where horses stood
In long and silent file,
Old Redbeard gaily rubbed his hands
And smiled a mysterious smile.

He counted the horses one by one,
And patted their ribs, approving; .
He counted and counted; with anxious haste
His silent lips were moving.

"That still is not the proper count,"
He said at last with regret.
"I've plenty of soldiers, and weapons, too,
But not enough horses yet.

"I've sent my grooms to the ends of the earth
To purchase all they are able;
They'll buy me the finest horses they see;
I've already a splendid stable.

"I'm waiting till the count's complete,
Then I'll attack—and free
My fatherland, my German folk
That loyally waits for me."

So spoke the King, but I cried out:
"Attack, old fellow, attack!
If your soldiers have not horses enough,
Let them ride on an ass's back!"

"One doesn't rush into attack,"
Redbeard replied with a smile;
"Rome was not built up in a day;
All good things take a while.

"Who comes not now, comes later on;
Oaks don't grow in a day;
And *chi va piano, va sano*,[21] my friend;
That's what the Romans say."

XVI

A jolt of the carriage woke me up,
But soon I slept again,
And dreamt of Redbeard, the ancient king,
Among his sleeping men.

Again we chatted and strolled about
Through each resounding hall;
He asked me this, he asked me that,
And bade me tell him all.

Not a syllable from the upper world
These many, many years,
—Since the Seven Years' War, not a single word
Had reached the monarch's ears.

He asked about Moses Mendelssohn,[22]
And Karschin; dropped a query
About old Countess Dubarry, too,
Louis the Fifteenth's dearie.

O King, I cried, how backward you are!
Many a year has passed
Since Moses died—Son Abraham, too,
Has long since breathed his last.

With Leah, Abraham begot
A fine son, Felix by name [23]
Who's gone quite far in the Christian world:
A conductor of great fame.

The aged Karschin is also dead,
And her granddaughter, Klencke,[24] is gone;
Her daughter, Helmine Chezy, though,
Has not as yet passed on.

As long as Louis the Fifteenth ruled,
Dubarry's life was gay.
By the time she went to the guillotine
She'd grown quite old and gray.

King Louis the Fifteenth died in bed,
His passing was serene;
The Sixteenth, though, was guillotined
With Antoinette, his queen.

The queen, as befits a royal wife,
Went with a brave demeanor;
Dubarry, though, shed tears and shrieked,
When they came to guillotine her.—

Redbeard suddenly stood still:
"By God, what does it mean?"
He looked at me with staring eyes,
"What is this guillotine?"

Guillotining—I explained—
Is a method we're now applying
To people of every circumstance:
It expedites their dying.

In this new method we employ
A newly-developed machine;
Monsieur Guillotin invented it,
So it's called the guillotine.

First they strap you to a board:
It drops—they quickly shove you
Between two posts—a three-cornered axe
Hangs directly above you;—

They pull a cord, then downward shoots
The spritely blade,—and crack!
Your head immediately drops
Into a waiting sack.

The king broke in on my words: "Shut up!
Enough of your machine!
God forbid that I should come
To use a guillotine!

"Strapped! The emperor, and his queen!
Strapped! Onto a plank!
That goes against all etiquette
And all respect of rank!

"And who are *you*, that you dare be
So intimate with me?
I'll clip your impertinent wings, young scamp!
Just wait, just wait and see.

"When I listen to the things you say
My very innards are stirred.
Your breath is itself a crown-offense;
High treason's in every word!"

Since Redbeard flew into such a rage,
And could only snarl and shout,
I, too, forgot to hold my tongue,
And my inmost thoughts burst out:

Sir Barbarossa!—I cried out loud—
You're a mythical creation.
Go, get some sleep! without your help
We'll work out our salvation.

The republicans would scoff at us
If a ghost with sceptre and crown
Came marching at the head of our ranks—
They'd laugh us out of town.

And I don't care much for your flag these days;
No longer am I thrilled
By your black-red-gold—I got sick of it
In the days of the Student Guild.

It would be best if you stayed at home
Here in your mountain-hall—
Considering how matters stand,
We need no king at all.

XVII

I wrangled with the king in dreams,
Only in dreams, of course,—
Awake, we answer majesty
With no such bold retorts.

Only while dreaming ideal dreams
Does the German dare impart
The German opinion he has held
So deep in his loyal heart.

We were passing a forest when I awoke;
The sight of all those trees,—
Their naked, wooden reality—
Expelled my fantasies.

The oak-trees gravely nodded their heads;
The birches, cautioning,
Shook their twigs—and I cried out:
Pardon, my dear old King!

Forgive, oh Redbeard, my hasty words!
I haven't your sensible mind.
My patience is short—but come, oh King,
On the fastest horse you can find!

And if you don't care for the guillotine,
We'll do it the old way again:
The rope for burghers and farmers in smocks;
The sword for noblemen.

But switch it around from time to time:
Let peasants die by the sword,
And let the nobility be hanged—
We're creatures all of the Lord . . .

Bring back the laws of Charles the Fifth,[25]
Set up the gallows again,
And divide the people in guilds and estates
As they were divided then.

Let the Holy Roman Empire rule,
Just as in ancient days;
Bring back its mouldiest trumpery,
And all its foolish ways.

The Middle Ages I'll endure,
No matter how dark they be—
If only from that hybrid thing
You'll promise to set us free;

From that new-fangled chivalry,
A nauseating dish
Of Gothic illusion and modern lie,
That's neither flesh nor fish.

We'll shut down all the theatres
And chase the clowns away
Who parody the olden times—
O King, we await your day!

XVIII

A mighty fortress is Minden town:
Its arms and bulwarks are fine.
But Prussian fortresses are not
Favorite places of mine.

We got there in the hour of dusk,
And when we rolled across
The old planks of the drawbridge groaned;
The dark moats gaped at us.

The lofty bastions glowered down
As though they expected war;
The great gate clattered open wide
And clattered shut once more.

Alas! my soul grew sorrowful,
As once Odysseus' soul
Grew dark when Polyphemus shoved
The rock in the cavern's hole.

A corporal neared, and asked our names
In a voice of brash defiance.
No-man's my name; I'm an oculist:
I open the eyes of giants.

I felt still worse when I got to the inn;
I had no appetite.
Went straight to bed—but I didn't sleep—
The bed-gear won the fight.

It was an ample feather-bed,
With curtains of damask-red;
The canopy of faded gold—
And a dirty fringe at the head.

Accursed fringe! that all night long
Robbed me of my repose!
Like the sword of Damocles it hung
Menacing over my nose.

It sometimes seemed a serpent's head
And I heard it hiss at me:
"You're *in* the fortress, and here you'll stay—
And never again be free!"

If only I were home—I sighed—
If I could be back there
In Paris with my darling wife
On the Faubourg Poissonière!

It seemed as though some eerie thing
Was passing over my head,
Just like a censor's icy hand—
And then my reason fled.

Policemen, draped in burial shrouds,
A crowd of ghosts, surrounded
My bed; and as they weirdly moved
A clang of fetters sounded.

Alas! the spectres dragged me off.
I found myself at last
Upon a steep and rocky wall:
There they bound me fast.

That evil, filthy canopy-fringe!
I found it here once more—
But it seemed to be a vulture now,
Of death-black feather and claw.

It looked like the Prussian eagle now,
And clutched me close, and ripped
The liver out of my gaping breast;
I groaned, and bitterly wept.

I'd been weeping long—when a rooster crowed
And the fevered vision fled.
I lay at Minden, in sweaty sheets,
With the tassel over my head.

I traveled on by special post;
And the first free breath I found
Was outside in the open air
On good old Bückeburg ground.

XIX

O, Danton, you were wrong indeed,
And paid for being wrong!
On his heels, on his feet, a man can take
His fatherland along.[26]

Half the duchy of Bückeburg
Was pasted to my boots;
Such muddy roads I've never seen
In all my wide pursuits.

When we reached the city of Bückeburg
I took the time to get down
And look at my grandfather's place of birth—
Hamburg was grandmother's town.

I reached Hanover close to noon,
And gave my boots a cleaning.
I went at once to see the town,
—I like my tours to have meaning.

My word! this is a pretty place!
The streets are very clean.
I saw some splendid buildings here—
A most imposing scene.

I especially liked a great wide square
Surrounded by buildings of state:
The king lives there, his palace is there—
It's a joy to contemplate!

(I mean the palace) At either side
Of the gate, a sentry stands.
Fierce and menacing redcoats watch
With muskets in their hands.

"This is Ernst Augustus' home," [27]
My Cicerone said;
"A high Tory lord, a nobleman:
He's old—but far from dead.

"His life is right idyllical—
No satellite can guard it
As well as the fear in our loving friends—
Spineless and chicken-hearted!

"I sometimes see him; and then he gripes
How deadening to the mind
The Kingship of Hanover is,
To which he's now confined.

"He finds the life too narrow here,
Being used to the British way;
He's plagued by the spleen; he's even afraid
He'll hang himself some day.

"He was stooped by the fire two days ago,
Awake before the sun;
He was cooking a cure for his ailing dogs,
Unhelped by anyone."

XX

From Harburg to Hamburg's an hour's ride;
Dusk had beaten me there.
The stars in heaven greeted me;
I felt the cool, mild air.

And when I opened mother's door
She nearly fainted for joy;
She clapped her wrinkled hands, and cried:
"My darling, darling boy!

"It has been all of thirteen years
Since you left home, my sweet.
You surely must be wild for food—
Now, what would you like to eat?

"I have some fish, and goose-meat, too—
And lovely oranges."
Then give me fish, and goose-meat, too—
And lovely oranges.

And while I ate with growing zest
Mother was gay as could be;
She asked me this, she asked me that;
Some questions embarrassed me.

"My darling boy! Now tell me the truth—
Are you well-tended in France?
Does your wife know how to manage the house?
Does she mend your shirts and pants?"

The fish is good, dear motherkin,
But 'twere better that no one spoke.
You really mustn't bother me now:
I might swallow a bone, and choke.

And when I'd devoured the excellent fish
She brought out the goose, and served me.
Again she asked me this and that;
Some of her questions unnerved me.

"My darling boy! in which of the lands
Do you find that life is cheerier?
Here or in France? And of these two folks
Which would you call superior?"

The German goose, dear motherkin,
Is good—but the Frenchmen do
A better job of stuffing geese;
Their sauces are better, too.

And when the goose had taken her bow,
The oranges came into sight.
They tasted so sweet—I'd never dreamed
They could give me such delight.

But mother cheerfully began
Her questions; and she harassed me
By bringing up a thousand things—
Some of her questions embarrassed me.

"My darling boy! And what are your views?
Do you still take note of the trends?
What party do you belong to now?
What sort of folks are your friends?

The oranges, dear motherkin,
Are good—and with genuine zeal
I swallow down the last sweet drop,
And lay aside the peel.

XXI

Hamburg, half of it burned away,
Is slowly being reborn;
The doleful city looks just like
A poodle halfway shorn.

So many streets are here no more
That I keep thinking of!
Where is the house in which I kissed
My first sweet kiss of love?

Where is the printer's where I took
My "Reisebilder" to press?
The oyster-cellar, where first I knew
An oyster's tenderness?

And the Dreckwall? where has the Dreckwall gone?
In vain I search the street!
Where's the pavilion, where I had
So many cakes to eat?

And the City Hall, in which were throned
The elders of the town?
Prey to the flames! The fire burned
Even the holiest down.

The people still were sighing with fear,
And with a mournful gaze
Recounted the terrible history
Of that gigantic blaze.

"It started in every quarter at once!
There was nothing but smoke and flame.
The high church-towers flared up wild
And, crashing, down they came.

"The old Exchange was burned to the ground,
Where once our fathers stood
And dealt with each other for centuries
As honestly as they could.

"The Bank, the city's silver soul,
And the book in which was listed
The bank account of every man—
Thank God! the fire missed it.

"Thank God! they raised a fund for us
In all the furthest lands—
An excellent business—eight million marks
Came pouring into our hands.

"The money filled our open hands—
It flowed from every nation;
We also accepted stores of food;
Rejected no donation.

"They sent us clothes and beds enough,
And bread, and meats, and soups!
The king of Prussia was kind enough
To offer us his troops.

"The material damage has been repaid,
That could be estimated—
But for the fright, the fright we felt,
We'll never be compensated!"

Dear people, I said to cheer them up,
You mustn't wail and weep;
Troy was a better city than yours,
Yet it fell in a blazing heap.

Dry your puddles, restore your homes,
And if you're set on vengeance
Let it take the form of better laws
And better fire-engines.

Go easy on pepper in mock-turtle soup;
And learn to scale your fish—
Unscaled carp, when it's cooked in grease,
Is not a healthy dish.

Turkey-cocks can't do much harm,
But you might be led to disaster
By the treacherous bird that laid its egg [28]
In the wig of the burgomaster.

This nasty bird's identity
It's needless to announce—
Whenever I remember him—
My lunch begins to bounce.

XXII

Even more striking than the town's
Was the people's transformation.
Like wandering ruins they walk around
In pain and tribulation.

The thin ones are even thinner now,
The fat ones even fatter;
The children are old, the older folk
Return to childish chatter.

Many that I'd left as calves
Were oxen when I found them;
Many goslings had grown into geese,
With haughty plumage around them.

Old Gudel looked like a siren still,
With her paint and powder and pearls;
She'd purchased teeth of dazzling white,
And a mop of pitch-black curls.

My friend, the stationer, had best
Preserved his youthful air;
He looks like John the Baptist, with
His halo of blonde hair.

I saw —— only from far,[29]
He swiftly fled from view;
I hear his mind was burned away,
But Biber'd insured it, too.

I saw my friend, the censor, again—
We met in the market place.
He was stooped, and wandering in a fog
With a troubled look on his face.

We shook hands, and his eyes were moist.
He felt such deep delight
At seeing his poet once again!
It was a moving sight—

I didn't find them all. Some friends
Had left this earthly shore.
Alas! my Gumpelino, too,[30]
Shall smile at me no more.

The noble fellow had lately died:
And now, with wings fullgrown,
He must be hovering—seraph-white—
Around Jehovah's throne.

In vain I sought through Hamburg's streets,
In every possible spot,
For the bent Adonis who hawked his cup
And porcelain chamber-pot.

Sarras, the faithful poodle's dead;
The heaviest loss in years!
If three-score writers passed away
Campe would shed less tears.

The population of Hamburg State
Consists—from its founding day—
Of Jews and Christians; the latter, too
Give very little away.

All of the Christians are pretty good,
They've good strong appetites, too.
And they're sure to pay up every bill
Even before it's due.

And as for the Jewish community,
It seems to have split in two:
The old ones pray in the synagogue,
And a temple houses the new.

The new Jews feast on pork, and stand
In constant opposition—
They're democrats; the old belong
To aristoscratchy tradition.

I love the old, I love the new,
But I swear by God above
There are certain fish we call smoked sprats
For which I've a greater love.

XXIII

The republic of Hamburg was never as great
As those of Venice and Florence;
But the oysters of Hamburg can't be beat—
They're best in the cellars of Lorenz.

When I went down there with good old Campe
The evening air was fine;
We were bent on wallowing once more
In oysters and Rhine wine.

A good crowd sat there; and I was glad
To find, among the others,
Many old cronies, like Chaufepié,
And many new-sworn brothers.

Here's Wille, whose face is a register;
His academic foes
Had signed inscriptions in that book
Too legibly—with blows.

Here was that thorough pagan, Fuchs,
A personal foe of Jehovah—
Devoted to Hegel, and also, perhaps,
To the Venus of Canova.

My Campe had turned Amphitryon,
And smiled in great delight;
Like a transfigured Madonna's now
His eyes were blessedly bright.

I ate and drank with zest, and thought:
"This Campe's a perfect gem—
There may be other good publishers—
But he's the best of them.

"Where another publisher, perhaps,
Would have let me starve in hallways,
This fellow even buys me drinks;
I'll have to keep him always.

"I thank the mighty Lord on high
Who made the sap of the vine,
And permitted such a publisher
As Julius Campe to be mine!

"I thank the mighty Lord on high
Whose glorious word gave birth
To oysters in the ocean-world
And wine of the Rhine on earth!

"He made the lemons grow, with which
Our oysters are bedewed—
Now, Father, see that I may well
Digest this evening's food!"

The Rhinewine always mellows me,
And soothes my strife-torn mind,
And kindles there a mighty urge,
An urge to love mankind.

It makes me leave my lonesome room;
It drives me from street to street;
I look for a garment soft and white,
A soul for my soul to meet.

At moments like these I nearly melt
With sadness and desire;
All cats are gray, all women then
Are Helens, and set me afire.

And as I came where the Drehbahn runs [31]
I saw the moon illumine
A woman, splendid and sublime,
A wondrously high-breasted woman.

Her face was round, and hale, and sound;
Her eyes were turquoise blue;
Her cheeks were like roses, like cherries her mouth—
And her nose was reddish, too.

Her head was covered with a white
And well-starched linen bonnet;
It looked like a crown, with towerlets
And jagged pinnacles on it.

She wore a white tunic down to her calves,
And oh! what calves they were!
The bases of two Doric columns
Couldn't be lovelier!

The most earthly unaffectedness
Could be read upon her face,
But her superhuman rear betrayed
She belonged to a higher race.

Stepping up to me, she said:
"Welcome to Elbe's shore—
After an absence of thirteen years—
I see you're the same as before.

"Perhaps you seek those lovely souls
Who often met you here
And revelled all night long with you
In a passed, a perished year.

"That hundred-headed hydra, Life,
Long since devoured them all—
The old times and the girls you knew
Are lost beyond recall!

"You'll find those pretty flowers no more,
That you loved when your heart was warm;
Here they bloomed—they are withered now,
And their leaves are ripped by the storm.

"Withered, stripped, and trampled down
By destiny's brutal feet—
My friend, such is the earthly fate
Of all that is lovely and sweet!"

Who are you?—I cried—you look at me
Like a dream that once I knew—
Majestic lady, where do you live?
May I accompany you?

At this the woman smiled and said:
"Sorry! but *I'm* refined;
I'm a respectable, moral sort;
Sorry! I'm not that kind.

"I'm not that kind of a mademoiselle,
A Loretta with open bodice—
Know then: I am Hammonia,
Hamburg's protecting goddess!

"You start, and even seem afraid;
You—such a valiant singer!
Are you still so anxious to come with me?
Well, then! no need to linger!"

But noisily I laughed, and said:
I'll come along—proceed!
I'll come along, though Hell's the place
To which your footsteps lead!

XXIV

How I got up her narrow stairs
I really couldn't say;
Perhaps a few invisible ghosts
Carried me part of the way.

Here in Hammonia's little room
The hours went swiftly by.
The goddess confessed, her opinion of me
Had always been quite high.

"You see," she said, "before your time
My heart was set afire
By one who praised the Messiah's works
Upon his pious lyre.

"My Klopstock's bust is standing yet [32]
On the bureau, there by the clock,
Though recently I've been using it
In place of a milliner's block.

"Now *you're* my pet; your picture hangs
On the wall above my bed.
And see, a fresh green laurel wreath
Adorns your handsome head.

"And yet, the way you've often nagged
My sons, I must admit,
Has sometimes deeply wounded me;
Let's have no more of it.

"I trust that Time has cured you of
Such naughty occupation,
And taught you even to look on fools
With greater toleration.

"But tell me! Winter's almost here—
What could have been your reason
For starting on a journey north
In such a draughty season?"

O, my goddess!—I replied,
Thoughts lie slumbering deep
Within the core of the human heart,
That may suddenly wake from their sleep.

On the surface things went pretty well,
But something within oppressed me,
And day by day that oppression grew—
Homesickness possessed me.

The air of France, that had been so light,
Now smothered me with its weight;
I had to breathe some German air
Or I would suffocate.

I longed for German tobacco-smoke,
For the fragrance of our peat.
My foot grew faint with eagerness
To step on a German street.

I longed to see my old lady again,[88]
And all through the night I'd sigh;
She lives beside the gate of the dam;
Lottchen lives nearby.

That old and noble gentleman [84]
I also longed to see;
He never failed to bawl me out,
Yet always took care of me.

"Stupid fellow!" he used to say.
Once more I wanted to hear it—
It always echoed like a song,
A sweet song, through my spirit.

I longed for the bluish chimney-smoke
That rises from German stoves;
For the nightingales of Saxony;
For quiet beech-tree groves.

I even hungered for those spots
Where grief had bowed me down;
Where once I dragged the cross of youth,
And wore a thorny crown.

I wanted to weep again, where once
My bitterest tears fell burning—
Love of country, I believe,
Is the name of this foolish yearning.

I do not like to speak of it;
It's only a disease;
Modest, I never permit the crowd
To see my agonies.

I have no patience with the bunch
That hopes to stir your heart,
By putting its patriotism on show
With every abscess and wart.

Shameless, shabby beggars are they
That kneel and whine for charity—
Give Menzel and his Suabians
A penny of popularity!

O, goddess mine, you've found me today
In a very sensitive state;
I'm somewhat ill, but if I take care,
I'll soon recuperate.

Yes, I am ill, and you could help
To raise my spirits some,
By serving a cup of good hot tea;
I'd like it mixed with rum.

XXV

She brewed some tea, mixed it with rum,
And poured a cup for me.
But she herself drank down the rum
Without a drop of tea.

Against my shoulder she leaned her head,
(The bonnet was somewhat crushed
As a result of her carelessness)
And she spoke in a tone that was hushed:

"Often I've anxiously thought of you
In Paris, that sinful place,
Living without a watchful friend
Among that frivolous race.

"You stroll along those avenues
And haven't at your side
A loyal German publisher
To be your mentor and guide.

"And it's so easy to be seduced!
Those boulevards are lined
With sickly sylphs; and all too soon
One loses peace of mind.

"Don't go back, but stay with us!
Here morals and breeding still stand—
And many a quiet pleasure blooms
Here in the fatherland.

"Stay with us in Germany;
   You'll find things more to your liking;
   You've surely seen with your own eyes
   That progress has been striking.

"And the censorship is harsh no more—
   Hoffmann grows milder with age;
   No more will he mutilate your books
   As he did in his youthful rage.

"You, too, are older and milder now—
   Less eager for a fight;
   You'll even see the bygone days
   In a more propitious light.

"To say that things were hopeless here
   Is gross exaggeration;
   You could break your chains, as they did in Rome,
   By self-extermination.

"The populace had freedom of thought,—
   The greatest number possessed it;
   Only the few who published books
   Were ever really molested.

"Lawless tyranny never ruled;
   Demagogues—even the worst—
   Never lost their citizenship,
   Without being sentenced first.

"And even in the hardest times
   Evil did not prevail—
   Believe me, no one ever starved
   In any German jail!

"So many fine examples of faith
   And kindness could be found
   Blossoming here in days gone by!
   Now doubt and denial abound.

"Practical, outward liberty
   Will one day drag to its doom
   The ideal that grew in our breasts—it was pure
   As the dream of the lily in bloom!

"Our beautiful poetry also dies,
    Today it's a flickering fire;
    Freiligrath's King of the Moors [85] goes down
    With the other kings that expire.

"Our grandsons will eat and drink enough,
    But their thoughtful silence is gone;
    The idyll is over, and in its stead
    A spectacle-play comes on.

"O, could you be silent, I'd open for you
    The book of destiny;
    In my magic mirrors I'd let you view
    Things that are to be.

"I'd like to show you what no one else
    Has seen before this day—
    The future of your fatherland—
    But ah! you'd give it away."

My god, oh goddess!—I cried, enrapt,
    Nothing could be so sweet!
    Show me the future of Germany—
    I am a man and discreet.

I'll pledge my silence by any oath
    That you may wish to hear;
    I guarantee my secrecy—
    Tell me, how shall I swear?

The goddess answered, "Swear to me
    In Father Abraham's way,
    When Eleazar prepared for his trip—
    Now heed whatever I say!

"Lift up my gown, and lay your hand
    Down here on my thigh, and hold it,
    And swear that this secret, in speech and in books,
    Shall never be unfolded."

A solemn moment! I felt as though
    The breath of a buried day
    Blew on me as I swore the oath,
    In the ancient patriarch's way.

I gravely lifted Hammonia's gown,
And laid my hands on her hips,
And vowed the secret would never escape
From my writing-quill or my lips.

XXVI

The rum must have reached Hammonia's crown—
Her cheeks became so red—
And with a sigh she turned to me
And sorrowfully said:

"I'm growing old; I was born on the day
That Hamburg rose from the ground.
As queen of the shellfish, here at the mouth
Of the Elbe, my mother was crowned.

"My father was a mighty king,
Carolus Magnus by name.
Friedrich the Great of Prussia had not
Such wisdom, power and fame.

"His coronation-chair is still
At Aachen; but the chair
On which he used to sit at night
Was left in mother's care.

"Mother willed this chair to me;
You see—it's old and faded;
But should Rothschild offer me all his wealth
I'd never agree to trade it.

"Do you see, there in the corner stands
A chair from an earlier day;
The leather is torn from its back, and moths
Have eaten the cushion away.

"But if you go up close and lift
The cushion from the chair,
You'll see an oval opening;
A pot is hidden there—

"It is a magic pot, in which
The magical powers brew;
Stick in your head, and future times
Shall be revealed to you—

"Germany's future, like waving dreams,
Shall surge before your eyes;
But do not shudder, if out of the mess
Foul Miasmas arise!"

She spoke, and laughed peculiarly,
But there was no fear in my soul;
With curiosity I ran
To stick my head in the hole.

The things I saw, I won't betray—
I promised never to tell.
I'm barely permitted to report:
God! O God! What a smell!

Against my will those cursed, vile
Aromas come to mind:
The startling stink, that seemed to be
Old cabbage and leather combined.

And after this—o God!—there rose
Such monstrous, loathsome stenches;
It was as though the dung were swept
From six and thirty trenches—

I know very well what Saint-Just said [36]
Of late to the Welfare Board—
Neither with attar of roses nor musk
Can the great disease be cured.

But all other smells were put to shame
By this prophetic scent—
No longer could my nostrils bear
That vile presentiment.

My senses swooned, and when I woke
I was still Hammonia's guest—
My head was resting comfortably
Upon her ample breast.

Her nostrils quivered, her lips were aglow,
Her look was a shower of lightning;
With a bacchanal hug of the poet, she sang
In an ecstasy fierce and frightening:

"I love you, stay in Hamburg with me;
We'll gaily eat and drink
The wines and oysters of today,
And forget tomorrow's stink!

"Put back the cover! and spare our joy
From the horrible smells below it—
I love you as never a woman before
Has loved a German poet!

"I kiss you—and your genius fills
My soul with inspiration;
And suddenly I'm overcome
By a grand intoxication.

"I feel as though I hear the song
Of watchmen on the street—
They sing a prothalamium,
My comrade-in-joy, my sweet!

"And now the mounted lackeys come,
With torches richly burning;
They dance the torch-dance solemnly,
Hopping, and waddling, and turning.

"Here come the worthy senators,
And the elders in their glory;
The burgomaster clears his throat
For a trial of oratory.

"The diplomatic corps appear
In dress befitting their stations;
With reservations, they wish us well
In the name of the border-nations.

"With rabbis and pastors arm in arm
God's delegation appears—
But alas! here comes Herr Hoffmann, too,
Wielding his censor-shears!

"The shears are rattling in his hand;
He comes with savage heart—
And cruelly cuts into your flesh—
It was the choicest part . . ."

XXVII

And in that night of miracle
Whatever else took place
I'll let you know another time,
In warmer Summer days.

Hypocrisy's old race, thank God!
Dissolves before our eyes.
It slowly sinks into the grave,
Killed by its cancer of lies.

There is a new race growing up:
Unrouged, unsinning youth!
Freedom of thought, and freedom of joy—
I'll let them know the truth.

They understand a poet's pride,
And know the worth of his art;
They bathe in the warmth of his sunlit mind,
And heed the pulse of his heart.

My heart is loving as the light,
And pure and chaste as fire;
The noblest of the graces tuned
The strings of my golden lyre.

This is the very lyre that once
My father made resound,
The late Lord Aristophanes
Whom the Graces loved and crowned.

Upon this lyre he sang a tale
That every schoolboy knows,
Of a Greek who sued for Zeus's child
And, winning her love, arose.[87]

In the previous chapter I made an attempt
To imitate the end
Of Aristophanes' "The Birds";
—It's the finest play he penned.

"The Frogs" is also excellent.
They're playing it in translation
Upon the stage of Berlin right now
For royal gratification.

The king's enchanted. That shows a taste
For the art of a day that's gone.
Father would laugh far more to hear
Our own frogs carrying on!

The king's enchanted. But were the bard
Alive, who wrote this play,
I'd stop him at Prussia's borderline
And warn him to turn away.

For the real Aristophanes things would be bad:
He'd soon be marched before us,
Clinking his chain, and accompanied
By a huge policemen's-chorus.

The crowd would soon be allowed to jeer
Instead of wagging its tail;
And soon the police would be aroused
To get on the poet's trail.

O king! I wish you very well,
And here's the advice I give:
Pay your respects to the poets who've died,
But spare the ones who live!

Do not offend the living bards;
They've weapons and conflagrations
More dreadful than all the lightnings of Jove
—Which were only a poet's creations.

Offend the gods, both old and new,
The whole Olympian lot,
And high Jehovah leading the rest—
But the poet—offend him not!

The gods, to be sure, are very hard
On wrongs that people do;
The fires of Hell are rather warm:
There one must fry and stew—

But there are certain saints, who pray
Until the sinner is freed;
Through gifts to churches, and requiems,
Heaven will intercede.

And Christ will descend on the final day
And break the Hell-gates down,
And though his judgment may be severe,
Some will be spared his frown.

But there are hells from whose confines
No amnesty avails—
No prayers will help, and even the word
Of our Redeemer fails.

Have you not heard of Dante's Hell,
The tercets that flamed from his pen?
He whom the poet imprisons there
Can never go free again—

No God, no Saviour, can free him from
This conflagration of rhyme!
Beware, lest we hold you in such a Hell
Until the end of time!

TRANSLATED BY AARON KRAMER

Songs of Protest

Du bist begeistert; du hast Mut

You are inspired to hardihood—
Ah, that is good!
Yet inspiration's not sufficient;
Remember, evil is omniscient.

The foe, I grant you, does not fight
For light or right.
But he is armed whatever happens;
His always are the heavier weapons.

So arm yourself, steady your hand,
And take your stand.
Aim well; and if the shot should carry,
Rejoice and let your heart make merry.

TRANSLATED BY LOUIS UNTERMEYER

THE SILESIAN WEAVERS   *Im düstern Auge keine Träne*

In gloomy eyes there wells no tear.
Grinding their teeth, they are sitting here:
"Germany, your shroud's on our loom;
And in it we weave the threefold doom.
  We weave; we weave.

"Doomed be the God who was deaf to our prayer
In Winter's cold and hunger's despair.
All in vain we hoped and bided;
He only mocked us, hoaxed, derided—
  We weave; we weave.

"Doomed be the king, the rich man's king,
Who would not be moved by our suffering,
Who tore the last coin out of our hands,
And let us be shot by his blood-thirsty bands—
  We weave; we weave.

"Doomed be the fatherland, false name,
Where nothing thrives but disgrace and shame,
Where flowers are crushed before they unfold,
Where the worm is quickened by rot and mold—
  We weave; we weave.

"The loom is creaking, the shuttle flies;
Nor night nor day do we close our eyes.
Old Germany, your shroud's on our loom,
And in it we weave the threefold doom;
  We weave; we weave!"

TRANSLATED BY AARON KRAMER

Ich hatte einst ein schönes Vaterland

I dreamed I had a lovely fatherland.
The sturdy oak
Grew tall there, and the violets gently swayed.
Then I awoke.

I dreamed a German kiss was on my brow,
And someone spoke
The German words: "I love you!" (How they rang!)
Then I awoke.

TRANSLATED BY AARON KRAMER

THE SLAVE SHIP   *Der Superkargo Mynher van Koek*

I

The supercargo Mynher van Koek
Sits in his cabin, counting;
He calculates his lading bills
And sees the profits mounting.

"The rubber's good, the pepper's good:
Three hundred barrels and sacks;
I've gold-dust and rare ivory—
But best is my cargo of blacks.

"I bought them on the Senegal,
Six hundred heads—all told.
Their flesh is hard, their sinews taut
As the finest iron mould.

"Whiskey, beads, and trinkets of steel
Were all the fortune I spent—
Should half of my cargo stay alive
I'll make eight hundred per cent.

"Should only three hundred blacks remain
When I get to Rio Janeiro,
I'll make three hundred ducats apiece
From the house of Gonzales Perreiro."

But all at once Mynher van Koek
Was roused from his reflection;
The ship-surgeon, van der Smissen by name,
Returned from his tour of inspection.

He's a skinny thing—red warts on his nose;
"Now tell me," the captain cries,
"Tell me, ship-surgeon, how do you find
My dear black merchandise?"

The doctor nods his thanks, and says:
"That's what I've come to announce—
Tonight the rate of mortality
Significantly mounts.

"A daily average of two have died,
But seven went today:
Four men, three women—I entered the loss
In the records right away.

"I looked the corpses over well,
For many a time these knaves
Pretend to be dead, because they hope
We'll toss them out on the waves.

"I took the irons off the dead,
And, as usual, gave an order
Early this morning, that every corpse
Should be cast out into the water.

"Sharkfish, whole battalions of them,
Shot swiftly up from the brine;
They love the Negro-meat so well!
They're pensioners of mine.

"Since first our ship put out to sea
They've stubbornly pursued;
These monsters catch the corpses' scent
With a sniffing hunger for food.

"It's a comical thing to see the sharks
Go snapping after the dead!
One of them tears at the rags, and one
At the legs, and one at the head.

"When everything's swallowed, they cheerfully stir
Around the vessel's planks,
And gape at me with sated eyes
As though to express their thanks."

But, sighing, the captain interrupts:
"How can I end this curse?
How can I keep the rate of death
From getting worse and worse?"

"Through their own fault," the surgeon sneers,
"Many succumb to death;
The air in the hold of the ship is foul
From their offensive breath.

"And many die because they're sad,
For they're kept in a boredom that kills;
A bit of music, dancing, and air,
Will cure them of all their ills."

"Splendid advice!" the captain cries,
"My dear old van der Smissen's
More clever than Aristotle was,
Who gave Alexander lessons.

"The Tulip Society's president
Has more than an average mind,
But when it comes to reasoning
You leave him far behind.

"Music! Music! the blacks shall dance
Here on the deck of the ship;
And whomever the hopping can't amuse,
Let him be cured by the whip!"

II

Many thousands of stars look out
From the high blue tent of the skies:
Longingly radiant, large and bright,
Like loyely ladies' eyes.

They gaze down into the endless sea
With its phosphorous purple hue;
Soft in the night the sleepless waves
Voluptuously coo.

There's not a sail on the slave-ship now;
It drifts unrigged and bare;
But lanterns glitter along the deck,
And music's in the air.

The helmsman plays a violin,
The doctor's trumpet sounds,
The cook plays flute, while a cabin-boy
Stands at the drum, and pounds.

A hundred Negroes, women and men,
Are whirling around—insane—
Shouting and hopping; at every leap
A rhythmic clatter of chains.

They stamp the boards with blusterous joy,
And many a naked beau
Embraces his beautiful Negro lass—
Between them a sigh of woe.

The hangman is *maître des plaisirs:*.
And, swinging left and right,
He's whipped the sluggish dancers on,
Driven them to delight.

And diddle-dum-dee and shnedderedeng!
The noise allures from the deep
The monsters of the water-world
That were lying sound asleep.

Many hundreds of sharks come close
With sleepy, half-shut eyes;
They stare up at the revelling ship
In wonder and surprise.

They know it's not their breakfast time,
And open wide their jaws—
Revealing rows of shiny teeth
As huge and sharp as saws.

And diddle-dum-dee and shnedderedeng—
No end to the exultations.
The sharkfish bite themselves in the tail—
So great is their impatience.

I think they don't like music much,
Like many of their gang.
"Trust no music-hating beast!"
Albion's bard once sang.

And shnedderedeng diddle-dum-dee—
There's never an end to the dance!
Mynher van Koek, at the bow of the ship,
Prayerfully folds his hands:

"Take pity, o Lord, in the name of Christ,
And let these sinners live!
You know they're stupid as cows, o Lord,
And if they enrage you—forgive!

"Spare their lives in the name of Christ
Who died for us all on the cross!
For unless three hundred heads remain
I'll suffer a terrible loss."

TRANSLATED BY AARON KRAMER

ANNO 1829 *Dass ich bequem verbluten kann*

Give me a fine wide plain, where I
May comfortably bleed to death!
Within this crowded world of trade
Oh do not let me gasp for breath!

They banquet well, they guzzle well,
Enjoy the blessings of the mole—
And show a generosity
No smaller than the poor-box hole.

They're always puffing on cigars.
Their hands in trouser-pockets rest;
And their digestion is first-rate—
Would they were easy to digest!

The spices that have made them rich
Are sold and savored everywhere;
And yet a rotten crawfish-smell,
Despite all spicing, fills the air.

O, that I saw gigantic wrong,
Unspeakable and bloody crime;—
But not this well-fed rectitude,
That always pays its bills on time!

To Lapland, or to Africa,
Or Pomerania—I would fly!
No matter to what distant land;
Take me along, you clouds on high!

Take me along!—They do not hear—
The clouds on high are wise indeed!
When voyaging above this town,
They hurry past with troubled speed.

TRANSLATED BY AARON KRAMER

ANNO 1839   *O, Deutschland, meine ferne Liebe*

Germany, distant love of mine!
When I remember you, I pine.
Gay France is dull—this flippant folk
Bears down my spirit like a yoke.

In witty Paris nothing rules
But Mind. O little bells of fools,
O bells of faith!—How dear, how sweet
You sound above the German street!

Courteous men! Yet I reply
To their *"Bonjour"* with jaundiced eye.
The rudest treatment I was given
In Germany, now seems like Heaven.

These smiling women! never still,
Forever churning—like a mill.
I'll take the German girls instead.
They never talk when they're in bed.

And here in France our whole life seems
To spin around, like frenzied dreams.
At home all things are in a groove,
As though nailed down—they scarcely move.

From far away I seem to hear
Night-watchman bugles, soft and clear;
Night-watchman songs are sweetly ringing,
And far-off nightingales are singing.

At home, in Schilda's oaken grove,
How well the poet thrived! I wove
My tender-hearted verses there,
Of moonlight and of violet-air.

TRANSLATED BY AARON KRAMER

TO GEORG HERWEGH *Herwegh, du eiserne Lerche*

Herwegh, you lark of iron,[1]
Up to the holy light of the sun
With clashing delight you've ascended!
Has the winter truly ended?
Has Germany's springtime truly begun?

Herwegh, you lark of iron,
You are so heaven-high of wing,
That earth has vanished from your eyes.
Only in your song arise
The blossoms of that vaunted Spring.

TRANSLATED BY AARON KRAMER

GERMANY [2] *Deutschland ist noch ein kleines Kind*

(WRITTEN IN THE YEAR 1840)

Germany's still a little child,
But the sun's his nursing-dame;
She does not feed him soothing milk,
She feeds him savage flame.

One grows up quickly on such food;
One's blood runs boiling mad.
You, neighbors' children—count to ten
Before you fight this lad!

He's a clumsy giant—he'll rip an oak
Out of the ground, like a weed,
And pound you till your heads are soft,
And till your buttocks bleed!

He is like Siegfried, that gallant youth
Around whom legends grew:
When he struck it with his sword,
The anvil broke in two.

Yes, you'll be a Siegfried, and by your sword
The hateful dragon will die;
Hurrah! how brightly your nurse, the sun,
Will laugh down from the sky!

You'll make the dragon's hoard your own,
When you have struck him dead.
Hurrah! how bright the golden crown
Will blaze upon your head!

TRANSLATED BY AARON KRAMER

OCTOBER 1849 [8] *Gelegt hat sich der starke Wind*

The wind's asleep, that howled so wild;
At home it's quiet as could be;
Germania, the great big child,
Plays happily around his Christmas tree.

Domestic joy's our main concern;
Whatever tempts beyond, we label
"Sin"—the doves of Peace return,
That used to make their nest within our gable.

The wood and stream rest cozily,
By gentle moonlight comforted;
But—on a sudden—can it be
A shot?—perhaps it is a friend, shot dead.

Perhaps, with weapon in his hand,
They came upon the hare-brained one.
(Not every lad can understand
As well as Flaccus—when it's time to run.) [4]

A shot. Is someone being fêted?
Fire-works lit to Goethe's glory? [5]
—The risen Sontag's celebrated
By rockets sounding off—the same old story!

And Franz Liszt, too, pops up once more;
He lives, he does not lie blood-red
On a Hungarian field of war;
No Russian, no Croatian left him dead.

The final trench of freedom fell,
And Hungary is bleeding, dying—
But Franz, Sir Franz, remained quite well;
His sabre, too—in his commode it's lying!

Franz is alive, and when he's old,
What tales of the Hungarian war
His children's children will be told!
"Thus stood I—and thus, thus my blade I bore!"

When someone speaks of Hungary
My German vest becomes too small;
A mighty tide wells up in me—
I hear the challenge of a bugle-call.

That myth of heroes, hushed so long,
Once more goes crashing through my soul:
The iron-savage hero-song
That tells us of the Nibelungen's fall.

The heroes' fate remains the same . . .
It is the very same old story;
There's only been a change in name,
Yet these are the same "Heroes crowned in glory."

There's little difference in their lot.
Though proud and free the banners fly,
Conforming to the ancient plot
The bestial forces win; the heroes die.

This time the ox and bear combined
Their brutal, overwhelming powers. [6]
You fall; but, Magyar, rest your mind!
—An ignominy even worse is ours.

For those were decent beasts, that broke
Your fortresses with manners fine;
While we are bowed beneath the yoke
Of heartless wolves, and common dogs, and swine.

They howl, and bark, and grunt—my nose
Can scarcely bear the victor's reek.
Poet, be still; your anguish grows—
You are so sick . . . 'twere wiser not to speak.

TRANSLATED BY AARON KRAMER

TENDENCY   *Deutscher Sänger, sing und preise*

German singers! sing and praise
German freedom—till your song
Takes possession of our souls,
And inspires us to goals,
As the noble *Marseillaise.*

No more Werthers [7] need be heard—
We have cooed and wooed too long—
Be your people's guide and rock—
Tell them that the hour has struck;
Speak the sword, the dagger word!

Do not be the tender flute,
The idyllic soul. Be strong.
Be the trumpet of the land!
Be the cannon—take your stand—
Shatter, thunder, blare, uproot!

Shatter, thunder, night and day—
Till you've righted every wrong!
Sing to waken, to incite!
—But be careful that you write
In the vaguest sort of way . . .

TRANSLATED BY AARON KRAMER

PROMISE *Nicht mehr barfuss sollst du traben*

> No more barefoot need you jog,
> German freedom, through the bog;
> For at last they've given you
> Shiny boots, and stockings, too.
>
> On your head you'll wear a warm
> Cap of fur in case of storm;
> This will help to guard your ears
> When the frosty winds are fierce.
>
> You are even banqueted—
> What a sumptuous future's spread!
> But do not let the foreign satyr
> Tempt you on—to vomit later!
>
> And do not swell with too much pride!
> Don't set all respect aside
> For the highest in command,
> And the Mayors of the land!
>
> TRANSLATED BY AARON KRAMER

THE EMPEROR OF CHINA [8] *Mein Vater war ein trockner Taps*

> My father was a dry old gawk,
> A sober soul, to hear him talk;
> But when I gulp old brandy down
> Then am I worthy of my crown.
>
> There must be magic in these cups:
> For every time I take my schnapps
> A vision rises in my room
> Of China standing all in bloom.
>
> The Middle Kingdom becomes a lawn
> With flowers aglow in the golden dawn.
> I almost am a man, and life
> Swells in the belly of my wife.

Abundance glitters all around,
And soon the sick grow hale and sound;
Confusius, wiseman of my court,[9]
Is gifted with the clearest thought.

The rye-bread of the soldier-boy
Becomes an almond-cake—O joy!
And all my empire's ragged clowns
Parade in silk and velvet gowns.

The mandarins—my noble knighthood—
Whose brains were seriously blighted,
Win back their youthful strength of yore,
And toss their braids about once more.

Religion's symbol and safe retreat,
The great Pagoda, is now complete;
The last of the Jews are sprinkled with water
And then receive the Dragon's Order.[10]

Gone is the spirit of revolution!
"We don't want a constitution;
We're satisfied with the stick, the kantshu!"
—Cry the noblest of the Manchu.

My court physicians seem to think
That it is bad for me to drink,
But, rest assured, my deep potation
Is in the interests of my nation!

And another, yet another cup!
Sheer manna's in each precious drop!
My people are happy, and kind of high;
"Hosanna!" is their joyous cry.

                    TRANSLATED BY AARON KRAMER

REASSURANCE   *Wir schlafen ganz, wie Brutus schlief*

Just as Brutus slept, we sleep—
But he awoke, and buried deep
In Caesar's breast the icy steel!
The Romans ate their kings with zeal.

We are no Romans: we like to smoke.
Tastes will vary with every folk.
Each in its way excels the rest:
I like the dumplings of Suabia best.

We're Germans: kindly souls. Our sleep
Is like the flowers'—wholesome and deep—
And when we awake, our throats are dry—
But it's not for princes' blood we cry.

We're firm as oak or linden-tree,
And such a race we are proud to be.
Where oak and linden touch the skies
No Brutus ever will arise.

And should such a Brutus among us rise,
He'd find no Caesar—he'd strain his eyes
In vain for Caesar everywhere;
The gingerbread we bake is rare.

We've six and thirty overseers
(That's not too many!) and each one wears
A star on his heart, to keep him from harm.
He can face the Ides without alarm.

We call them Fathers, and Fatherland
Is the name we place upon that land
Which princes rule by inherited right;
And sausage with sauerkraut's our delight.

Whenever Father takes the air,
Our heads bow: reverently bare;
No Roman murderers' hideaway
Is Germany, where children play.

TRANSLATED BY AARON KRAMER

ADAM THE FIRST   *Du schicktest mit dem Flammenschwert*

You sent forth, with their swords of flame,
The guards of your heavenly city,
And chased me out of Paradise
With neither justice nor pity.

I trudge along beside my wife
Toward regions far and strange;
But I have fed on wisdom's fruit,
And this you cannot change.

You cannot steal what I have learned:
How weak you are, and small,
Trying to prove, with thunder and death,
That you are Lord of all!

Oh, God! How wretched is this deed,
This awful condemnation!
I call it worthy of heaven's dean,
A brilliant inspiration!

I'll never yearn for Paradise;
Your Eden wasn't much:
I found some lovely trees, whose fruit
I was not allowed to touch.

My freeman's right must be complete!
If I should ever feel
The slightest limit—Heaven would be
A Hell, and a Bastille!

TRANSLATED BY AARON KRAMER

1649—1793—???? [11]   *Die Britten zeigten sich sehr rüde*

The British were rude and most unpolished
When their royal lord was to be abolished.
In Whitehall Charles unsleeping passed
The night that was to be his last.
Before his window mockery sang,
And on his scaffold the hammers rang.

The French showed scarcely better grace:
Louis Capet was borne by them,
In a hansom, to the judgment place;
No *calèche de remise* was given him—
Which, under the old rules, would be
More fitting to his majesty.

It was even worse for Marie Antoinette,
For she was given just a *charrette;*
No *chambellan*, nor *dame d'atour*,
But a *sans-culotte* accompanied her.
With a sneer upon her Hapsburgian lip
The widow took her final trip.

The British and French are a heartless clan;.
But the German is a gentleman:
He's very kind, and kind he'll stay
Even when it's time to slay.
The German will forever be
Respectful toward His Majesty.

With six fine horses, draped in black,
Drawing his carriage at the crack
Of a lamenting coachman's whip,
On which the loyal tears shall drip—
Just so shall our king to the block be led
And respectfully be deprived of his head.

TRANSLATED BY AARON KRAMER

KING DAVID   *Lächelnd scheidet der Despot*

Smiling, kings give up their breath;
For they know that with their death
Someone else will shout commands,
And enslavement never ends.

Wretched folk! like horse and bull,
Harnessed to the plough, they pull—
And whoever will not bow
Breaks his neck beneath the plough.

David, when his time is done,
Whispers to Prince Solomon:
"Apropos of Joab, too—
Whom I recommend to you—

"Many years I've sought relief
From the thorn of this brave chief,

But I never dared molest him,
Bitterly though I detest him.

"You, my son, are wise and young,
Reverent toward God, and strong;
And with no distress at all
You'll accomplish Joab's fall."

TRANSLATED BY AARON KRAMER

HYMN   *Ich bin das Schwert, ich bin die Flamme*

I am the Sword, I am the Flame.

I've lighted your way in the darkness, and when the fight began, battled ahead in the front lines.

Here round about me lie the bodies of my friends, but the victory was ours. The victory was ours, but here round about lie the bodies of my friends. Amid the wild paeans of triumph sound the chants of the funeral rites. But we have time neither for grief nor for rejoicing. The trumpets sound anew, fresh battles must be fought—

I am the Sword, I am the Flame.

TRANSLATED BY AARON KRAMER

Hebrew Melodies

PRINCESS SABBATH   *In Arabiens Märchenbuche*

In Arabia's book of fables
We are shown enchanted princes
Who may now and then recover
All their former manly beauty.

Thus the wild and hairy monster
Changes to a royal prince:
Brightly dressed, with lavish jewels,
Blowing on a flute, enamored.

But the magic-time runs out,
And we suddenly discover
All his high and regal grandeur
Turning into something monstrous.

Here I sing of such a prince.
He is known as Israel.
Words of witchcraft have transformed him,
Turning him into a dog.

As a dog, with dog-ideas,
All week long he goes on scraping
Through life's excrement and sweepings,
To the mocking jeers of street-boys.

But on every Friday evening,
At the hour of dusk, the magic
Suddenly grows weak; the dog
Once again becomes a person.

Human, and with human feelings.
With uplifted head and heart,
Clean, and festively attired,
Enters he his father's dwelling.

"Greetings, oh beloved dwelling
Of my mighty royal father!
Jacob's tents, upon your sacred
Entrance-posts I press my lips."

Through the house mysteriously
Moves a whispering and a weaving:
The invisible Creator
Thrills the silence with his breathing.

Silence! Just the seneschal
(Or the "sexton"—as we call him)
Hurries nimbly to and fro,
Setting all the lamps afire.

Comfort-pledging golden candles,
How they glisten, how they glimmer!
Proudly, too, flare up the tapers
On the ramparts of Almenor.[1]

And before the ark, in which
Rests the Torah, overhung
With a costly silken cover,
Glittering with precious jewels—

There, beside his praying-table,
Stands the congregation's singer;
Tidy man, who shrugs the shoulders
Of his cloak coquettishly,

While he fumbles at his neck,
Just to show how white his hand is,
Pressing thumb against the throat,
Index-finger on the temple.

Hums quite softly to himself,
Till, at last, exulting loudly,
He lifts up his voice, intoning:
Lecho daudi likras kallah! [2]

Lecho daudi likras kallah—
Lover, come, the bride awaits you,
She who soon shall lift the cover
From her bashful countenance!

This inspired song of marriage
Was created by the noble,
Greatly-honored minnesinger,
Don Jehuda ben Halevy. [3]

In this song he celebrated
The event of Israel's wedding
To the lady Princess Sabbath,
Who is called "The Silent Princess."

Pearl and flower of all beauty
Is the princess. Not more lovely
Was the fabled Queen of Sheba,
Bosom friend of Solomon,

Who, an Ethiope blue-stocking,
Hoped to dazzle with her wit,
And, with all her clever riddles,
Finally became fatiguing.

Princess Sabbath, though, who surely
Is tranquillity in person,
Hates intensely all debating
And contention of the mind.

She is startled and repelled
Both by trampling, noisy Passion,
And by Pathos, storming forward
With its loosened hair aflutter.

Modestly the silent princess
Hides her tresses in her cap;
Meek as a gazelle she gazes,
Blossoms slender as the myrtle.

She allows her sweetheart all
But the smoking of tobacco—
"Sweetheart, smoking is forbidden,
For today's the holy Sabbath.

"But this noon, as compensation,
There shall smoke for you instead
A repast that's truly godlike—
Noon today you'll feast on sholet!" [4]

Sholet, lovely spark of heaven,
Daughter of Elysium!
Thus would sound the ode of Schiller,
Had he ever tasted sholet.

Sholet is the dish of heaven,
Whose immortal recipe
God himself once gave to Moses
Long ago upon Mount Sinai,

Where the Lord made manifest
All His good religious dogma,
And the holy ten commandments,
Writ in characters of lightning.

Sholet is the true creator's
Kosher banquet of ambrosia,
Rapture-bread of Paradise;
And, compared with such refreshment,

Nothing more than devil's filth
Are the platters of ambrosia
Eaten by the false Greek gods,
Who were masquerading devils.

Dines the prince on such a dinner,
Then he glows as though transfigured,
And his waistcoat he unbuttons,
And with blissful smile declares:

"Is that not the Jordan rushing?
Are those not the desert-fountains
Down in Bethel's vale of palms,
Where the camels once encamped?

"Is this not the little herd-bell?
Are those not the fattened wethers
Which the herdsman drives at evening
Down the hill of Gilead?"

But the lovely day is flitting,
While the curse's evil power
Comes on speedy feet of shadow—
And the noble prince laments;

For he feels as though a witch's
Ice-cold fingers clutch his heart.
Now the shivers drizzle through him
Of a doggish transformation.

Princess Sabbath hands her golden
Box of spices to the prince.
Slowly he inhales it—thirsting
For one final drink of fragrance.

Then the princess pledges him
With a parting-drink—he swallows
Hastily, and in the goblet
Only a few drops remain;

Sprinkles them upon the table,
Then he takes a little wax-light,
And he dips it in the wetness,
Till it crackles and goes out.[5]

TRANSLATED BY AARON KRAMER

PROLOGUE: The Rabbi of Bacherach   *Brich aus in lauten Klagen*

Burst forth in loud complaining,
Oh mournful martyr-song
That I have been restraining
Within my soul so long!

Like flame the lyrics flower
In every heart that hears;
I've spoken, with all my power,
The pain of a thousand years.

The great and the small, and even
Cold lords begin to cry;
And girls and flowers are grieving;
And stars shed tears in the sky.

And the tears flow on forever,
Southward in silent ranks;
They flow to the Jordan river,
And overrun the banks.

TRANSLATED BY AARON KRAMER

DISPUTATION   *In der Aula zu Toledo*

Fanfares ring across the Aula
Of Toledo, braying loud;
To the tournament of minds
Comes the motley-colored crowd.

This is not a worldly joust,
Here's no flash of iron arms—
Sharp, scholastically pointed,
It's the word alone that harms.

None here battles for his lady
Like a young and gallant knight—
Holy capuchins and rabbis
Are the heroes of this fight.

Here, instead of shiny helmets,
Sabbath-lids and cowls appear;
Scapularies, arbekanfess [6]
Are the armor that they wear.

Who's the genuine Creator?
Is it Israel's rigid Lord,
For whose glory Rabbi Judah
Of Navarre takes up the sword?

Or is it the three-fold Master
Whom all Christian souls adore,
In whose name St. Francis' guardian,
Brother Joseph, wages war?

Through the logic of conclusions,
And by reason's mighty weight,
And quotations out of authors
Not a foe would dare debate,

That his God's the rightful godhead
Each of them shall try to show,
By reducing *ad absurdum*
The position of his foe.

This is certain: that whichever
Shall at last be overthrown,
Must acknowledge the religion
Of the victor as his own.

That the Jew with holy water
Shall be sprinkled and baptized,
While the Christian, vice versa,
Shall be duly circumcised.

And eleven bold companions
Stand by each disputing chief,
Pledged to share his destiny,
Whether it be joy or grief.

That their guardian's sure to triumph
Every friar is convinced:
Holy water-tubs are waiting
For the Hebrews to be rinsed.

Sprinkling-brush is swung already,
And the incense-barrels gleam—
While the cutting-knives are whetted
By the opposition's team.

In the hall, prepared for battle,
Stands each army at its bounds,
And the restless crowd is waiting,
Pressing for the signal-sounds.

There, among a rush of servants,
Canopied by golden lace,
Sit the king and queen; how childlike
Are the features of her face:

A diminutive French pugnose;
Mischief titters in her eyes;
But the ever-smiling rubies
Of her mouth can hypnotize.

Beautiful and fickle blossom—
May the hand of God be mild!—
Torn up from the Seine's bright valley,
And transplanted, luckless child,

To the Spanish Grandee's garden,
To this hard soil: when she came
She was known as Blanche of Bourbon—
Doña Blanca's now her name.

Pedro is the king; the Cruel
Is a nickname people add;
But today his thoughts are gentle,
And he's really not so bad.

Smiles good-naturedly at nobles,
And his conversation sparks;
While the Jews and Moors are honored
With a few polite remarks.

These, the knights who have no foreskin,
Are the king's pet sycophants;
They command his mighty armies,
They administer finance.

There's a sudden crash of drums,
And the trumpets loudly bruit
The beginning of the battle,
The devotional dispute.

First the guardian of St. Francis
In a pious wrath breaks out:
Alternates repulsive whining
With a vulgar, blustering shout.

In the names of Holy Ghost,
Son and Father, he keeps ranting
Execrations at the rabbi,
Evil seed of Jacob's planting.

For in such a controversy
Devils hide within the Jew;
They provide him clever answers,
Whispering his every cue.

Having driven out the devils
Through the might of exorcism,
Next the monk makes use of dogma,
Rolling off the catechism.

He explains: that in the Godhead
Is contained a Trinity—
Which, on suitable occasions,
Turns to One Divinity—

It's a miracle that only
One can recognize who's risen
Out of reason's heavy bondage
And the bleakness of its prison.

He explains: how in the city
Bethlehem, was brought to bed
Virgin Mary, she who never
Gave away her maidenhead.

How the Lord of Heaven lay there
In the crib, and at his side
Stood a calf and ox—two cattle
Looking up, beatified.

How the beadles of King Herod
Chased him forth from Nazareth
Into Egypt, and how later
He endured the pangs of death

At the hand of Pontius Pilate,
Who delivered the decree
Goaded on by wicked Hebrews,
By the hateful Pharisee.

He explains: how Christ ascended
From the grave in which he lay,
And went soaring up to Heaven
On the third, the blessed day.

How upon the proper moment
He shall once again arrive
And at Josaphat pass judgment
On the perished and alive.

"Shudder, Jews, before the Master!"
Cried the monk, "whom you have torn,
Whom you've driven to destruction
With your blows and crowns of thorn!

"That was you—the tribe of hatred,
Jews, who drove Him to the grave—
Always you've assassinated
The Redeemer come to save.

"Israelites, you are a carcass
In whose heart the demons dwell;
And your bodies are a barracks
For the cavalries of Hell.

"Thomas of Aquinas says it,⁷
Erudition's giant ox,
(So they call him) he's the very
Fountain of the orthodox.

"Israelites, you are hyenas,
Jackals, wolves who dig up graves,
To uncover human corpses
Which your vulture spirit craves.

"Jews, oh Jews, you're hogs, baboons,
Every vile and bloody beast,
Crocodiles, rhinoceri,
Vampires flying to a feast.

"You are hoopoo, horn-owl, raven,
Bat, and basilisk, and owl;
You are creatures of black midnight,
Gallows'-bird, and carrion-fowl.

"You are vipers, yea, and blind-worms,
Crawling things of hate and lust,
Rattle-snakes and poison toads;
Christ will trample you to dust.

"Or, bewitched ones, would you rather
Bring your wretched souls to grace?
From the synagogue's black malice
Flee unto the holy place?

"Flee to love's illumed cathedral,
Where, within the blessed basin,
You'll be washed by wells of pardon—
That's what you should stick your face in—

"There you'll wash away old Adam
And the sins that made him black;
Clean your bosom of its mouldy
Grudge that gathered ages back!

"Don't you hear Him? It's your new name
That He thunders from the sky—
Let the vermin of your trespass
On the breast of Jesus die!

"Love's our God, a gentle lamb;
On the cross his life was spilt
To atone for us, and purchase
Expiation for our guilt.

"Love's our God, our precious Saviour,
Jesus Christ his own true name,
Always humble and forgiving—
And we strive to be the same.

"That's why we are all so gentle,
Calm, and affable, and mild;
Never wrangling—in the image
Of the Lamb Who Reconciled.

"Some day we shall be transfigured
Up in Heaven, and we'll walk
Blessed there among the angels,
Holding each a lily-stalk.

"There, instead of cowls, we'll wear
Gowns of muslin and brocade,
Gowns of silk, with golden tassels,
Ribbons, too, in every shade.

"Bald no more! Around each forehead
Curls shall flutter—golden curls;
And our hair'll be neatly braided
By the most delightful girls.

"There, in the domains of Heaven,
Wider cups shall be in use
Than the goblets here on earth,
Sparkling with the vineyard's juice.

"On the other hand, a lady's
Little mouth will undergo
Quite a shrinkage from the mouthpiece
Of the woman here below.

"We'll enjoy Eternity
With a drink, a laugh, a kiss;
And we'll carol Hallelujah
In an ecstasy of bliss."

So the Christian ceased. His brothers
Were convinced, beyond a doubt,
Light had filled each Hebrew heart,
And they dragged the basins out.

But the Hebrews shook, and vilely
Sneered—preferring to stay dry.
Rabbi Judah of Navarre
Now was ready to reply:

"To manure my soul's dry acre
For your seed, you've bravely flung
Such abusive words upon me,
All those cart-loads full of dung.

"Everyone exploits the method
Once he finds it to be good,
And, instead of chiding you,
I express my gratitude.

"We could scarcely be attracted
By the dogma of the Three,
We who have been multiplying
From our very infancy.

"Still, it's modest to imagine
That within your God are rolled
Three divinities—six thousand
Godheads ruled the men of old.

"This Divinity called Jesus
Is a God unknown to me;
And the Virgin, too, I never
Have been privileged to see.

"For the hardships that twelve hundred
Years ago he may have met
In Jerusalem, I give you
My assurance of regret.

"Whether Hebrews caused his murder
It is difficult to say,
Since the chief *corpus delicti*
Three days later flew away.

"Just as doubtful is the story
That he was our Lord's relation,
Since the latter had no children,
Judging by our information.

"As a poor lamb's-tail our Master
Never perished for mankind;
He's no gentle little driveller,
Little philandropic mind.

"Ours is not the God of love;
Never does he bill and coo,—
For he is a God of thunder,
And a God of vengeance, too.

"Unrelenting falls the lightning
Of his wrath on sinful ones,
And the evils of the fathers
Often fall upon the sons.

"Our God is a living God,
And on high he marches free
Thriving in his halls of Heaven
Through each vast eternity.

"And our God's a healthy God;
He's no feeble fairy-tale,
Like the shadows of Cocytus,
Or like wafers—thin and pale.

"Mighty is our God. He carries
Sun and moon and constellations;
With a frown he shatters thrones,
Blots out the most haughty nations.

"And he is a giant God—
David sings: There is no test
Fit for measuring His greatness—
Earth's a footstool for his rest.

"Our God is a music-lover,
Favors festive songs and strings;
But he thinks that pigs are grunting
Every time a church-bell rings.

"In the ocean lives a fish,
And Leviathan's his name—[8]
Every morning, for an hour,
God comes down and joins his game.

"On the Ninth of Ab, however,[9]
They must rest, for on that day
Ashes fill his holy temple;
He's too peevish then for play.

"Fins as mighty as King Og [10]
Has Leviathan—a tail
Huge as any full-grown cedar—
He's a hundred miles of whale.

"But his flesh is delicate;
Turtle-meat is tougher fare;
On the day of resurrection
God will lead the banquet-prayer.

"All the pious souls appointed,
Both the wise and just, shall savor
On that day the tender fish
Foremost in our Master's favor.

"Part will bathe in garlic gravy,
While the rest will bathe in wine;
Matelottes,[11] with spice and raisins,
Never tasted so divine.

"Little radish-bits will swim
In the spicy garlic sauce—
Brother Joseph, I may wager
That you'll gobble down this course.

"And the brown, the raisin gravy,
Brother Joseph, is so nice,
It will teach your little belly
All the bliss of Paradise.

"Little monk, now heed my counsel!
What God stews is really stewed!
Offer up your aged foreskin;
On Leviathan be renewed."

So the rabbi, grinning darkly,
Spoke seductively, enticing,
And the Jews, with grunts of rapture,
Brandished high their tools of slicing,

Set to scalp the friars' foreskins
Forfeit as the victor's right—
Truthful *spolia opima* [12]
Won in this peculiar fight.

But the monks refused to yield their
Fathers' creed, and be bereft
Of their foreskins, too; they'd never
Stand for such a brutal theft.

When the rabbi finished speaking,
The Crusading Christian shrilled
More of insult—every sentence
Was a chamber-pot, well-filled.

Then, still holding back his passion,
Patiently the Jew replied;
Though his heart was boiling over,
Still he kept his rage inside.

He made reference to the Mishna,[18]
Commentaries, dissertations;
And he turned to Tausves-Yontof [14]
For some very apt quotations.

But what blasphemous rebuttal
Did he swallow from the friar!
That one said: The Tausves-Yontof
Ought to feed the devil's fire!

"That's the end, oh God!" and now
Dreadfully the rabbi screamed;
Gone was all his show of patience;
In his eyes a frenzy gleamed:

"Now the Tausves-Yontof's worthless?
What *is* worthy? Shame! oh shame!
Lord, avenge the evil deed!
Punish them, who mock your name!

"For the Tausves-Yontof, God,
That is You! Hurl sword and fire!
For the honor of Your Name
Smite the holy book's denier!

"Let the black abyss engulf them
Just like Korah's evil lot,
That of old rebelled against you
Rioting and deep in plot.

"Punish, oh my God, the crime!
Thunder now your finest thunder!
As at Sodom and Gomorrha
Pitch and brimstone piled them under!

"Strike the Capuchins, oh Lord,
As you struck at Pharaoh's head,
He who bitterly pursued us
When we swiftly packed and fled.

"After this Mizrayim monarch,[15]
Knights—a hundred thousand—came
Armor-clad, from dread yadaim
Rose their sharp-edged swords aflame.

"Then, beneath your outstretched yad
Each and every knight was smitten,
Swallowed by the Red Sea water,
Pharaoh, too—a helpless kitten.

"Strike the Capuchins, oh Lord,
Let the shameless blackguards learn
That the lightnings of your fury
Still can blast the sky, and burn.

"Then I'll sing the praise and glory
Of your triumph, and I'll beat
Kettle-drums, like Miriam, and
Dance the madness from my feet."

Now the monk flared up with fury,
From his mouth the thunder burst:
"May the Lord be *your* destruction,
Execrable and accursed!

"Belial and Astaroth—[16]
All your devils I defy—
Lucifer and Beelzebub—
Filthy godhead of the fly.

"I can brave your evil spirits,
All your hellish tricks are wasted;
For in me is Jesus Christ;
Of his body I have tasted.

"Better than Leviathan,
Jesus is my favorite food,
Better than the garlic sauce
Which the devil may have stewed.

"Oh, instead of wrangling with you
I would see you stew and roast—
You and all your brave companions
On the warmest burning-post!"

Thus the joust for God and credo
Roars along: insulting, grave;
But the champions all in vain
Shriek and scold and snort and rave.

Twelve embittered hours are gone,
And the end's no closer yet;
Till the audience grows weary,
And the ladies bathe in sweat.

Now the Court is also restless;
Yawning chambermaids are seen.
Questioning, the monarch turns
To his beautiful young queen:

"Tell me, what is your opinion?
Which one of the two is right?
Would you say that Brother Joseph
Or the Jew has won the fight?"

Doña Blanca looks at him,
And, as though she weighs her choice,
Rubs her hand across her forehead,
And at last she finds her voice:

"Which is right I hardly know—
But, to tell the truth, I think
That the rabbi and the friar,—
That they both—forgive me—stink."

TRANSLATED BY AARON KRAMER

BELSHAZZAR [17]   *Die Mitternacht zog näher schon*

The deep of night is coming on;
In still repose lies Babylon.

But high in the castle of the king
The royal train is revelling.

High in the lordly chamber there
Belshazzar feasts on lordly fare.

His retinue sit in a glittering line
And empty their goblets of sparkling wine.

The goblets clink, the puppets applaud;
It rings like a song to the arrogant lord.

He drinks, and his cheeks begin to glow;
Within him the flames of mutiny grow.

And blindly he's carried away by the flame;
And he slanders God with a sinful name.

And he shamelessly struts, and savagely rants,
With a roar of applause from his sycophants.

Then haughtily the monarch cries;
A slave flies out, and back he flies.

On his head are vessels of gold design
Plundered from Jehovah's shrine.

And with sinful hand the King takes up
A holy goblet, filled to the top.

And hastily he drains it dry,
And with foaming mouth he utters a cry:

"Hear how I mock you, Almighty One!
It is I that am King in Babylon!"

But scarcely died the dreadful word;
The breast of the King was strangely stirred

The laughter ceased; and in the hall
A deathly stillness came over all.

And see! and see! on the wall of white
A hand like a man's began to write;

And wrote, and with letters of fire seared
The wall, and wrote, and disappeared.

The monarch sat and stared ahead,
With shaking knees, and pale as the dead.

Cold sat the courtiers, chilled to the bone,
And made no sound, were still as stone.

The Magi came, yet of them all
Not one could interpret the words on the wall.

But ere the sun rose up again,
Belshazzar was murdered by his men.

TRANSLATED BY AARON KRAMER

DONNA CLARA *In dem abendlichen Garten*

In the evening-shadowed garden
Walks the great Alcalde's daughter;
From the castle, darkly towering,
Roll the drums and blare the trumpets.

"I am weary of the dances,
Weary of the flattering speeches,
Weary of the knights who neatly
Match my beauties with the sunshine.

"All things are to me a burden
Since the moon's rays lighted for me
That same Knight, whose lute, spell-binding,
Nightly draws me to my window.

"As he stood there, slender, daring,
And his eyes shot fiery glances
From a face of noble pallor,
Almost a St. George I held him!"

Musing thus walked Donna Clara,
Eyes downcast and all unseeing,
Till she raised them to behold her
Unknown, handsome, knightly stranger.

Clasping hands and whispering passion
To and fro they move in moonlight;
Gently Zephyr comes to meet them,
Roses greet, speech-dowered by magic.

The enchanted roses greet them,
Liveried red, as Love's own heralds.
"Tell me, tell me, my Belovèd,
Why thy cheek so sudden flushes."

" 'Twas the flies that stung, Belovèd,
And I hate these flies in summer
With a hate as deep as though they
Were a mob of long-nosed Hebrews."

"Waste not words on Jews or midges,"
Spake the Knight in tones caressing.
From the almond trees there fluttered
Myriad hosts of snowy blossom.

Myriad hosts of snowy blossom
Poured their fragrance on the evening.
"Tell me, tell me, my Belovèd,
Is thy whole heart given to me?"

"Yea, I love thee, my Belovèd,
I will swear it by that Saviour
Whom the Jews, of God accursèd,
Once did slay in treacherous malice."

"Waste not words on Jews or Saviour,"
Spake the Knight in tones caressing.
Far away, as in a vision,
Swayed white lilies, bathed in moonlight.

Gleaming lilies, bathed in moonlight,
Gazed upon the starry heavens.
"Tell me, tell me, my Belovèd,
Was thine oath not falsely sworn me?"

"Naught in me is false, Belovèd,
Even as in my breast there floweth
No blood-drop of Moorish tincture,
Nor the unclean blood of Hebrews."

"Waste not words on Moors or Hebrews,"
Spake the Knight in tones caressing,
And towards a grove of myrtles
Leads he the Alcalde's daughter.

With love's soft and subtle meshes,
Secretly hath he ensnared her!
Short their words and long their kisses,
And their hearts were overflowing.

Sweet and melting is the bride-song
Sung by Philomel the gentle;
In the grasses close about them
Fireflies bear the bridal torches.

In the grove the silence deepens,
Naught is heard save furtive rustlings
Of the discreet myrtle-branches,
And the breathing of the blossoms.

Roll of drums and blare of trumpets
Ring out sudden from the castle.
Clara wakens and withdraws her
From her lover's arm encircling.

"Hark, they call for me, Belovèd,
Yet before we part, oh tell me,
Tell me thy dear name, Belovèd,
That so long thou'st hidden from me!"

And the Knight, with merry laughter,
Kissed the lady's lily fingers,
Kissed her lips and kissed her forehead,
Ere he made her answer slowly:

"I, Senora, your Belovèd,
Am the son of the renowned,
Famed, and scripture-learned Rabbi,
Israel of Saragossa!"

TRANSLATED BY M. M. BOZMAN

THE NEW ISRAELITE HOSPITAL IN HAMBURG [18] *Ein Hospital für arme, kranke Juden*

A hospital for sick and needy Jews,
For the poor sons of sorrow thrice accursed,
Who groan beneath the heavy, threefold evil
Of pain, and poverty, and Judaism.

The most malignant of the three the last is:
That family disease a thousand years old,
The plague they brought with them from the Nile valley—
The unregenerate faith of ancient Egypt.

Incurable deep ill! defying treatment
Of douche, and vapour-bath, and apparatus
Of surgery, and all the healing medicine
This house can offer to its sickly inmates.

Will Time, the eternal goddess, in compassion
Root out this dark calamity transmitted
From sire to son?—Will one day a descendant
Recover, and grow well and wise and happy?

I know not. Let us praise and bless him meanwhile,
Whose tender heart so lovingly and wisely
Sought to allay such woes as can be softened,
Upon the wounds a kindly balsam dropping.

The dear, good man! He builded here a refuge
For troubles that the art of the physician
(Or Death, at worst!) could heal, providing fully
For pillows, soothing draughts, and careful tendance.

He was a man of deeds and did his utmost:
Gave to good works, when life had reached its evening,
The wage of his laborious days, humanely
Finding refreshment after toil in mercy.

He gave with open hand—yet alms more costly
Fell from his eyes: tears fair and very precious,
With which he often wept the vast and hopeless
Incurable affliction of his brothers.

TRANSLATED BY MARGARET ARMOUR

JEḤUDA BEN HALEVY Four Selections

I. THE TALMUDIC SCHOLAR

Yes, his father led him early
To the teachings of the Talmud,
And within it he uncovered
The Halacha, this tremendous

Fencing-school, in which the leading
Babylonian logicians
Used to carry on their prize-fights
With the pride of Pumpeditha.

In this school Jehuda gathered
All the skills of controversy:
And his mastery was later
Proven by the book "Cosari."

But the sky pours down upon us
Two quite different kinds of light:
Both the blinding light of day,
And the milder moonlight—so,

So the Talmud also shines
Twofoldwise, and its two beacons
Are Halacha and Haggadah.
Fencing-school I called the first—

But the second, the Haggadah,
I prefer to call a garden,
A fantastic sort of garden,
Comparable to that other,

Which, according to the legend,
Sprouted once in Babylon—
Queen Semiramis' garden,
The eighth wonder of the world.

Queen Semiramis, who'd gotten
All her teaching, as a child,
From the birds, and who had always
Kept a number of their traits,

Would not think of promenading
On the ground, among us mammals;
So she got to work, and planted
Her own garden in the air—

High up on colossal pillars
Sparkled cypresses and palms,
Golden oranges, and fountains,
Flower-beds, and marble gods,

All adroitly, soundly linked by
Numberless suspension bridges
Fashioned in the form of creepers,
On whose top the birds would rock—

Huge, exotic, solemn birds—
Thinkers, too profound to sing;
While around them fluttered tiny
Sparrow people, gaily trilling—

All of them in highest rapture
As they breathed the fragrant air
Which had never been polluted
By the stench and steam of earth.

The Haggadah is a garden
Of an air-child's fancy, too;
And whenever young Jehuda
Found himself confused and deafened

By the neverending quarrels
In Halacha: arguments
Over the annoying egg
Which a hen had laid one feast-day,

Or about some other matter—
Just as weighty—he'd escape,
And refresh his weary mind
In the blossoming Haggadah—

Where were lovely old traditions,
Angel fairy-tales and legends,
Quiet histories of martyrs,
Festive hymnals, words of wisdom,

Humorous hyperboles;
—But the whole place throbbed with zeal,
Glowed with zeal—oh, how it glowed,
What a garden of abundance!—

And Jehuda ben Halevy's
Noble heart each time would yield
To the fierce, mysterious sweetness,
To the wondrous joy of sorrow

And the fabulous vibrations
Of that blessed, secret world,
Of that mighty revelation
Which we know as poetry.

And the craft of poetry,
Radiant knowledge, graceful power,
Which we call the lyric art,
Wrought itself upon his senses.

And Jehuda ben Halevy
Learned to be not just a scribe,
But a master craftsman, too,
And a truly mighty poet.

Yes, he was a mighty poet,
Star and torch atop his time,
Flame and beacon for his people;
A miraculous, gigantic

Pillar of ignited song
Which was carried at the head of
Israel's sorrow-caravan
Through the wilderness of exile.

II. HIS LADY

Love, to live, must have a lady,
And for troubadours of love
Such a lady was as vital
As is butter to the bread.

And the hero of this poem,
Our Jehuda ben Halevy,
Also had his love, but she
Was a very different sort.

This was not another Laura,
She whose eyes (o mortal stars!)
Caused that famous conflagration
In a church, upon Good Friday—

Nor was this a Chatelaine,
Dressed up in the bloom of youth,
Who presided over tourneys
And conferred the laurel-crown . . .

For the one our rabbi worshipped
Was a sad, a wretched darling,
Yea, the image of destruction—
And her name—Jerusalem.

Even in his early childhood
She had been his only sweetheart:
Even then his soul had quivered
At the word Jerusalem.

Young Jehuda stood and listened,
Purple flame upon his cheek,
When a pilgrim reached Toledo
From the far-off eastern lands

And reported: how forsaken
And defiled was now that town
Where the prophets' fiery footprints
Still illumined every street . . .

Not an ordinary pilgrim
Was this man, whose eyes looked out
With a thousand-year-old sorrow
As he sighed: "Jerusalem!

"She, the thriving holy city,
Has become a wilderness,
Where the satyr, werewolf, jackal
Carry on their wicked business—

"Snakes and birds of midnight nestle
In the weatherbeaten walls:
From the windows' airy arches
Foxes comfortably gaze.

"Here and there one sometimes catches
A bedraggled desert-slave
Pasturing his hunch-backed camel
In the high, wild-growing grass.

"On the noble heights of Zion
Where the golden feasts were held—
Whose magnificence bore witness
To the Lord's unequalled pomp,—

"There, all overgrown with weeds,
Stand the solitary ruins;
And they watch us with such sorrow
One can almost hear them weep.

"It is said that once a year,
On the fatal Ninth of Ab,
They do actually weep—
And with tears in my own eyes

"I once watched the heavy drops
Trickling from those giant stones,
And I heard the lamentations
Of the temple's broken pillars." . . .

Such religious pilgrim-stories
Wakened in the youthful breast
Of Jehuda ben Halevy
Great love for Jerusalem.

III. THE CASKET AND THE PEARLS

Many were the pearls' adventures.
Nothing very special happened
To the box, though: Alexander
Kept that treasure for himself.

In it he had locked the poems
Of divine, ambrosial Homer
Whom he loved above all singers:
And at night the casket stood

By his bedside—while he slumbered,
Radiant visions of the heroes
Rose up out of it, and glided
Spectrally across his dreams.

Other ages, other birds—
I, I also used to treasure
Homer's songs about the deeds
Of Achilles, of Odysseus.

In those days my hope was rosy,
And my soul so full of sunshine—
Vine-leaves garlanded my brow,
And I heard the fanfares ringing—

No. No more of that—now broken
Lies my coach of victory,
And the panthers that once drew it
Now are dead, as are the women

Who, with kettle-drum and cymbal,
Danced around me: and, in sorrow,
Cripple's sorrow, I myself
Waltz about—no more of that—

No. No more—it was the story
Of the box of old Darius,
And I somehow started thinking:
Were the box in my possession,

And did not distress compel me
To convert it into cash,
I would lock away in it
All the poems of our rabbi,—

All the feast-songs, elegies
Of Jehuda ben Halevy,
The ghasels, the travelogues
Of his pilgrimage—I'd hire

Expert zophars to transcribe them
On the most expensive parchment
And I'd lock away these writings
In the little golden casket.

This I'd place upon the table
Near my bed, and when my friends
Would arrive, and be astounded
By the splendor of the chest,

By the matchless bas-reliefs
So diminutive, yet perfect,
And be dazzled by the huge
Precious stones encrusted on it—

Smiling, I would say to them:
This is but the unwrought shell
Which confines a nobler treasure—
In this little box there lie

Diamonds whose radiance mirrors
And is mirrored by the sky,
Rubies with a blood-red glow,
Turquoises that have no blemish,

Also emeralds of promise,
Pearls, far purer than those others
Which the blackguard Smerdis proffered
Long ago to Queen Atossa,

And which later ornamented
All those notabilities
Of our moon-encircled planet:
Cleopatra, and Thais,

Priests of Isis, Moorish princes,
And the queens of Spanish kings,
And at last the much-respected
Lady Baron Salomon—

Those world-famous pearls are nothing
But the colorless saliva
Of a wretched oyster, dying
At the bottom of the ocean.

But the pearls within this casket
Were created by a noble
Human soul, that is far deeper,
Chasms deeper than the ocean—

Since they are the teardrop pearls
Of Jehuda ben Halevy,
Which he shed for the destruction
Of his dear Jerusalem—

Pearls of tears that, linked together
On the golden thread of rhyme,
Came from poetry's gold-smithy
In the pattern of a song.

This rare song of teardrop pearls
Is the famous lamentation
Sung in all the tents of Jacob
Scattered through the universe,

Each year on the Ninth of Ab,
On the anniversary day
Of Jerusalem's destruction
By Vespasian's bloody legions.

Yes, it is the song of Zion,
Which Jehuda ben Halevy,
Dying in the holy ruins
Of Jerusalem, intoned—

Barefoot, in the ragged vestments
Of a penitent, he sat
On the fragment of a pillar;—
And his hair, an aged forest,

Tumbled down upon his breast,
Shading in mysterious fashion
That poor melancholy face
And those strange, phantasmal eyes—

Thus he sat and thus he sang,
Like a seer from other ages—
Just as if old Jeremiah'd
Newly risen from the grave—

And his song's wild notes of grief
Almost tamed the feathered creatures,
And the vultures fluttering nearer
Listened, almost sympathetic—

But there came a saucy Arab
Galloping along that road,
Rocking high upon his stallion,
Brandishing a shiny lance—

And he thrust its deadly point
Through the breast of the poor singer,
And away he swiftly galloped
Like a winged silhouette.

Calmly flowed the rabbi's blood,
Calmly he intoned his song
To the last note, and his final
Death-sigh was Jerusalem!—

There's a certain age-old legend
Claiming that that saracen
Was in fact no wicked earthling
But an angel in disguise

Who had been dispatched from Heaven
To transport God's favorite
From this earth, and, without pain,
Bring him to the Blessed Land.

There, the story goes, a welcome
Was awaiting him, prepared
Solely in the poet's honor:
A most heavenly surprise.

Festively the choir of angels
Came to meet him with their music,
And the hymns they sang to greet him
Were his own enraptured verses,—

First they did the wedding-anthem,
Followed by the Sabbath chant
With its well-loved melodies
—Such exultant, magic notes!

Little angels blew on oboes,
Others played the violin,
Strummed a viol, or beat time
On the kettle-drums and cymbals.

And the music rang so sweetly,
And so sweetly did it echo
Through the spacious halls of Heaven:
Lecho daudi likras kallah.

IV. A NIGHTINGALE OF GOD

Yes, the noblest hearts were pierced:
Like Jehuda ben Halevy,
Moses Ib'n Esra perished,
And Gabirol, too, was slain—

Our Gabirol, minnesinger
Pledged by song unto the Lord,
That religious nightingale
Whose beloved rose was God—

That pure nightingale, Gabirol,
Warbling love-songs tenderly
In the darkness of that gothic
Medieval midnight-time!

Undisturbed, unterrified
By the spectres and grimaces,
By the waves of death and madness
Haunting mankind in that night—

This, our nightingale, was thinking
Only of its godly sweetheart,
For whose sake it sobbed its passion,
Whom its song of praise exalted!—

Thirty Springs Gabirol witnessed
Here upon the earth, yet fame
Loudly trumpeted the glory
Of his name through all the lands.

In Corduba, near his dwelling,
Lived a Moslem, and this man
Also thought himself a poet,
And was jealous of Gabirol.

When he'd hear the genius singing
Instantly his gall would rise,
And the sweetness of those lyrics
Turned to bitterness in him.

He enticed the hated Jew
To his house one evening, slew him,
And concealed the bleeding corpse
In the earth, behind his dwelling.

But behold! in just the spot
Where the body had been buried
Soon a fig-tree blossomed forth
Of the most amazing beauty.

Strangely shapen were its fruits,
And of strangely seasoned sweetness,
And whoever tasted them
Sank into a dreamy transport.

There were many words and whispers
Of this tree among the people,
Till at last the rumor traveled
To the Caliph's noble ears.

After his own tongue had tasted
Of the fig-phenomenon,
He appointed men to study:
Whence the fruit and what the meaning?

Summary proceedings followed.
Sixty bamboo-strokes were planted
On the fig-tree owner's bottom;
Thus he answered for the outrage.

After this they ripped the fig-tree
From the earth with all its roots,
And before them lay the body
Of our mutilated singer.

Splendid was his burial,
Loud his brothers' lamentation;
That same day was hanged the Moslem
On the gallows of Corduba.

TRANSLATED BY AARON KRAMER

NOTES

꠸ *Poems and Ballads*

1. '*Thalatta! Thalatta!*' This was the jubilant cry of the Greeks (the sea! the sea!) when, during the retreat in their unfortunate campaign against Artaxerxes, they finally saw the sea.

2. '*Suabian poets' school*' A group of contemporary poets, most of them mediocre.

3. '*In Dresden I saw a poor old dog*' Allusion to Ludwig Tieck, the Romantic poet and story teller. In the following stanzas, the allusions are to the death of Goethe, and to Eduard Gans, the distinguished philosopher of law.

4. *Childe Harold* This is an elegy on the death of Byron, author of "Childe Harold's Pilgrimage."

5. *Faibish* A Yiddish name, which Heine playfully derives from Phoebus.

6. '*He has also clipped some sovereigns*' Reference to the practice of debasing currency by clipping.

7. *Thanatos* The Greek god of Death.

8. *Kaddish*   The Hebrew prayer for the dead.

9. '*the Baden board*'   The governing body of Baden was one of the most vigorous opponents of German liberalism.

10. '*a cousin*'   Heine's old friend, later a relative by marriage, Rudolph Christiani.

11. '*Stuttgart's punisher of lust*'   Heine's old bête noire, the critic Wolfgang Menzel.

12. '*precious poet-soul*'   Ludwig Uhland, see pp. 334–7.

ぞ➤ *Germany: A Winter's Tale*

1. *Hoffmann von Fallersleben* (1798–1874) Author of "Deutschland, Deutschland über alles" and many other poems, he was persecuted by the German authorities.

2. *Zollverein* or customs union lasted from 1834 till the Franco-Prussian War; it was founded as an instrument for the unification of the German states.

3. *Carolus Magnus* Charlemagne.   *Karl Mayer* Unimportant German poet belonging to the so-called Suabian school, the constant object of Heine's bitter attacks.

4. *Körner* Theodor Körner (1791–1813), soldier and patriotic poet during the wars against Napoleon.

5. *The spiked helmet* was introduced by order of King Frederick William IV in 1842.   *Johanna de Montfaucon* Romantic play by August von Kotzebue.   *Fouqué, Uhland, Tieck* Romantic poets.

6. '*the bird that I despise*'   The Prussian eagle.

7. '*the black men . . .*'   The 'Dunkelmänner' or obscurantists of Cologne who, under the leadership of J. van Hooghstraaten and the renegade Pfefferkorn, waged war on the humanists, who responded in the famous satire, "Epistolae Virorum Obscurorum," to which Ulrich von Hutten contributed.

8. '*His power of elocution*'   Interest in completing the construction of the cathedral of Cologne was reawakened during the Napoleonic era. King Frederick William IV of Prussia made a speech at the laying of the foundation stone in 1842.

9. '*the king of the tailors*'   In these iron cages were exposed the bodies of the Anabaptists of Münster after their execution in 1536.

10. *'stones at Biberich'* Reference to the quarrel between Hesse-Nassau and Hesse-Darmstadt, in the course of which the latter obstructed the right arm of the Rhine, near Biberich, by unloading a cargo of stones, ostensibly intended for the Cologne cathedral. *Nicholas Becker*, during the Franco-German difficulties in 1840, in which there was talk of annexation of the Rhine provinces by the French, composed a patriotic and provocative ballad.

11. *Alfred de Musset*, the French poet, replied to the above ballad with his "Le Rhin allemand, réponse à la chanson de Becker."

12. *Hengstenberg* A very conservative Berlin theologian.

13. *George Harris* See Heine's description of Paganini, pp. 614–21.

14. *'the Emperor's risen again'* Napoleon's body was transferred from St. Helena to Paris in 1840, and interred in the Dôme des Invalides on December 15.

15. *'forest of Teutoburg,'* where in 9 A.D. the Cheruscan leader Hermann or Arminius defeated three Roman legions led by Varus.

16. *Neander* Johann Augustus Wilhelm Neander, church historian.   *Charlotte Birch-Pfeiffer* Writer of pot-boilers.   *Friedrich von Raumer* Historian.   *Ferdinand Freiligrath* German political poet, who later turned reactionary.   *Father Jahn* Reactionary leader of the gymnastics movement.

17. *Schelling* Friedrich Wilhelm Joseph von Schelling (1775–1854), German philosopher of the idealistic school. Heine discusses him in his "Religion and Philosophy in Germany."   *Cornelius* Peter Cornelius, contemporary painter.   *'cacatum. . . .'* 'Excrement is not painting.'

18. *Kolb* Gustav Kolb, editor of the Augsburg "Allgemeine Zeitung," to which Heine contributed.

19. *Sisyphus* According to Greek legend, Sisyphus, king of Corinth, was punished for his wickedness, after his death, by having to roll up hill a huge marble block, which always rolled down again as soon as it reached the top.   *Danaid* The Danaides, for murdering the sons of Aegyptus, were punished in Hades by being compelled to pour water into a sieve.

20. *Redbeard* Barbarossa, epithet of the Holy Roman Emperor Frederick I (1121–1190).

21. *'chi va piano, va sano'* Italian proverb: 'haste makes waste.'

22. *Moses Mendelssohn* The famous Jewish philosopher, whom Heine praised in his "Religion and Philosophy in Germany"

(see pp. 684–5). *Anna Luise Karsch* A mediocre poet. *Marie Jeanne Dubarry* Mistress of Louis XV.

23. *Felix* Felix Mendelssohn-Bartholdy, the great composer. He was baptized in his childhood.

24. *Klencke* Caroline Luise von Klencke was a fashionable author of the early nineteenth century. *Helmine Chezy* A popular writer.

25. *Charles the Fifth* The laws introduced in 1532 by Charles V were marked by their extreme cruelty.

26. *'Danton . . .'* When Danton was advised to flee France, he is said to have exclaimed: "Leave France? Does a man carry his fatherland on the soles of his shoes?"

27. *Ernst Augustus* Son of George III of England, became King of Hanover in 1837, and immediately discarded the constitution.

28. *'the treacherous bird'* The Prussian eagle. The allusion is to the invitation which was extended by Prussia to Hamburg to join the customs union.

29. The dash stands for Dr. Adolf Halle, Therese Heine's husband. He went insane. *Biber* Owner of an insurance firm which went into bankruptcy after the fire.

30. *Gumpelino* Lazarus Gumpel, banker, and character in Heine's "Baths of Lucca."

31. *Drehbahn* Popular street in Hamburg.

32. *Klopstock* Friedrich Gottlob Klopstock (1724–1803), author of "The Messiah."

33. *'my old lady'* Heine's mother. *Lottchen* His sister.

34. *'that old and noble gentleman'* Heine's uncle, Solomon Heine.

35. *King of the Moors* One of Freiligrath's compositions.

36. *Saint-Just* said: "You don't cure the social sickness with musk and attar of roses."

37. In Aristophanes' comedy, "The Birds," Peisthetairos marries Basilea, after having founded the new Cloud-Cuckoo-Land.

ࣙ Songs of Protest

1. *Georg Herwegh* (1817–1875) German political poet and revolutionary.

2. *Germany*   This poem was occasioned by the imminent possibility of war between France and Germany.

3. *October 1849*   Aftermath of the Revolution of 1848, and the suppression of the Hungarian uprising against the Habsburg monarchy.

4. *Flaccus*   An allusion to the flight of Horace at the Battle of Philippi.

5. *'Goethe's glory'*   Centennial celebration of Goethe's birth. *'Risen Sontag'*   The celebrated actress and singer Henriette Sontag returned to the stage after a twenty years' retirement.

6. *'The bear . . .'*   Russia came to the assistance of Austria against Hungary.

7. *Werther*   Hero of Goethe's "Sorrows of Young Werther."

8. *The Emperor of China*   Frederick William IV of Prussia.

9. *Confusius*   The philosopher Schelling who had been brought to Berlin by the King. Obviously, a pun!

10. *'the great Pagoda'*   The cathedral of Cologne, the construction of which had been recommenced.   *'the Dragon's Order!'* The Order of the Swan, which was renewed in 1843.

11. *1649, 1793*   The years in which Charles I of England and Louis XVI of France were respectively executed.

ঙ Hebrew Melodies

1. *Almemor*   The raised dais from which the Biblical portions are read in the synagogue.

2. *'Lecho daudi likras kallah'*   'Come, my beloved, let us welcome the Bride.' The opening verses of the great Sabbath eve hymn, not composed, as Heine thought, by Jehudah Halevi, but by Solomon Alkabez.

3. *Don Jehuda ben Halevy*   More correctly, Jehudah Halevi, one of the foremost Hebrew poets (1085–1140).

4. *sholet*   Sometimes called *sholnt*, traditional Jewish pudding, prepared especially for the Sabbath. In this stanza, Heine is parodying the famous lines from Schiller's "Ode to Joy," which Beethoven set to music in his Ninth Symphony.

5. This is a description of the "Habdalah" ceremony, with which Jews usher out the Sabbath.

6. *arbekanfess* More correctly, *Arbah Kanfos,* or 'four corners'—so called from the four-cornered garment to which were attached the fringes, "that ye may look upon it, and remember all the commandments of the Lord." ("Numbers," chap. 15.)

7. *Thomas of Aquinas* The greatest of Christian scholastic philosophers (1225–1274).

8. *Leviathan* See Psalm 105.

9. *'Ninth of Ab'* A day of mourning for all Jews, commemorating the destruction of the Temple by Vespasian.

10. *King Og* "For only Og, King of Bashan, remained of the remnant of the Rephaim (giants)." ("Deuteronomy," 3.)

11. *matelotte* A spicy meat stew.

12. *spolia opima* Latin: war-booty consisting of weapons.

13. *Mishna* The commentary on the laws of the Bible, one of the main portions of the Talmud.

14. *Tausves-Yontof* More correctly, *Tosafoth Yomtob,* a commentary on the "Mishna," by Yomtob Lipman Heller (1597–1654)—actually three hundred years later than the reputed date of this disputation.

15. *Mizrayim* Hebrew: Egypt.   *yadaim* Plural of *yad:* 'hand.'

16. *Belial, Astaroth, Beelzebub* Heathen divinities of Palestine.

17. *Belshazzar* See the "Book of Daniel," chap. 5.

18. The New Israelite Hospital in Hamburg was founded by Solomon Heine in 1840.

INDEX OF
FIRST LINES IN GERMAN

Ade, Paris, du teure Stadt 179
Als ich, auf der Reise, zufällig 80
Am blassen Meeresstrande 98
Am Fenster stand die Mutter 92
Am Himmel Sonn und Mond und
  Stern' 170
Am Kreuzweg wird begraben 79
An dem stillen Meeresstrande 110
Anfangs wollt ich fast verzagen 58
Auf diesem Felsen bauen wir 112
Auf Flügeln des Gesanges 71
Aus meinen grossen Schmerzen 74
Aus meinen Tränen spriessen 70

Brich aus in lauten Klagen 268

Das Fräulein stand am Meere 112
Das ist der alte Märchenwald! 53
Das ist der böse Thanatos 153
Das Kloster ist hoch auf Felsen
  gebaut 140
Das Meer erglänzte weit hinaus 84
Dass du mich liebst, das wusst ich 110
Dass ich bequem verbluten kann 249

Den Strauss, den mir Mathilde
  band 168
Denk ich an Deutschland in der
  Nacht 134
Der Abt von Waltham seufzte
  tief 136
Der Brief, den du geschrieben 107
Der Hans und die Grete tanzen
  herum 59
Der junge Franziskaner sitzt 126
Der König Harald Harfagar 128
Der Schmetterling ist in die Rose ver-
  liebt 104
Der Superkargo Mynher van
  Koek 245
Der Tod das ist die kühle Nacht 90
Der Traumgott bracht mich in ein
  Riesenschloss 78
Der Vorhang fällt, das Stück ist
  aus 154
Der Wind zieht seine Hosen an 83
Des Weibes Leib ist ein Gedicht 163
Deutscher Sänger, sing und
  preise 254

Deutschland ist noch ein kleines
    Kind 251
Die Britten zeigten sich sehr rüde 258
Die holden Wünsche blühen 108
Die Linde blühte, die Nachtigall
    sang 73
Die Lotosblume ängstigt 72
Die Mitternacht zog näher schon 281
Die Rose, die Lilie, die Taube, die
    Sonne 70
Die schlanke Wasserlilie 105
Doch die Kastraten klagten 89
Donna Clara! Donna Clara! 61
Draussen ziehen weisse Flocken 132
Du bist begeistert, du hast Mut 243
Du bist gestorben und weisst es
    nicht 152
Du bist wie eine Blume 88
Du hast Diamanten und Perlen 88
Du liebst mich nicht, du liebst mich
    nicht 73
Du schicktest mit dem Flammen-
    schwert 257
Du schönes Fischermädchen 82

Ein Fichtenbaum steht einsam 74
Ein Hospital für arme, kranke
    Juden 285
Eine starke, schwarze Barke 129
Erstorben ist in meiner Brust 167
Es fiel ein Reif in der Frühlings-
    nacht 119
Es kommt der Tod—jetzt will ich
    sagen 176
Es stehen unbeweglich 71
Es träumte mir von einer Sommer-
    nacht 172
Es war ein alter König 107
Es war mal ein Ritter trübselig und
    stumm 68

Gekommen ist der Maie 03
Gelegt hat sich der starke Wind 252
Gesanglos war ich und beklom-
    men 116

Herwegh, du eiserne Lerche 251
Herz, mein Herz, sei nicht beklom-
    men 86

Hör ich das Liedchen klingen 76
Ich bin das Schwert, ich bin die
    Flamme 260
Ich bin nun fünfunddreissig Jahr
    alt 162
Ich bins gewohnt, den Kopf recht
    hoch zu tragen 67
Ich grolle nicht, und wenn das Herz
    auch bricht 73
Ich hab dich geliebet und liebe dich
    noch! 76
Ich hab im Traum geweinet 78
Ich hab in meinen Jugendtagen 148
Ich halte ihr die Augen zu 113
Ich hatte einst ein schönes Vater-
    land 244
Ich lieb eine Blume, doch weiss ich
    nicht welche 103
Ich liebe solche weisse Glieder 117
Ich mache jetzt mein Testa-
    ment 165
Ich seh im Stundenglase schon 169
Ich stand gelehnet an den Mast 66
Ich stand in dunkeln Träumen 85
Ich wandle unter Blumen 106
Ich weiss nicht was soll es be-
    deuten 79
Ich wollt, meine Schmerzen er-
    gössen 86
Ihr guten Christen, lasst Euch
    nicht 119
Ihr Lieder! Ihr meine guten
    Lieder! 97
Im düstern Auge keine Träne 244
Im nächtgen Traum hab ich mich
    selbst geschaut 55
Im Traume war ich wieder jung und
    munter 154
Im traurigen Monat November
    wars 181
Im Wald, in der Köhlerhutte,
    sitzt 144
Im wunderschönen Monat Mai 69
In Arabiens Märchenbuche 263
In dem abendlichen Garten 282
In dem Schlosse Blay erblickt
    man 146
In der Aula zu Toledo 268

In Gemäldegalerieen 102
In meiner Erinnrung erblühen 108

Jüngstens träumte mir: spazieren 117

Keine Messe wird man singen 156

Lächelnd scheidet der Despot 259
Lehn deine Wang an meine Wang 71
Leise zieht durch mein Gemüt 103
Lieb Liebchen, leg's Händchen aufs
Herze mein 57

Manch Bild vergessener Zeiten 75
Mein Kind, wir waren Kinder 87
Mein Tag war heiter, glücklich meine
Nacht 168
Mein Vater war ein trockner
Taps 255
Meine gute, liebe Frau 162
Meiner goldgelockten Schönen 127
Mensch, verspotte nicht den
Teufel 85
Mich locken nicht die Himmel-
sauen 159
Mich ruft der Tod—Ich wollt, o
Süsse 157
Mir träumt': ich bin der liebe Gott 90
Mit deinen blauen Augen 106
Morgens steh ich auf und frage 57

Nach Frankreich zogen zwei Grena-
dier 60
Nicht mehr barfuss sollst du tra-
ben 255

O, Deutschland, meine ferne
Liebe 250

Sag mir, wer einst die Uhren er-
fund 105
Sag, wo ist dein schönes Liebchen 90
Schaff mich nicht ab, wenn auch den
Durst 114
Schöne Wiege meiner Leiden 58
Schwarze Röcke, seidne Strümpfe 95
Sie floh vor mir wie'n Reh so
scheu 111
Sie haben mich gequälet 77

Sie haben dir viel erzählet 74
Sie liebten sich beide, doch keiner 85
Spätherbstnebel, kalte Träume 109
Sterne mit den goldnen Füsschen 108
Still ist die Nacht, es ruhen die
Gassen 84

Täglich ging die wunderschöne 145
Tannenbaum, mit grünen Fingern 95
Thalatta! Thalatta! 99

Überall wo du auch wandelst 115
Und als ich so lange, so lange
gesäumt 75

Vergiftet sind meine Lieder 77
Verlass Berlin, mit seinem dicken
Sande 116
Verletze nicht durch kalten Ton 166
Verlorner Posten in dem Freiheits-
kriege 155
Vor dem Dome stehn zwei Män-
ner 129

Während ich nach andrer Leute 114
Was treibt dich umher, in der Früh-
lingsnacht? 104
Was treibt und tobt mein tolles
Blut? 55
Wenn dich ein Weib verraten hat 132
Wenn ich an deinem Hause 83
Wenn ich, beseligt von schönen
Küssen 113
Wenn ich in deine Augen seh 70
Wenn junge Herzen brechen 161
Wenn zwei von einander scheiden 77
Wie die Nelken duftig atmen! 106
Wie dunkle Träume stehen 88
Wie langsam kriechet sie dahin 158
Wie neubegierig die Möwe 111
Wir sassen am Fischerhause 81
Wir schlafen ganz, wie Brutus
schlief 256
Wir standen an der Strasseneck 115
Wo wird einst des Wander-
müden 166

Zu dem Wettgesange schreiten 66